BECOMING
CONVERSANT
WITH THE
EMERGING
CHURCH

Zondervan Books by D. A. Carson

BECOMING
CONVERSANT
WITH THE
EMERGING
CHURCH

*Understanding a Movement
and Its Implications*

D. A. CARSON

ZONDERVAN®

GRAND RAPIDS, MICHIGAN 49530 USA

ZONDERVAN.COM/
AUTHOR**TRACKER**

Becoming Conversant with the Emerging Church
Copyright © 2005 by D. A. Carson

Requests for information should be addressed to:
Zondervan, *Grand Rapids, Michigan 49530*

Library of Congress Cataloging-in-Publication Data

Carson, D. A.
    Becoming conversant with the emerging church : understanding a movement and
its implications / D. A. Carson.
        p. cm.
    Includes bibliographical references and indexes.
    ISBN-10: 0-310-25947-9 (pbk.)
    ISBN-13: 978-0-310-25947-3 (pbk.)
    1. Postmodernism—Religious aspects—Christianity.   2. Non-institutional
churches. I. Title.
    BR115.P74C37 2005
    262—dc22   2005000360
                                                                           CIP

Interior design by Tracey Walker

Printed in the United States of America

06 07 08 09 10 11 12 • 16 15 14 13 12 11 10 9 8

This book is gratefully dedicated to
JoyJoy

CONTENTS

PREFACE

A simplified form of the substance of this book was first delivered as three Staley Lectures at Cedarville University in February 2004. I would like to thank the president and faculty who welcomed me so warmly, and the numerous students who went out of their way to engage thoughtfully with what I was saying.

As I attempt to make clear in the opening chapter, the "emerging (or 'emergent') church" movement, though scarcely a dozen years old, exerts an astonishingly broad influence. An entire literature has sprung up, with those on the inside quoting and supporting one another in publications and conferences. In other words, a self-identity has already been established. Nevertheless, the diversity of the movement, as well as its porous borders, ensure that I have not found it easy to portray it fairly. I have tried to be accurate in description and evenhanded in evaluation. Even so, I must underscore the fact that when I am forced (for the sake of avoiding endless qualifications) to resort to generalization in order to move the discussion along, one can almost always find some people in the movement for whom the generalization is not true, and others who do not think of themselves as belonging to the emerging church movement who nevertheless share most of its values and priorities. (Also, let it be noted that some of the leaders feel that this has not yet reached the dimensions of a movement and prefer to call it a "conversation.")

I have tried to avoid too much technical discussion. The flavor of the lecture series has not been entirely removed. In reality that means this book will probably frustrate some readers in opposite ways: some will find the treatment of postmodernism to be too elementary, and perhaps others will find parts of it heavy going. The notes will help the former, and I hope that rereading will help the latter. But the book is several times longer than the manuscript of the lectures. The brevity of the latter meant that I could not indulge in detailed documentation or introduce a lot of nuances and exceptions. Owing not least to the fact that some emerging church leaders have criticized the lectures, in various blogs, for such omissions, I have tried in this book to fill that gap as much as possible.

Whenever a Christian movement comes along that presents itself as reformist, it should not be summarily dismissed. Even if one ultimately decides that the movement embraces a number of worrying weaknesses, it may also have some important things to say that the rest of the Christian world needs to hear. So I have tried to listen respectfully and carefully; I hope and pray that the leaders of this "movement" will similarly listen to what I have to say.

I would like to thank Jonathan Davis and Michael Thate for compiling the indexes.

Soli Deo gloria.

D. A. Carson
Trinity Evangelical Divinity School

Chapter 1

THE EMERGING CHURCH PROFILE

What Are We Talking About?

When I have mentioned to a few friends that I am writing a book on the emerging church, I get rather diverse reactions.

"What's that?" one of them asked, betraying that his field of expertise does not encourage him to keep up with contemporary movements.

"Are you going to focus primarily on Acts, or are you going to include the Pauline and other epistles?" queried another, presupposing that I am writing about the church as it "emerged" in the first century—since, after all, I teach in a New Testament department at a seminary.

Another colleague, known for his worldwide connections, asked, "How did you become interested in the difficult and challenging questions surrounding the emergence of the church in the Two-Thirds World?" After all, the last hundred years have witnessed remarkable stories of "emergence" in Korea, many parts of sub-Saharan black Africa, Latin America, certain countries of Eastern Europe (especially Ukraine, Romania, and Moldova), and elsewhere.[1]

---

[1] To mention only one book with "emergence" or a cognate in the title, see Mark T. B. Laing, *The Indian Church in Context: Her Emergence, Growth and Mission* (Delhi: Indian Centre for Promoting Christian Knowledge/Pune: Centre for Mission Studies, 2002).

The responses are sensible enough, since "emerging" and related terms are words that have been applied to these and other circumstances,[2] including some fairly esoteric discussions in the philosophy of science. But during the last dozen years, "emerging" and "emergent" have become strongly associated with an important movement that is sweeping across America, the United Kingdom, and elsewhere. Many in the movement use "emerging" or "emergent" (I will use the two words as equivalents) as the defining adjective for their movement. A dozen books talk about "the emergent church" and "stories of emergence" and the like.[3] One website encourages its patrons in "emergent friendship," which turns out to refer, not to friendship that is emerging, but to the importance of friendship in the movement—thus confirming that "emergent" is, for those in the movement, a sufficient label of self-identification, so that "emergent friendship" is formally akin to, say, "house church friendship" or "Baptist friendship."

At the heart of the "movement"—or as some of its leaders prefer to call it, the "conversation"—lies the conviction that changes in the culture signal that a new church is "emerging." Christian leaders must therefore adapt to this emerging church. Those who fail to do so are blind to the cultural accretions that hide the gospel behind forms of thought and modes of expression that no longer communicate with the new generation, the emerging generation. The National Pastors Convention and the Emergent Convention were held simultaneously in San Diego in 2003; of the three thousand pastors who attended, 1,900 chose the more traditional forum, the NPC, while 1,100 chose the other.

Before attempting to outline its emphases, I should stress that not only is the movement amorphous, but its boundaries are ill-defined. Doubtless many (I have no idea how many) of the thousand pastors at the Emergent Convention did not (at that time, anyway) consider themselves part of the

---

[2] For instance, tying the word to the early church, Arthur G. Patzia has written *The Emergence of the Church: Context, Growth, Leadership and Worship* (Downers Grove, IL: InterVarsity Press, 2001).

[3] I will provide bibliography as we go along.

emerging church: they were exploring, aligning themselves perhaps with some aspects of the movement but not with others. By contrast, one reason why the movement has mushroomed so quickly is that it is bringing to focus a lot of hazy perceptions already widely circulating in the culture. It is articulating crisply and polemically what many pastors and others were already beginning to think, even though they did not enjoy—until the leaders of this movement came along—any champions who put their amorphous malaise into perspective.

So it is not surprising that many books and articles that do not identify themselves as part of the emerging church movement nevertheless share its core values and thus belong to it without the label. One thinks, for instance, of Pete Ward's *Liquid Church*[4] or an essay by Graham Kings that analyzes evangelicalism in the Church of England.[5] Some months ago I was speaking to a group of several hundred pastors in Australia and used the emerging church movement in America as illustrative of something or other. None of the pastors to whom I was speaking had heard of the movement, but quite a number of them described churches near them that reflected exactly the same values. In Great Britain, churches of the Baptist Union used to emphasize "believing" before "belonging"—reflecting their historical roots in the believers' church tradition. But today the leaders of the Baptist Union encourage its member churches to reverse the priorities: first "belonging," then "believing." This parallels the priorities of the emerging church movement, even though the "emerging church" rubric has made only marginal headway on that side of the Atlantic.

From these diverse tendencies I infer that the emerging church movement is probably slightly smaller than some of its leaders think, and perhaps also substantially larger than some of its leaders think. Indeed, one

---

[4] Peabody, MA: Hendrickson, 2002.

[5] "Canal, River and Rapids: Contemporary Evangelicalism in the Church of England," *Anvil* 20 (2003): 167–84. In Kings's analysis, conservative evangelicals are like canals, with everything tamed and channeled; charismatics are like rapids, uncontrolled and dangerous. Guess which ones are like proper rivers?

perceptive observer has suggested that talk about "the emerging church" is already out of date, since the emerging church has already emerged.[6]

What Characterizes the Movement?

1. Protest

It is difficult to gain a full appreciation of the distinctives of the movement without listening attentively to the life-stories of its leaders. Many of them have come from conservative, traditional, evangelical churches, sometimes with a fundamentalist streak. Thus the reforms that the movement encourages mirror the protests of the lives of many of its leaders.

Probably the place to begin is a book of *Stories of Emergence*.[7] The book tells fifteen such stories, and the first interesting fact about this list is who is in it. Of course, many of the self-identified leaders of the emerging church movement are here, people such as the late Mike Yaconelli (the editor), Spencer Burke, and Brian McLaren. But the list also includes people who, though they may be sympathetic to the movement, would not think of themselves as part of it. Chuck Smith Jr., for instance, in some ways belongs to another generation and another movement. Frederica Mathewes-Green left a childhood in Roman Catholicism and young adulthood in feminism and Episcopalianism for the Orthodox Church; she is one of several exceptions in the book.

Most of these "stories of emergence" have in common a shared destination (namely, the emerging church movement) and a shared point of origin: traditional (and sometimes fundamentalist) evangelicalism. What all of these people have in common is that they began in one thing and "emerged" into something else. This gives the book a flavor of protest, of

---

[6] Rob Moll, "Has the Emergent Church Emerged?" published on LeadershipJournal.net, at http://www.christianitytoday.com/leaders/ newsletter/2003/cln31230.html. For samples of emerging church movement websites, see http://www.emergentYS.com and http://www.emergentvillage.com. Already, however, the sites are legion, and I will refer to a few of them later in this book.

[7] Mike Yaconelli, ed., *Stories of Emergence: Moving from Absolute to Authentic* (El Cajon, CA: emergentYS / Grand Rapids: Zondervan, 2003).

rejection: we were where you were once, but we emerged from it into something different. The subtitle of the book discloses what the editor sees as common ground: *Moving from Absolute to Authentic.*

Some examples may clarify what the book is trying to accomplish. Spencer Burke's account of his emergence is entitled "From the Third Floor to the Garage."[8] Burke used to sit in a plush third-floor office, serving as one of the pastors of Mariners Church in Irvine, California—"a bona fide megachurch with a 25-acre property and a $7.8 million budget."[9] Every weekend 4,500 adults use the facilities, and the church ministers to 10,000 people a week. But Burke became troubled by things such as parking lot ministry. ("Helping well-dressed families in SUVs find the next available parking space isn't my spiritual gift.")[10] He became equally disenchanted with three-point sermons and ten-step discipleship programs, not to mention the premillennial, pretribulational eschatology in which he had been trained.

After eighteen years of ministry, things began to come apart for Burke. Sensing his unrest, the senior pastor asked Burke to start a Saturday evening service in which he could "try new ideas and put a postmodern spin on the message."[11] At first this went well, and new folk started to attend. Nevertheless, he began to feel even more unsettled, partly because he still felt the services were "cross-wired" (some elements very modern, others very postmodern) and partly because he felt less and less connected to the rest of the church's program. So eventually he resigned "and drove home to my 700-square-foot beach shack. Five years later, here I sit"[12]—or more precisely, he often sits in its garage, which he converted to a makeshift office.

The half-decade of separation has enabled Burke to crystallize why he had to leave Mariners: "I've come to realize that my discontent was never with Mariners as a church, but contemporary Christianity as an institution."[13]

---

8 Ibid., 27–39.
9 Ibid., 28.
10 Ibid.
11 Ibid.
12 Ibid., 29.
13 Ibid.

Burke organizes the causes of his discontent under three headings. *First,* he has come to reject what he calls "spiritual McCarthyism."[14] Under this rubric he includes three things. He rejects the style of leadership that belongs to "a linear, analytical world"[15] with clear lines of authority and a pastor who is CEO. Spiritual McCarthyism, Burke asserts, is "what happens when the pastor-as-CEO model goes bad or when well-meaning people get too much power."[16] Similarly, he has "become increasingly concerned about the power certain evangelical personalities have over popular opinion." He writes, "Call me crazy, but it seems like many of my church friends live on every word that comes from the mouths of the evangelical leaders of the world more than on every word that proceeds from the mouth of God."[17] And finally, these authority structures are quick to brand anyone a "liberal" who questions the received tradition.

> Challenge an accepted belief or confess doubt and you're the equivalent of a card-carrying communist. Brows furrow. Eyes narrow. Lips purse. Want to earn a place on the Colorado Springs . . . er, I mean, Hollywood black list? Admit your uncertainty about homosexuality as a biblically condemned sin. Want to be branded as a traitor in your own church? Admit your ambivalence about a denomination-defining symbol such as baptism.[18]

History, Burke argues, has shown Christians to be wrong about many things: slavery, whether women could vote or own property, and much more. "Given a less-than-stellar track record, is it really so heretical to think that the evangelical church may be wrong about homosexuality as well? Isn't it wise to ask the what-if question from time to time, if for no other reason than to test our contemporary application of Scripture?"[19] Similarly for communion:

> Growing up I heard about the dangers of "drinking the cup in an unworthy manner"—how the Lord's Supper was only for professing Christians. The proof text, of course, was always 1 Corinthians 11:29: "For anyone who eats

---

[14] Ibid.
[15] Ibid.
[16] Ibid., 30.
[17] Ibid., 31.
[18] Ibid., 30.
[19] Ibid.

and drinks without recognizing the body of the Lord eats and drinks judgment on himself." Since most Christians assume that all humanity is doomed apart from Christ, just how much would taking the elements affect a so-called unbeliever's fate? Would they go to hell twice? Or might it be a powerful first experience with the story of Christ? In a subculture where Spiritual McCarthyism has taken hold, those aren't good questions to ask.[20]

"To me," writes Burke, "Spiritual McCarthyism is about idolatry—about finding righteousness in something other than Christ. Every time I put on a mask for the sake of my reputation and career, I'm guilty of a sin far more serious than not believing whatever I'm supposed to believe."[21] As Jesus challenged the religious establishment of his day, we must do the same. "Spiritual McCarthyism, meanwhile, promotes exactly the opposite. It encourages people to orchestrate their lives to avoid censure and minimize risk. In short, it teaches people to live in fear—to put up and shut up. Fear, intimidation, and control shouldn't be the defining hallmarks of Christianity."[22]

The *second* cause of Burke's discontent is what he calls "spiritual isolationism."[23] Under this heading he includes the pattern of many churches moving from the city to the suburbs. Sometimes this is done under the guise of needing more space. Nevertheless, he insists, there are other motives. "It's simpler for families to arrive at church without having to step over a drunk or watch drug deals go down in the alley. Let's be honest: church in the city can be messy. Dealing with a homeless man who wanders into the service shouting expletives or cleaning up vomit from the back steps is a long way from parsing Greek verbs in seminary."[24] Indeed, megachurches out in the suburbs sometimes construct entire on-campus worlds, complete with shops and gyms and aerobics centers.

Another form of "spiritual isolationism" in Burke's view is the kind of "separation" that does not do a number of things that most people do. In 1977 Burke moved from a conservative Baptist church to Berkeley, California, where he joined a Christian commune. He was stunned when the

---

[20] Ibid., 30–31.
[21] Ibid., 31.
[22] Ibid.
[23] Ibid., 32.
[24] Ibid.

man assigned to disciple him met him at a local eatery and ordered a beer. A year later, Burke was asked to photograph Chuck Colson, and he noticed a pipe on the dresser of Colson's hotel room. Questioned, Colson said he had been given it by the C. S. Lewis Foundation. "I was devastated," Burke writes. "In just one afternoon, I lost two pillars of the faith."[25] Eventually this sense of dislocation between the culture and evangelical expectations became too much for him—the more so since, even while he was at Mariners, Burke continued to inhabit the art world.

> It was so bizarre to sip wine at a gallery opening of my photography on Saturday night then slap on a suit and preach Sunday morning. When the gallery folks found out I was a pastor, they were stunned. Likewise, my friends at church struggled to understand the arts community I belonged to.... Both sides had cloistered themselves away for so long, they no longer had the words—or even the desire—to communicate with each other.[26]

The *third* cause of his discontent Burke labels "spiritual Darwinism"[27]—climbing up the ladder on the assumption that bigger is better. The zeal for growth easily fostered "a kind of program-envy.... Looking back, I spent a good part of the 1980s and '90s going from conference to conference learning how to ride high on someone else's success."[28] To shepherd a congregation was not enough; the aim was to have the fastest-growing congregation. "It was survival of the fittest with a thin spiritual veneer."[29]

While still serving as a pastor at Mariners, Burke went on a three-day silent retreat with author-priest Brennan Manning and was horrified to be told not to read any books during this time, not even the Bible. Despite his anger and confusion, however, Burke experienced something of an epiphany:

> And yet as I sat there fuming, a strange thing happened. I felt like I could see Jesus standing there asking to come and be with me. In my anger, I refused. I could barely even look at him. Still, there he stood. When I finally relented, he sat down next to me and gently wrapped his arms around me. He didn't say anything; he just held me in my pain.

---

[25] Ibid., 33.
[26] Ibid., 33–34.
[27] Ibid., 34.
[28] Ibid.
[29] Ibid., 35.

In that moment, I realized that God could handle severe honesty. Authenticity, in all its messiness, is not offensive to him. There is room for doubt and anger and confusion.

There was room for the real me.[30]

This experience led Burke into what he calls "The Search for Authentic Expression."[31] It also led him to newfound authors: Thomas Merton, Henri Nouwen, St. Teresa of Avila. The more he read of their works, the more he felt he should leave the professional ministry. Now, in his garage, he judges that he is still serving the church, but in a different way: "By choosing to live out the questions in my heart, I'm able to dialogue with people in a way I never have before. I no longer consider myself a tour guide. I'm a fellow traveler and, as Robert Frost said, 'That has made all the difference.'"[32]

In 1998 Burke started TheOoze.com. The name of the active chat room is designedly metaphorical: Burke intends this to be a place where "the various parts of the faith community are like mercury. At times we'll roll together; at times we'll roll apart. Try to touch the liquid or constrain it, and the substance will resist. Rather than force people to fall into line, an oozy community tolerates differences and treats people who hold opposing views with great dignity. To me, that's the essence of the *emerging* church."[33] For several years, TheOoze hosted "a learning party called Soularize," where members of the "online community" shared with each other—and in 2001 they went out on a limb and offered a Native American potlatch—i.e., "a spiritual ceremony of gift giving and grace giving"[34]—as part of the conference. "More and more, my heart is about creating safe places for leaders to ask questions and to learn from each other."[35]

Obviously it would be rather time-consuming to devote as much space to the other contributors to *Stories of Emergence*. Nevertheless, it is vital to observe what these stories have in common and yet how divergent they are. The editor, Mike Yaconelli, sets the stage with an introduction that is his

---

[30] Ibid.
[31] Ibid., 36.
[32] Ibid.
[33] Ibid., 36–37.
[34] Ibid., 37.
[35] Ibid., 38.

own story, which he entitles "The Illegitimate Church."[36] "I've never lost my love" for the "Church with a capital C," he writes, but as far as the institutional church is concerned, he has been "appalled, embarrassed, depressed, angry, frustrated, and grieved" because of it.[37] When he was pastor of a church, he was told he wasn't really a pastor: he had no seminary degree, he had been kicked out of two Bible colleges, and the congregation was shrinking. He longed for rest, for a God "for whom friendship was enough, a God who was happy to be with me. I just wanted God to like me and to believe I was a legitimate minister of the gospel."[38]By the age of fifty he was tired and frustrated. In desperation, after reading a book by Henri Nouwen,[39] he spent time in a community called "L'Arche"—and found himself at home.

> I realized the modern-institutional-denominational church was permeated by values that are contradictory to the Church of Scripture. The very secular humanism the institutional church criticized pervaded the church structure, language, methodology, process, priorities, values, and vision. The "legitimate" church, the one that had convinced me of my illegitimacy, was becoming the illegitimate church, fully embracing the values of modernity.[40]

Those values include efficiency, pretending, doing. Returning to his church, which, he writes, was still tiny but had been transformed, he began to see things change. Instead of "editing" their services, members read publicly what they like, and others interrupted the sermon to ask questions, while someone else might suggest a better illustration to end the sermon. They didn't talk about sin much any more—perhaps twice in twelve years since L'Arche, Yaconelli writes—not because they did not believe in sin, but because they already knew all about sin and addiction to sin, and what they needed now was grace: "We don't have to talk about sin. It's a given. What we're all longing for is good news."[41] And no longer did they talk in propo-

---

[36] Ibid., 12–22.
[37] Ibid., 14.
[38] Ibid., 16.
[39] *In the Name of Jesus* (New York: Crossroad, 1993).
[40] Ibid.
[41] Ibid., 18.

sitions: they told stories, not least stories that admitted their own failures, and stories that disclosed their interaction with God.

Ultimately these stories "are not about what happened. They're about what's going on inside us. They're about the deep hiding places in us that show up and reveal not only us, but God's fingerprints on our lives."[42] And the stories are "always unfinished, partial, under construction, never over."[43] Stories, after all, are easy to remember; more importantly, they are "the most effective way to combine complicated and difficult-to-explain truth into simple, understandable bites of reality we can grasp."[44] These Christians saw the gospel as story and believed "quite simply that Church is the place where we share our stories. Are these the stories of the emerging postmodern church? I hope not. I hope, instead, they are the stories of an increasing number of people who are trying to be the Church at this moment knowing full well that the next moment the Church may look very different."[45]

Todd Hunter[46] was formerly the director of Vineyard USA, working with young Christian leaders, especially church planters. He began to notice that the questions being asked by unbelievers were changing: "Is there truth?" "How can one know it given our human fallibilities?" "How certain can we be about truth?" "Is all truth inherently good?" "Are there ways of knowing truth beside the absolutist, foundationalist ways we were taught? If so, what does this mean for apologetics, theology, and church history?"[47]

Hunter left the Vineyard in 2000 to plant a new church for postmoderns. "Postmodernism," he writes, "has made me into a postreductionist."[48] Influenced by Stanley J. Grenz and John R. Franke,[49] he has come to see how important it is not to live in the wrong story. All of us live in some

---

[42] Ibid., 20.

[43] Ibid.

[44] Ibid., 21.

[45] Ibid., 21–22.

[46] "Entering the Conversation," 40–54.

[47] Ibid., 43.

[48] Ibid., 46.

[49] *Beyond Foundationalism: Shaping Theology in a Postmodern Context* (Louisville: Westminster John Knox Press, 2000).

sense of story or other, and the most important thing is to live in God's story, the story-line of the Bible itself.

> [T]he gospel of the Kingdom invites us into a large, all-encompassing story; the stories of Adam and Eve, Israel, and the church were always intended to be lived in. Living there is a huge privilege. Choosing to live outside God's story has serious ramifications (a wasted life and hell come immediately to mind).[50]

In other words, Hunter wants to avoid the "say-a-prayer-so-that-when-you-die-you-can-go-to-heaven" reductionism.[51] He does not view himself as having arrived at an entirely new position, but as "touching down gently on the way to a proper landing,"[52] and in this context he doesn't want to be either "a faddish embracer of postmodernity or an unthinking critic of modernity."[53] He does not want to abandon the truth-claims of the gospel, but sees himself as a critical realist: a realist, because he insists there is reality outside human speech (i.e., words can have extra-textual referentiality; they can refer to something outside the speech act itself), but a critical realist, because "the only access we have to this reality lies along the spiraling path of the knower and the thing known."[54]

More rapidly: As a youth pastor, Tony Jones moved from a program mentality toward a pattern of ministry that focuses on pastoral care, theological reflection, contemplative prayer, and intergenerational community.[55] The influences that moved him in this direction were Nancey Murphy's teaching on postmodern theology at Fuller Seminary, some exposure to Lakota culture, and in the late 1990s, involvement with a group then called Young Leaders Network (now Emergent).

Chris Seay asserts that his grandfather was a 1950s revivalist and his father "a Swindoll-esque pastor."[56] Rebelling against the form but not, he

---

[50] "Entering the Conversation," 48.

[51] Ibid., 49.

[52] Ibid., 50.

[53] Ibid.

[54] Ibid., 53.

[55] "Toward a Missional Ministry," 56–72.

[56] "I Have Inherited the Faith of My Fathers," 74–84, esp. 77.

says, the substance ("The essentials [as stated in the Apostle's Creed] haven't changed"),[57] and against his first pastoral responsibility ("the meanest people you'll find outside of hell"),[58] and discovering "the beautiful objections to modernity articulated by a few French philosophers and the philosophy of generational characteristics,"[59] not to mention the writings of Stanley Hauerwas—Seay established University Baptist Church in Waco, Texas. He sees his role as "pastor as storyteller":

> Modern ... attempts to tie each passage off neatly into propositional statements that capture truth are backfiring and emerging generations see through the charade of our modern forms of exegesis. We are not simply autonomous knowers given the ability to decipher truth for others. Jesus understood that it's not only the truth that changes us, but also the *journey* of seeking truth.[60]

This is especially so, Seay says, because the world is "reembracing eastern thought like that of the Hebrews,"[61] which was given to storytelling, as Jesus' example shows us. In the past, Western Christianity held that knowledge is power: "salvation is most often assessed by one's ability to regurgitate the propositions about Christ and faith. In theological terms this is called metanoia, the cognitive switch that turns in our head ushering us into salvation."[62] The gospel became a set of propositions. But the real gospel is "everything—the whole story of God for whole people."[63] Moreover, we need less linear thinking and more circular thinking along the "Hebraic" model of Ecclesiastes—and more Web-style thinking, which works by association.

> The Web-oriented thinking style is connected, but with no predictable pattern. Like the book of Proverbs, it's a lesson in random or chaos thinking. We often describe people that think and speak this way as chasing rabbits or joke

---

[57] Ibid., 77.
[58] Ibid.
[59] Ibid.
[60] Ibid., 79.
[61] Ibid.
[62] Ibid., 80.
[63] Ibid., 81.

that they have attention deficit disorder. Thinking in nonlinear patterns is not dysfunctional. Visualize the way you surf the Web, and you'll see this thinking pattern. Each page that you see offers numerous options as does each succeeding page. Then imagine browsing the Internet in a linear format that offers one choice on each page. It would be an underwhelming experience. This is what many Web-oriented thinkers experience in our churches, sheer boredom with no intellectual or spiritual challenge. Isn't the essence of the gospel about bending, becoming all things to all people? This is an area that will require an immediate change in the emerging church. Please, consider the ways you communicate and the reasons your stories fail to connect.[64]

In 1999, Seay began Ecclesia, a church in the arts district of Houston. He concludes:

My own journey has brought me from the trappings of Baptist revivalism to a spiritual center in the arts district. I'm on the move, but, unlike Abraham, God has blessed me with the wisdom and encouragement of my fellow travelers. Emergent is a gathering of wanderers. We are searching for a home in an age of rapid transition. It's possible that a set of ideals will not ever bring us stability. Instead that assurance seems to be rooted in community, love, and relationship. Imagine that! A reformation built around mission and relationship instead of thoughts, systems, and ideals.

Thank you, Emergent.[65]

The stories I have summarized so far are in the section of Yaconelli's book called "Stories of Ministry Crisis." The two other sections are "Stories of Worldview Crisis" and "Stories of Faith Crisis." I heartily urge anyone who wants to understand the emerging church movement to read the book right through. Although there are protests against feminism (Frederica Mathewes-Green),[66] Lutheranism (Gregory R. Baum),[67] and Communism (Parush R. Parushev),[68] the dominant protest in these stories is against culturally conservative forms of evangelicalism.

---

[64] Ibid., 82.
[65] Ibid., 84.
[66] "Twice Liberated: A Personal Journey through Feminism," 132–45.
[67] "Emerging from the Water," 192–203.
[68] "Faith that Matters in a Culture of Ghosts," 204–18.

This sense of protest is similarly clear in the book by Dave Tomlinson, *The Post-Evangelical*, published a few years ago in Britain and now available in America.[69] Some of the protest is against evangelicalism's perceived failure to interact with other traditions, and against the middle-class conservatism with which it is often allied. But the heart of Tomlinson's thesis is that the post-evangelicals are shaped by a different culture from that which helped to shape evangelicalism. This is the shift from modernism to postmodernism. Evangelicals think about the integrity and credibility of their faith in the culture of modernism; post-evangelicals think about the integrity and credibility of their faith in the culture of postmodernism.

Tomlinson's personal move was from the Brethren Church through Pentecostalism to the house church movement (very large in England) to his present focus on post-evangelicalism. In his case, this includes Tuesday night meetings of a rather different form of church: the lounge bar of a South London pub, named Holy Joe's. The atmosphere is relaxed: people can drink or smoke, participate as much or as little as they like in the worship evenings—which place a high value on contemplation, candle, symbols, ambient music—and if they don't like it, they can move off to the main bar. There are also many Bible study evenings. Tomlinson is quick to add that Holy Joe's, although it is meeting a need that many churches have not addressed, is not necessarily the way ahead for post-evangelicals, merely an example of how one particular group of post-evangelicals is working out their faith communally.

That thought gives us a segue to a second dominant characteristic of the emerging church movement.

2. Protest against Modernism

The difficulty in describing the emerging church movement as a protest against modernism is partly one of definition: neither modernism nor postmodernism is easy to define. Even experts in intellectual history disagree on their definitions.

One important though minority view is that "postmodernism" is not a useful label at all because the phenomena that go by that name are nothing

---

[69] London: SPCK, 1995; North American edition: El Cajon, CA: emergentYS / Grand Rapids: Zondervan, 2003.

other than the fruit of late modernism.[70] In part I agree with this, because it is difficult to imagine postmodernism without modernism. Postmodernism begins with many of the assumptions of modernism (as I will show a little later), but heads off in a different direction. Reacting against the worst evils of modernism, it turns around and devours its parent, refusing to recognize its own origins.[71] Moreover, both modernism and postmodernism are far too stereotyped in a lot of popular discussion; *reductionism* is the name of the game. By showing the common threads of development, the worst reductionisms are avoided. Nevertheless, the changes that have taken place in Western culture during the last half-century are both complex and significant. Are they better summarized with the label "postmodernism" or with the label "late modernism"? In terms of understanding the organic development, I suppose "late modernism" is the better term, while in terms of understanding the changes in epistemology in the popular culture, "postmodernism" is preferable—and of course both are open to the charge of being confusingly reductionistic, as we shall see.

Another group of people use the label "postmodern" to focus on some axis or other of culture that has exploded in rampant growth. For Andy Crouch, a nonemerging Christian, postmodern culture is rampant consumerism, fed both by greed and the ideal of uncontrolled individualism: we can entertain ourselves as we like, buy what we like, and choose as we like, and the ideal is having enough money to satisfy our most esoteric whims. In his analysis, this postmodernism is an extension of modernism: postmodernism is "ultramodernism." But the same consumerist mental-

---

[70] See, for example, Thomas C. Oden, *After Modernity ... What? Agenda for Theology* (Grand Rapids: Zondervan, 1990); Michael Horton's chapter, "Better Homes & Gardens," in *The Church in Emerging Culture: Five Perspectives,* ed. Leonard Sweet (El Cajon, CA: emergentYS / Grand Rapids: Zondervan, 2003), 105–38; and especially the elegant discussion of Harold Netland, *Encountering Religious Pluralism: The Challenge to Christian Faith and Mission* (Downers Grove, IL: InterVarsity Press, 2001), esp. 55–91.

[71] That is why I elsewhere call postmodernism the bastard child of modernism: the genetic descent can scarcely be denied, but from the perspective of the parent this child is illegitimate. For full discussion, see my *The Gagging of God* (Grand Rapids: Zondervan, 1996).

ity that inspires the Vehicle Assembly Building at Cape Canaveral inspires the Mall of America in Bloomington, Minnesota.[72] A certain kind of sacramentalism, Crouch argues, is urgently needed: baptism "offers the only way into true postindividualism, the Eucharist offers the only way into true postconsumerism."[73]

The majority view, however, is that the fundamental issue in the move from modernism to postmodernism is *epistemology*—i.e., how we know things, or think we know things. Modernism is often pictured as pursuing truth, absolutism, linear thinking, rationalism, certainty, the cerebral as opposed to the affective—which in turn breeds arrogance, inflexibility, a lust to be right, the desire to control. Postmodernism, by contrast, recognizes how much of what we "know" is shaped by the culture in which we live, is controlled by emotions and aesthetics and heritage, and in fact can only be intelligently held as part of a common tradition, without overbearing claims to being true or right. Modernism tries to find unquestioned foundations on which to build the edifice of knowledge and then proceeds with methodological rigor; postmodernism denies that such foundations exist (it is "antifoundational") and insists that we come to "know" things in many ways, not a few of them lacking in rigor. Modernism is hard-edged and, in the domain of religion, focuses on truth versus error, right belief, confessionalism; postmodernism is gentle and, in the domain of religion, focuses on relationships, love, shared tradition, integrity in discussion. In my view, it is this epistemological contrast between the modern and the postmodern that is most usefully explored, as it touches so many other things, and I will return to it in the fourth and fifth chapters of this book.

How then do those who identify with the emerging church movement think about these matters? Although some would agree with Crouch in seeing consumerism as a major evil of our age, they would not call that

---

[72] See, for example, Crouch's essay "Life After Postmodernity," in Sweet, *The Church in Emerging Culture: Five Perspectives*, 62–95.

[73] Ibid., 82. This is because those who are baptized belong to another, and thus cannot pander to individualism, while all who participate in the Eucharist "get the same portion" (p. 83): there is no hierarchy of money, buying power, or self-idolatry.

"postmodern," as he does. The majority of emerging church leaders see a very clear contrast between modern culture and postmodern culture and connect the divide to questions of epistemology. Some (as the testimonies I've related suggest) think that we are in a postmodern culture and therefore ought to be constructing postmodern churches. A few acknowledge that not everything in postmodernism is admirable and therefore want to maintain some sort of prophetic witness against postmodernism at various points while eagerly embracing the features of postmodernism that they perceive as admirable.

Brian McLaren, probably the most articulate speaker in the emerging movement, has emphasized, in both books and addresses, that postmodernism is not antimodernism. By this he means that in many ways modernism is not dead, and the prefix "post" means "flowing on from or coming after."[74] Properly understood, "the term [post-] suggests continuity as well as discontinuity: A postpubescent adolescent, for example, still occupies the same name, lives in the same family, carries on the same story, and is at heart the same person as the prepubescent and pubescent boy. A postgraduate student similarly doesn't become anti-intellectual."[75] (Frankly, I find McLaren's discussion a bit confusing, because it jumps categories.)[76]

---

[74] See, for instance, his substantive response to Crouch's essay in Sweet, *The Church in Emerging Culture: Five Perspectives*, 66.

[75] Ibid.

[76] The prefix "post-" simply means (according to the unabridged Webster's) "(a) *after in time, later, following,* as in *post*graduate, *post*glacial; (b) *after in space, behind,* as in *post*axial." True, "postglacial" does not mean "antiglacial," but since it comes *after* the glacial period, it refers to a period that can no longer be called "glacial." Similarly, a "postgraduate" is no longer an undergraduate: the individual has gone beyond graduation. To say that he is nevertheless not now an anti-intellectual is to introduce irrelevancies to the expression, in precisely the same way that postglacial neither affirms nor denies that the percentage of oxygen in the atmosphere in both the glacial and the postglacial periods may be the same. A prepubescent, pubescent, and postpubescent lad doubtless still belongs to the same family and "carries on the same story," but that is irrelevant to the expression, which focuses on pubescence—and there is nothing in the expression

The telling point for McLaren and most of the other leaders of the emerging church movement is their emphasis on the discontinuity as over against the continuity with modernism. When McLaren speaks through the lips of Neo, the postmodern Christian protagonist of his two best-known books, he can use "post-" as a universal category to highlight what he does *not* like: "In the postmodern world, we become postconquest, postmechanistic, postanalytical, postsecular, postobjective, postcritical, postorganizational, postindividualistic, post-Protestant, and postconsumerist."[77] A rapid reading of those books shows how much what McLaren thinks "a new kind of Christian" *should* be like today is determined by all the *new things* he believes are bound up with postmodernism: hence "a new kind of Christian."

For almost everyone within the movement, this works out in an emphasis on feelings and affections over against linear thought and rationality; on experience over against truth; on inclusion over against exclusion; on participation over against individualism and the heroic loner. For some (as in the subtitle of Yaconelli's book), this means a move from the absolute to the authentic. It means taking into account contemporary emphases on tolerance; it means not telling others they are wrong. It underscores the

---

itself that hints at the degree of continuity or discontinuity of characteristics *outside* the semantic domain of the expression. Thus "postmodern" refers to something after the period of the modern. To say that continuities persist in the broader stream of culture is to assert a mere truism—but they do not persist in the shift from whatever it is that constitutes "modernism" to whatever it is that constitutes "postmodernism," or else we cannot usefully say that we have arrived at *post*modernism. In other words, for a term like postgraduate McLaren jumps outside the "graduate" category to deny an intellectual/anti-intellectual antithesis, but with postmodern he wants to insist that there are continuities between modernism and postmodernism in the "modern" domain itself. But of course, if language means anything, insofar as modernism persists, we are *not* in a postmodern situation; conversely, if it is true that we live in postmodern times, then we no longer live in modern times.

[77] Brian D. McLaren, *A New Kind of Christian: A Tale of Two Friends on a Spiritual Journey* (San Francisco: Jossey-Bass, 2001), 19. The successor to this book is *The Story We Find Ourselves In: Further Adventures of a New Kind of Christian* (San Francisco: Jossey-Bass, 2003).

importance of narrative—both life-narrative (as believers and unbelievers alike tell their stories) and in Bible study and preaching.[78]

Yet in some quarters of the emerging church movement the argument has moved beyond debates about epistemology to debates about social history. In a workshop called "Pluralism Revisited," presented at the 2004 Emergent Convention in Nashville,[79] McLaren says he has changed: he has come to think that social history is more important than intellectual history. At the end of World War II, many European thinkers, mired in the debris of war, began to ask penetrating questions about modernity, about the Enlightenment that had spawned modernity. Once these questions were put on the table, they could not be limited to the Holocaust or the barbarities of Stalin. They asked, Who gave Europeans the right to conquer and possess Africa, North America, South America? What gives us the right to destroy the earth to satisfy our greed?

Their conclusion (which McLaren thinks is accurate, though incomplete) was that the common element was an abounding confidence, grounded in their metanarratives (their "big stories" that constrained their interpretation of all their little stories). In the United States, confidence was grounded in a conviction of white supremacy and visions of manifest destiny. In keeping with that, McLaren says, the confidence of Christianity and the confidence of colonialism were intertwined.

Regardless of the cogency or otherwise of this analysis, what must be recognized is that many sophisticated treatments of epistemology include discussion of social history as part of the necessary framework of intellectual history. One cannot escape the primacy of epistemology in the turn to the postmodern. Social history exposes part of the challenge, but social history itself raises (as far as its bearing on postmodernism is concerned) essentially epistemological questions.

Much of McLaren's aim in his writing and lecturing is to explode the certainties that he feels have controlled too much of the thinking of West-

---

[78] See, for example, Walter Wangerin Jr., "Making Disciples by Sacred Story," *Christianity Today* 48/2 (February 2004), 66–69.

[79] I was unable to attend, but a colleague kindly sent me a CD of the workshop. Copies of the CD based on this workshop at the Emergent Convention 2004 are available from PSI, Inc. at 1-800-808-8273.

ern Christian people in the past. His discussion, in other words, is in the domain of epistemology, whether he accesses that domain through social history or some other route. But there is a danger in constantly exploding the certainties of the past: if we are not careful, we may be left with nothing to hang on to at all. Recognizing the danger, McLaren in this lecture takes the next step by providing us with two definitions that control his ensuing discussion (and these definitions keep recurring in his writing).

The first of his definitions is of *pluralism*. He does not focus on *empirical pluralism*, which simply describes the diversity that is actually here, diversity approved by God in the vision of Revelation 5: the people redeemed by Christ are drawn from "every tribe and language and people and nation" (5:9; cf. also the Day of Pentecost). Rather, he focuses on *philosophical pluralism*, the stance that asserts that no single outlook can be the explanatory system or view of reality that accounts for all of life. Even if we Christians think we have it, we must immediately face the diversities among us: are we talking about Baptist views of reality? Presbyterian? Anglican? And which Baptist? Philosophical pluralism denies that any system offers a complete explanation.

The second definition is of *relativism*. At one time relativism had primary influence in the field of aesthetics: it was the theory of aesthetics that denied absolutism and insisted that aesthetics is *relative* to the people holding particular stances regarding what constitutes beauty. Nowadays, relativism dominates the fields of religion and morality as well. It is the theory that denies absolutism and insists that morality and religion are *relative* to the people who embrace them. Lest Christians think none of this applies to them, McLaren draws attention to the ethnic cleansing of the Old Testament, to David's many wives, to injunctions against wearing gold rings.

If both philosophical pluralism and relativism are given free play, McLaren asserts, it is difficult to see how one can be faithful to the Bible. Yet absolutism cannot be allowed to rule: the criticism of absolutism is too devastating, too convincing, to permit it to stand. So McLaren puts forth his solution: "emergent thinking," better known, perhaps, as integral thinking.[80] McLaren uses a number of illustrations, some better than others. A

---

[80] Here McLaren is leaning on Ken Wilber, *The Marriage of Sense and Soul: Integrating Science and Religion* (New York: Broadway Books, 1998).

tree does not simply grow up, but adds a layer at a time, and the accumulation of layers is what enables it to grow. Each layer embraces everything that went before. It is a bit like learning to read. The ability *emerges*, embracing the old and moving on by acquiring the new.

So perhaps a culture plagued by absolutism needs a dose of relativism to correct what is wrong with it—not so much a relativism that utterly displaces what came before, but a relativism that in some sense embraces what came before, yet moves on. If absolutism is the cancer, it needs relativism as the chemotherapy. Even though this chemotherapy is dangerous in itself, it is the necessary solution. So our culture has become post-colonial, postmodern, post-totalitarian. How then shall we think of the gospel in a post-colonial, postmodern, post-totalitarian way?

It is no solution, McLaren asserts, to propose a "metanarrative," the Christian metanarrative, because even if there is a sense in which we want to invite people into the Bible's story line, in a postmodern world the word "metanarrative" has all the associations of "propaganda." For postmoderns, it smacks of absolutism. So how shall we approach this challenge?

McLaren comes back to the central issues that are more typically his central concerns—the destruction of the absolutism that he finds endemic to a lot of old-fashioned Western confessionalism—and he returns to the topic by coming through a side door. He asks us to answer two questions. First, were the Muslims wrong to destroy the Buddha shrines in Afghanistan? Most of us would answer yes. Second, were they wrong to do so in Jesus' name? If we say yes—i.e., if we say that our belief in Jesus contributes to the conclusion that the destruction was wrong—then are we not tacitly admitting that Christianity is not the total explanation of reality? Moreover, Christianity has its own horrible barbarities to account for: McLaren reminds us of the grievous sins against the native peoples of the Americas, whether conquests by Juan Pizarro and other Spanish conquistadors or the wretched events described in *Bury My Heart at Wounded Knee*.[81] From this line of reasoning, McLaren affirms that absolutism is simply not the answer.

So where to go? If absolutism is not the answer and absolute relativism is not the answer, what is the Christian way ahead? Here McLaren finds himself heavily indebted to the short work by Jonathan Wilson, *Living Faith-*

---

[81] By Dee Alexander Brown (New York: Henry Holt & Co., 1971).

fully in a Fragmented World: Lessons for the Church from MacIntyre's After Virtue,[82] a book which, as its subtitle suggests, owes a great deal to the ideas of philosopher Alasdair MacIntyre.[83] This is surely what we want: we want to learn to live faithfully in a fragmented world. Absolutism plays by one set of rules. *Real* pluralism is like a large field where many games are being played, each game observing its own rules. This sort of pluralism is coherent. But we live in a *fragmented* world: we are playing golf with a baseball, baseball with a soccer ball, and so forth. This is not *real* pluralism; it is fragmented existence.

Doubtless a few small, coherent, communities exist—Hasidic Jews, perhaps, or the Amish—who manage to play by one set of rules, but the rest of us are mired in fragmentation. As a result, there is no coherence, no agreement on where we are going, no *telos,* no goal. Our accounts of what we are doing maintain the lingering use of the older absolutist language, while we find ourselves, not in genuine pluralism, but in fragmentation. In North America we have a memory of absolutist totalitarian Christianity and experience fragmentation. So our choice is whether to go back to this absolutist heritage or forward to something else. Can we weave a fabric that is not totalitarian and absolutist but avoids absolute relativism? The former returns us to the barbarities and is unconvincing in a postmodern age; the latter simply leaves us open to the marketers, for there is no coherent defense against them.

The way ahead, McLaren suggests, is very helpfully set out in a large book by David J. Bosch.[84] Toward the end of the book, Bosch lists eight perspectives that speak to our situation and give us some direction:

(1) Accept co-existence with different faiths gladly, not begrudgingly. It is not their fault if they are alive.

(2) Dialogue presupposes commitment to one's position, so it is surely not a bad thing to listen well. Dialogue should be congruent with confidence in the gospel.

---

[82] New York: Morehouse Publishing, 1998.

[83] *After Virtue: A Study in Moral Theory*, 2nd ed. (Notre Dame, IN: University of Notre Dame, 1984 [1981]).

[84] *Transforming Mission: Paradigm Shifts in Theology of Mission* (Maryknoll, NY: Orbis, 1991).

(3) We assume that the dialogue takes place in the presence of God, the unseen Presence. In such dialogue we may learn things, as Peter does in Acts 10–11. Similarly, Jesus learns from his interchange with the Syrophoenician woman.

(4) Missional dialogue requires humility and vulnerability. But that should not frighten us, for when we are weak, we are strong. It is surely right, for instance, to acknowledge earlier atrocities committed by Christians, even as we remain careful not to diss those earlier Christians.

(5) Each religion operates in its own world and therefore demands different responses from Christians.

(6) Christian witness does not preclude dialogue.

(7) The "old, old story" may not be the true, true story, for we continue to grow, and even our discussion and dialogues contribute to such growth. In other words, the questions raised by postmodernism help us to grow.

(8) Live with the paradox: we know no way of salvation apart from Jesus Christ, but we do not prejudge what God may do with others. We must simply live with the tension.

McLaren ended his lecture by asserting that conservatives complain that liberals are relativistic and liberals complain that conservatives are absolutist. But history teaches us that if we give either party its head, we are in a great deal of trouble. In any case, the way ahead is with neither extreme, but with a *reasonable* confidence.

A brief question-and-answer period followed McLaren's workshop. Two of the questions are worth reporting here: (1) **Q:** Our culture largely associates intolerance with absolutism, and tolerance with relativism. Is there a better way ahead? **A:** McLaren thinks that the best treatment of this difficult question is that found in the book by Miroslav Volf, *Exclusion and Embrace.*[85] (2) **Q:** How are we to respond to the issue of homosexuality? **A:** McLaren asserts that there is no good position, because all positions

---

[85] I have myself warmly commended Volf's book, even though I take issue with him here and there: cf. D. A. Carson, *Love in Hard Places* (Wheaton, IL: Crossway, 2002).

hurt someone, and that is always bad. Moreover, homosexuality may be seventy-five different things. By way of analogy, consider schizophrenia, which, though it is a complex and not uncommon disease, is not mentioned in the Bible. The closest thing to it in the Bible, phenomenologically, is demon-possession. But are we prepared to say that every instance of schizophrenia should be labeled demon-possession, so as to preserve biblical categories? Similarly, contemporary homosexuality is a complex phenomenon, and it is not entirely clear that what we mean by homosexuality in any particular instance entirely lines up with what the Bible says about homosexuality. McLaren insists that by such cautions he is *not* making a judgment on homosexuality itself, one way or another, but on how to treat people.

I have taken this much space to summarize one of McLaren's recent workshops, partly because most sides would agree that McLaren is the emerging church's most influential thinker (or, at the very least, one of them) and partly because this workshop shows something else, something somewhat more innovative among emerging thinkers. I am not referring to McLaren's handling of social history and the social construction of knowledge: that is not particularly innovative, even though it is a reasonable popularization of what others in the field have written. Rather, while most leaders of the emergent movement set up a relatively simple antithesis—namely, modernism is bad and postmodernism is good—McLaren is careful in this piece to avoid the obvious trap: many forms of postmodern thought do in fact lead to some kind of religious relativism, and McLaren knows that for the Christian that is not an option. He clearly wants to steer a course between absolutism and relativism, and he is more careful on this point than some of his peers.

Nevertheless, for McLaren, absolutism is associated with modernism, so that every evaluation he offers on that side of the challenge is negative. Indeed, it is difficult to think of a single passage in any of the writings of the emergent leaders that I have read that offers a positive evaluation of any element of substance in modernism. But McLaren does not connect relativism with postmodernism. He appears to think of relativism as something more extreme (perhaps postmodernism gone to seed?), while postmodernism itself becomes the uncritiqued matrix in which we must work out our theology. So while he dismisses absolute religious relativism (it cannot be said that he critiques it; rather, he recognizes that as a Christian he cannot finally go down that avenue), I have not yet seen from McLaren, or anyone else in the emerging church movement, a critique of any substantive element of postmodern thought. At this juncture I write with neither praise nor blame: I am merely trying to portray the thought of the emerging church movement as accurately as I can.

3. Protesting on Three Fronts

As we have seen, the emerging church movement is characterized by a fair bit of protest against traditional evangelicalism and, more broadly, against all that it understands by modernism. But some of its proponents add another front of protest—namely, the seeker-sensitive church, the megachurch. Sometimes these three protests are hard to disentangle, but this third element carries special interest.

The degree to which this element stands out varies considerably. It is certainly present, for instance, in the construction of Dan Kimball.[86] His recent book is praised by not a few pastors in the seeker-sensitive tradition,[87] doubtless because Kimball casts his work, in part, as the way forward to reach a new generation of people who have moved on, generationally and culturally, from the kinds of people who grabbed the attention of the seeker-sensitive movement three decades ago. Although there are differences, the emerging church leaders, like the seeker-sensitive leaders in their time, are motivated, in part, by a desire to reach people who do not seem to be attracted to traditional approaches and stances—and the seeker-sensitive movement is now old enough to be one of the "traditional" approaches. Pastors in the seeker-sensitive tradition, then, tend to see in the emerging church leaders a new generation of Christians doing the sort of thing that they themselves did a generation earlier.

Kimball's book sets out how to go after the post-seeker-sensitive generation. Much of his material goes over common ground. He offers a kind

---

[86] *The Emerging Church: Vintage Christianity for New Generations* (El Cajon, CA: emergentYS / Grand Rapids: Zondervan, 2003).

[87] E.g., John Ortberg, formerly of Willow Creek, and Rick Warren of Saddleback.

of popular profile of what he thinks postmodernism embraces:[88] it accepts pluralism, embraces the experiential, delights in the mystical, and is comfortable with narrative, with what is fluid, global, communal/tribal, and so forth. Kimball then turns to how we should go about things rather differently. This includes an appendix on post-seeker-sensitive worship. Here we must have much more symbolism and a greater stress on the visual. We should have crosses and candles. There might be an entire communion service without a sermon. The entire geography of the room may be different, with the possibility of different groups within the assembly engaging in different things at a time, and perhaps someone going off for a while to a quiet desk for a bit of journaling. The entire experience should be multisensory; the prayer corner may well burn incense. "Worship in the emerging church," Kimball writes, "is less about looking out for what is on the cutting edge and more about moving back into our spiritual center with Jesus as our sole focus."[89]

Kimball offers us antithetical visions of modern preaching and postmodern preaching.[90] In modern preaching, the sermon is the focal point of the service, and the preacher serves as the dispenser of biblical truths to help solve personal problems in modern life. Sermons emphasize explanation—i.e., explanation of what the truth is. The starting point is the Judeo-Christian worldview, and biblical terms like "gospel" and "Armageddon" do not need definition. The biblical text is communicated primarily with words, and this preaching takes place within the church building during a worship service.

By contrast, Kimball writes, in the (postmodern) emerging church movement, the sermon is only one part of the experience of the worship gathering. Here the preacher teaches how the ancient wisdom applies to kingdom living; the preacher emphasizes and explains the experience of who the truth is. The starting point is the garden of Eden and the retelling of the story of creation and of the origins of human beings and of sin (cf.

---

88 See, for instance, his chart in *The Emerging Church,* 61.
89 Ibid., 169.
90 See especially his chart, ibid., 175. Many of the clauses in the following lines come from Kimball's book.

Acts 17:22–34). Biblical terms like "gospel" and "Armageddon" need to be "deconstructed and redefined." The scriptural message is communicated through a mix of words, visual arts, silence, testimony, and story, and the preacher is a motivator who encourages people to learn from the Scriptures throughout the week. A lot of preaching takes place outside the church building in the context of community and relationships. Such preaching will be deeply theocentric rather than anthropocentric, and care should be taken not to insult people's intelligence.

What cannot be overlooked in Kimball's book, I think, is how much of his analysis is specifically directed against churches in the seeker-sensitive tradition. For example, some of his suggestions—such as insistence that sermons should be theocentric and not anthropocentric, that they should not insult the intelligence of the hearers, that instruction in the Word should go on throughout the week and not be confined to public services on Sunday, and that we should aim for kingdom living—one could as easily find in Reformed exhortations, perhaps in the pages of a magazine such as *Modern Reformation*.

Other parts of Kimball's advice, of course, could not similarly be aligned. Yet the fact that so much of what he has to say *can* be aligned with many serious (and not just Reformed) voices within traditional evangelicalism suggests that most of the time the "implied reader" of his book is not the more traditional evangelical church, but seeker-sensitive churches. In Kimball's view, they, too, are out of step with the culture and fall under the curse of modernism. Moreover, it must be said that if, as we have seen, several of Kimball's individual suggestions as to the way ahead are reminiscent of stances taken within parts of traditional evangelicalism, the structure of his thought, taken as a whole, is distinctively postmodern.

This business of protesting on more than one front at the same time is very clearly seen in a document prepared by a church in the Chicago area that wishes to align itself with the emerging church movement. In its search for a "lead pastor" (no one in the emerging church movement refers to a "senior pastor"), the church authorized a "Forward Development Team" to develop a long-term proposal for the church, along with guidelines for the hiring of any new pastoral staff. The three purposes of the church became three Cs: celebrating, connecting, and coaching. The lead pastor should have a clear understanding of the emerging church culture, and experience of it.

The document includes pertinent quotations from Dan Kimball (whose work I have just abbreviated) and other authors[91] and admirably sets forth the goal of reaching the completely unchurched. But for our purposes, it is the threefold typology of the document that captures our interest at this point. The document distinguishes traditional evangelicals, pragmatic evangelicals, and emerging evangelicals.

—The traditional evangelicals are "Mostly traditional and 'modern' in their thinking and approach to ministry, including traditional Biblical exposition, hymns, and some more contemporary music"; "Often have traditional buildings with pews, organ, pulpit, religious symbols"; "Illustrated locally in Moody Church, Arlington Heights Evangelical Free Church, Harvest Bible Church, or Trinity Evangelical Divinity School"; "Tend to be preferred by people with church backgrounds."

—The pragmatic evangelicals mostly have "Baby Boomer values in their thinking and approach to ministry, including seeker-sensitive focus, highly polished services, and emphasis on meeting people at their points of need"; "Buildings more like theaters with no religious symbols evident"; "Illustrated locally in Willow Creek Community Church"; "Tend to be preferred by people with Baby Boomer values."

—By contrast with both groups, the emerging evangelicals "Mostly are contemporary in their thinking and approach to ministry, including an emphasis on worship, both traditional hymns and contemporary music, active participation, authentic relationships, and reaching out to their communities"; "Multipurpose buildings that often serve as community centers, but are able to be turned into worship settings where technology, art, and even candles and liturgical symbols can be used to create a sense of mystery and awe"; "There are no examples in the Palatine area although the Chapel in Northern Illinois and Axis (at Willow Creek) have the concept. But there is a quickly increasing number of growing emerging churches in other parts of the country"; "Tend to be preferred by people who want relationships, community, and equipping, along with a place to

---

[91] E.g., Robert Lewis and Rob Wilkins, *The Church of Irresistible Influence* (Grand Rapids: Zondervan, 2001); Brian D. McLaren, *The Church on the Other Side* (Grand Rapids: Zondervan, 2000).

serve and worship but in smaller settings. Seem best able to reach post-modern people who distrust the church."[92]

Even when emerging church theorists do not specifically distinguish seeker-sensitive evangelicals from more traditional evangelicals, the antithe-ses and paradigms they provide show that they wish to distance themselves from both. In his book *Post-Modern Pilgrims*, Leonard Sweet argues that ministry in the twenty-first century has more in common with the first century than with the modern world that is collapsing all around us.[93] Although Sweet warns us not to embrace a postmodern worldview,[94] his solution, argued in four chapters, is that twenty-first-century ministry should be experiential, participatory, image-driven, and connected—generating the acrostic EPIC, which has become a bit of a mantra.

Sometimes the stereotyping of the contrast between modern ministry and postmodern ministry is charged with rather stunning extremes, extremes that capture the sweep of the protest. Consider, for example, the following chapter headings from one recent book:

3. Communication: From Print to Cultural Transmission
4. History: From Ahistorical to Tradition
5. Theology: From Propositionalism to Narrative
6. Apologetics: From Rationalism to Embodiment
7. Ecclesiology: From Invisible to Visible
8. Being Church: From Market to Mission
9. Pastors: From Power to Servanthood
10. Youth Ministers: From Parties to Prayer
11. Educators: From Information to Formation
12. Spiritual Formation: From Legalism to Freedom
13. Worship Leaders: From Program to Narrative
14. Artists: From Constraint to Expression

---

[92] All of the quotations in the preceding paragraph come from in-house documents of the church to which I have referred.

[93] *Post-Modern Pilgrims: First Century Passion for the 21st Century World* (Nashville: Broadman & Holman, 2000).

[94] Ibid., xvii.

15. Evangelists: From Rallies to Relationships
16. Activists: From Theory to Action[95]

In short: the whiff of protest in the emerging church movement is everywhere. It can be usefully analyzed along three axes: against what is perceived to be a personally stifling cultural conservatism, against modernism and its incarnation in modern churchmanship, and against modernism's incarnation in seeker-sensitive churches.

What Should We Be Asking?

This is but a sketchy introduction to the emerging church movement. Many more books and articles might usefully be summarized;[96] indeed, some of them will be discussed in the following chapters. But before pressing on, it

---

[95] Robert E. Webber, *The Younger Evangelicals: Facing the Challenges of the New World* (Grand Rapids: Baker, 2002).

[96] Apart from books already mentioned, see, among others, Spencer Burke with Colleen Pepper, *Making Sense of Church: Eavesdropping on Emerging Conversations about God, Community, and Culture* (El Cajon, CA: emergentYS / Grand Rapids: Zondervan, 2003); Brian D. McLaren, *More Ready Than You Realize: Evangelism as Dance in the Postmodern Matrix* (Grand Rapids: Zondervan, 2002); Joseph R. Myers, *The Search to Belong: Rethinking Intimacy, Community, and Small Groups* (El Cajon, CA: emergentYS / Grand Rapids: Zondervan, 2003). There is also a list of books on postmodern theology that overlap with the more pragmatically oriented literature of the emerging church movement itself. Sometimes these are written within a heritage that seeks some sort of continuity with historic orthodoxy, and sometimes not. Works in these categories that are worth reading include Robert C. Greer, *Mapping Postmodernism: A Survey of Christian Options* (Downers Grove, IL: InterVarsity Press, 2000); Stanley J. Grenz, *Renewing the Center: Evangelical Theology in a Post-Theological Era* (Grand Rapids: Baker, 2000); David J. Lose, *Confessing Jesus Christ: Preaching in a Postmodern World* (Grand Rapids: Eerdmans, 2003); John W. Riggs, *Postmodern Christianity: Doing Theology in the Contemporary World* (Harrisburg, PA: Trinity Press International, 2003); Kevin J. Vanhoozer, ed., *The Cambridge Companion to Postmodern Theology* (Cambridge, UK: Cambridge University Press, 2003).

will prove helpful to take stock of what we have learned so far and then reflect on the questions we should be asking.

From these opening pages—the summaries of the stories of many of the leaders of the emerging movement, and the survey of some of their publications—one point stands out rather dramatically. To grasp it succinctly, it is worth comparing the emerging church movement with the Reformation, which was, after all, another movement that claimed it wanted to reform the church. What drove the Reformation was the conviction, among all its leaders, that the Roman Catholic Church had departed from Scripture and had introduced theology and practices that were inimical to genuine Christian faith. In other words, they wanted things to change, not because they perceived that new developments had taken place in the culture so that the church was called to adapt its approach to the new cultural profile, but because they perceived that new theology and practices had developed in the church that contravened Scripture, and therefore that things needed to be reformed by the Word of God. By contrast, although the emerging church movement challenges, on biblical grounds, some of the beliefs and practices of evangelicalism, by and large it insists it is preserving traditional confessionalism but changing the emphases because the culture has changed, and so inevitably those who are culturally sensitive see things in a fresh perspective.[97] In other words, at the heart of the emerging reformation lies a perception of a major change in culture.

---

[97] In an essay posted on a blog, David M. Mills ("The Emergent Church—Another Perspective: A Critical Response to D. A. Carson's Staley Lectures," at http://kevincole.blogspot.com/2004_04_01_kevincole_archive.html) protests that this analysis is an oversimplification. After all, "Changes in philosophy, science, politics, technology, art, education and historiography were beginning to change the way that people thought about their religion, and Luther himself is an illustration of that shift." Luther's "plea for reform is itself enmeshed in a specific time and place within Western culture, and the changes he calls for are bound up with other changes taking place at that time. To ignore those factors is to misrepresent the nature of the Protestant Reformation." Mills's protest is simultaneously true and irrelevant to my argument. It is true in that any major societal change inevitably runs along several axes. It is irrelevant because that

This does not mean that the emerging church movement is wrong. It means, rather, three things.

First, the emerging church movement must be evaluated as to its reading of contemporary culture. Most of its pleas for reform are tightly tied to its understandings of postmodernism. The difficulty of the task (granted the plethora of approaches to postmodernism) cannot exempt us from making an attempt.

Second, as readers will have already observed from the survey provided by this chapter, the appeals to Scripture in the emerging church literature are generally of two kinds. On the one hand, some emerging leaders claim that changing times demand that fresh questions be asked of Scripture, and then fresh answers will be heard. What was an appropriate use of Scripture under

---

point is not disputed between us. The question, rather, is what the Reformers themselves judged to be the *primary* problem, and what appeals they made at the heart of their solution. The primary problem, as they saw it, was not that the culture had changed and the (Roman Catholic) Church had failed to adapt, even getting some of its own Scriptures wrong along the way, but that the Church had itself moved lamentably far from Scripture, and the solution lay in a return to Scripture. It is impossible to find in the writings of, say, Brian McLaren, an utterance akin to that of Luther at the Diet of Worms: "Since then your Majesty and your lordships desire a simple reply, I will answer without horns and without teeth. Unless I am convicted by Scripture and plain reason [note: this is a pre-Enlightenment appeal to reason]—I do not accept the authority of popes and councils, for they have contradicted each other—my conscience is captive to the Word of God. I cannot and I will not recant anything, for to go against conscience is neither right nor safe. God help me. Amen" (see Roland Bainton: *Here I Stand: A Life of Martin Luther* [Nashville: Abingdon, 1950], 183). Cf. Mark D. Thompson, *A Sure Ground on Which to Stand: The Relation of Authority and Interpretive Method in Luther's Approach to Scripture* (Carlisle, UK: Paternoster, 2004). Similar things can easily be demonstrated from John Calvin, Ulrich Zwingli, and other Reformation leaders. This is not to say that the Reformation leaders got everything right but simply to point out that the fundamental analysis of the problem and the primary appeal to the solution are very different in the Reformation and in the changes demanded by the emerging church movement.

modernism is no longer an appropriate use of Scripture under postmodernism. On this gentler reading of evangelicalism's history, traditional evangelicals are not accused of being deeply mistaken for their own times, but of being rather out of date now, not least in their handling of the Bible. On the other hand, the emerging church's critique of modernism, and of the evangelicalism that modernism has produced, is sometimes (not always) so bitter that evangelicalism's handling of Scripture can be mocked in stinging terms. (Recall Spencer Burke's treatment of the Lord's Supper in 1 Corinthians 11, for instance.) This is not meant to imply that this is true of all emerging pastors.

Third, granted that the emerging church movement is driven by its perception of widespread cultural changes, its own proposals for the way ahead must be assessed for their biblical fidelity. In other words, we must not only try to evaluate the accuracy of the emerging church's cultural analysis, but also the extent to which its proposals spring from, or can at least be squared with, the Scriptures. To put the matter differently: Is there at least some danger that what is being advocated is not so much a new kind of Christian in a new emerging church, but a church that is so submerging itself in the culture that it risks hopeless compromise?

Even to ask the question will strike some as an impertinence at best, or a tired appeal to the old-fashioned at worst. I mean it to be neither. Most movements have both good and bad in them, and the next chapter highlights some of the things I find encouraging and helpful in the emerging church movement. If the four subsequent chapters are more critical, it is partly because my "take" on contemporary culture is a bit removed from theirs, partly because the solutions I think are required are somewhat different from theirs, partly because I worry about (unwitting) drift from Scripture, and partly because this movement feels like an exercise in pendulum swinging, where the law of unintended consequences can do a lot of damage before the pendulum comes to rest.

But first, some things for which to be grateful.

Chapter 2

EMERGING CHURCH
STRENGTHS IN READING
THE TIMES

Because the emerging church movement is remarkably diverse, penetrating criticisms that apply to one part of it are sometimes inappropriate to some other part. The same caveat must be applied to assessments of the movement's strengths. The things I find encouraging and hopeful in the movement are not found everywhere in the movement. If I indulge in generalizations now and then, my generalizations will apply equally to commendations and criticisms.

Reading the Times

The emerging church movement honestly tries to read the culture in which we find ourselves and to think through the implications of such a reading for our witness, our grasp of theology, our churchmanship, even our self-understanding.

For many reasons, as the world has shrunk it has also become more diverse. Better put, as rapid and relatively inexpensive travel has increased, as increased mobility has utterly transformed patterns of migration (some of it bound up with refugee status), as instant communications demand that we know a little more about other parts of the world, somehow the world seems smaller—but we have also become more aware of the sheer diversity of cultures that make it up. This in turn has led to introspection where we live, because our own culture is rapidly changing, owing in part to immigration, in part to the sweeping tides of history. Endless nostalgia for "the good old days" (often a masked appeal for reactionary conservatism combined with intellectual laziness) is no answer. Of course there are important things that need to be conserved, but there are also changes that, for good or ill, cannot be held back, any more than Canute could check the incoming tide. These changes must not only be understood, but must be understood with reference to what the Bible says, with reference to the gospel, with reference to what Christian discipleship means. The emerging church movement is responding to these changes and is trying to think through their implications.

This should not threaten us. Even within the first Christian generation, the church *emerged* (that word again) from a Jerusalem-bound Jewish body to an international community made up of Jews and Gentiles all over the Roman Empire and beyond. Naturally, some of the changes that such expansion brought about were unique. After all, the movement was not only from a Jewish-bound locus to a mixed-race locus, but from a canon of Scripture (which we call the Old Testament) to fresh revelation bound up with the advent, ministry, death, resurrection, and ascension of the Lord Jesus—and with the books that bore initial witness to him (collectively known as the New Testament). The kinds of cultural changes we face today may be rapid and extensive, but by and large Christians are not claiming new revelation that drives a reconsideration or reevaluation of earlier revelation. That is what makes the changes in the New Testament period unique.

Yet this does not mean that there are no lessons about cultural change to be learned from the New Testament. When the apostle Paul preaches evangelistically in a Jewish synagogue in Pisidian Antioch (Acts 13), he sounds rather different than he does when he is preaching evangelistically to intellectually trained pagans in Athens (Acts 17:16–34). In the case of the first group, the apostle presupposes that his hearers are familiar with the Old Testament story line and believe it: there is one God, who created everything; the fall threw the human race into sin and decay; the Jewish race began with God's sovereign call of Abraham and Sarah; in the fullness of time, God disclosed the law to Moses at Mount Sinai; with increasing intensity God promised a coming redeemer, a "messiah" (an "anointed one"); and so on. All of this is common ground, so Paul devotes most of his preaching to proving that Jesus really is the promised Messiah. But when he deals with biblically illiterate pagans (regardless of how intellectually gifted they are), the apostle finds himself in the place where he must begin a lot farther back if he is to make sense of who Jesus is. He begins with the fact that there is but one God, that he is the Maker of everything, that he does not need his creation but that all of his creation is continually dependent on him, that he is not a mere tribal deity. Sin must be explained, and Paul chooses to render his explanation in terms of idolatry.

Many have spelled out these and other differences between the two evangelistic addresses, of course.[1] Strictly speaking, the different cultures (the synagogue leaders in Pisidian Antioch and the Mars Hill philosophers in Athens) do not represent a change in *one* culture, but the differences experienced by one man, Paul the apostle, as he moves from place to place. Our closest analogy today, I suppose, is the Christian (often a missionary) who moves from one culture to another and has a lot to learn in order to present the gospel fairly and effectively within the new culture. The extra feature that all of us experience today is the speed of change: cultural shifts sometimes take place so rapidly within one locale that the people there experience the sense of dislocation the missionary feels when going from one culture to another. Nowadays we stay home, but our own culture changes.

Just as the apostle understood that his moves from culture to culture brought implications for how he went about his preaching (even though his constant resolution was to preach Christ crucified, 1 Corinthians 2:1– 5), and just as thoughtful missionaries learn the same lesson as they step from one culture into another, so also must the church of God when it stays home and the culture in which it is embedded changes. That is something the emerging church movement understands.

We have not always grasped how much the culture in which we are embedded shapes our understanding and outlook. Elsewhere I have mentioned how, in my office at Trinity, C. S. Lewis's famous words about Aslan hang above my head: my wife's needlepoint has been nicely framed to set out the utterance, "He is not a tame lion." One day a Korean, newly arrived to enter our Ph.D. program, sat for the first time in my office, making his

---

[1] My own attempt is found in D. A. Carson, "Athens Revisited," in *Telling the Truth: Evangelizing Postmoderns*, ed. D. A. Carson (Grand Rapids: Zondervan, 2000), 384–98.

first contact with our department. I could see his eyes flitting upward from my face to the hanging on the wall behind me, then back to my face. I suddenly realized that although most of our European-American students would recognize the quotation and its source, this Korean, quite understandably, could not be expected to be familiar with literature written in English. I wondered what he'd make of it, and so I offered him no help: we simply continued our conversation about doctoral seminars and the like. Finally he screwed up his courage, pointed to the hanging with the words "He is not a tame lion," and asked me directly, "Is that you, sir?" And of course, in a flash I remembered that, as a Korean, he would have had bred into him a Confucian outlook on education: the teacher was way up there, the student was way down the scale. The differences in our respective backgrounds guaranteed that the two of us would interpret the six words from C. S. Lewis in very different ways.

Or consider a joke such as the following:

A group of chess enthusiasts checked into a hotel and were standing in the lobby discussing their recent tournament victories. After about an hour, the manager came out of the office and asked them to disperse.

"But why?" they asked as they moved off.

"Because," he said, "I can't stand chess nuts boasting in an open foyer."

Imagine the tortuous explanations you would have to undertake to explain this story to someone who has learned English fairly fluently as a second language, but who knows little of American pop music and the odd pleasure of complex English puns.

To put the matter a different way: To understand particular forms of discourse, it is necessary to have more than a superficial knowledge of the language of the discourse. One requires some grasp of the *culture* in which the language is embedded in addition to the language itself. Those associated with the emerging church movement are trying to read our changing times and make the necessary adjustments so as to be able to communicate the gospel to what is, in substantial measure, a new culture. The postmodern ethos tends to be anti-absolutist, suspicious of truth claims, and wide open to relativism. It tends to adopt therapeutic approaches to spirituality, and—whether despite the individualism of the Western heritage or perhaps even because of it—it is often attracted to communitarian wholeness.

Other elements of contemporary culture are often fastened on by emerging church leaders, of course; I have merely listed a few common and isolated features.[2] My point is that regardless of one's analysis of the contemporary culture, virtually all sides admit it is changing rapidly. Given that reality, it is surely as commendable to read the changing culture in which we live and make appropriate adjustments as it is for missionaries to read a new culture they have entered, or as it is for Paul to read the changes in culture as he moves to different locales around the Empire. Certainly this is far more commendable than a cultural conservatism that acts as if the culture with which we are most comfortable (usually the one in which we grew up) is the only culture acceptable to thinking Christians, and perhaps to God himself.

Pushing for Authenticity

In the first chapter we noticed that Mike Yaconelli's *Stories of Emergence* was subtitled *Moving from Absolute to Authentic*. Whether or not this is a fair antithesis, the emphasis on authenticity—authentic Christian faith, authentic spirituality, authentic Christian obedience—is surely commendable.

We might wonder whether corporate worship is any more "authentic" just because there are candles or centers for journaling. Certainly we must try to think through such matters fairly. But which of us can safely deny that a fair proportion of what goes on in many traditional evangelical churches—whether corporate worship, small-group Bible studies, and even prayer times—feels disturbingly *in*authentic at times?

You know the kind of inauthenticity I have in mind. We may go through meeting after meeting, and all of it is reassuringly familiar, but we do not come out saying, in effect, "Surely we have met with the living

---

[2] To cite one more work: A recent D.Min. project that studies high school students in a major metropolitan suburb concludes that they learn visually, are drawn to experiences, desire meaningful relationships, and are hugely tolerant of others. See Richard P. Wager, "Hearing with Their Eyes and Seeing with Their Hearts: Ministry to the Senior High Bridger Generation" (D.Min. project, Trinity Evangelical Divinity School, 2001).

God!" We start attending meetings because it is a habit, or because it is the right thing to do, or because we know that the means of grace are important, but not out of a heart-hunger to be with God's people and to be fed from God's Word. Sermons are filled with mere clichés. There is little intensity in confession, little joy in absolution, little delight in the gospel, little urgency in evangelism, little sense of privilege and gratitude in witness, little passion for the truth, little compassion for others, little humility in our evaluations, little love in our dealings with others. To expose such inauthenticity is a good thing; to hunger for authenticity in all our existence, not least our walk with God and with other Christians, is also a good thing.

Nor is this simply a matter of how *we* feel about the church. The fact of the matter is that the new generation coming along has less attachment to any church, so there is very little sense of duty or obligation to continue attending unless there is a burning sense of reality about the enterprise. That is the theme of a couple of recent books that deserve to be widely read. Purists may raise eyebrows at this or that theological point, but these two books are saying something that deserves to be heard. "Live such good lives among the pagans," the apostle Peter writes, "that, though they accuse you of doing wrong, they may see your good deeds and glorify God on the day he visits us" (1 Peter 2:12). The theme of the first book is that on one sense churches should be deliberately provocative; they should make people long for God.[3]

> One of the key themes of this book is that unless there is something about church, or Christians, or Christian faith that intrigues, provokes or entices, then all the evangelism in the world will fall on deaf ears. If churches cannot convey a sense of "reality" then all our "truth" will count for nothing. . . . Churches need to become provocative, arresting places which make the searcher, the casual visitor, want to come back for more.[4]

The issue is *not* gimmicks or entertainment, carefully orchestrated to attract a crowd addicted to entertainment, but a profound sense of reality, of authentic knowledge of God, manifested in goodness and transformed living. When emerging church leaders foster the kind of authenticity that

---

[3] Graham Tomlin, *The Provocative Church* (London: SPCK, 2002).

[4] Ibid., 10–11.

builds a contagious church thoughtful Christians will be grateful for their unease with the superficial and their passion for what is real.

Recognizing Our Own Social Location

During the last two or three decades many people have written books and articles on the changing culture of America, and most of us are well aware of the rapid developments. But many of us somehow remain under the illusion that we Christians live *outside* these cultural changes. We therefore address the changes from a kind of independent bastion of impregnability. In other words, we observe the changes in the culture and strategize about how to respond faithfully to them, but these changes are all happening *out there*, in the culture—but not in us. In short, many Christians have yet to come to grips with the fact that *we ourselves* are part of this rapidly changing culture, and we cannot help but be influenced by it.

As we read the biblical text and read the culture, we ourselves have a social location. The more radical forms of reader-response theory, fed by postmodern hermeneutics, insists that the social location of the readers is the single most important factor in determining their conclusions as they read. Such a stance holds that any interpretation—whether of a text or a culture—says more about the social location of the readers than it does about the text or the culture. This rather extreme stance I shall happily criticize in the fourth and fifth chapters of this book. Yet there is some insight in the postmodern insistence that the readers themselves are socially located and that this social location plays a contributing role in their interpretations. There are ways in which that role can be reduced or disciplined or even harnessed, as we shall see, but there is no way it can be eliminated. We are finite beings, and our knowledge is always partial. Even the fact that I am writing this and you are reading this in English betrays one small part of our social location: we are speakers/writers/readers of English, and language is one part of the cultural matrix.

One thing this observation entails, of course, is that we are most likely to be closest to the objective truth of the text if we encourage people with different backgrounds and social contexts to contribute to the discussion as to what the text means. By bringing our different backgrounds and presuppositions to the text, each group is more likely to overcome its own hermeneutical blind spots.[5] This does *not* mean that each reading is as valid as every other reading, which is what the more radical wing of postmodernism avers: to this point, too, I shall return. But it *does* mean that all of us inevitably interpret things out of a particular framework.

Leaders in the emerging church movement are among the people who rightly recognize this point, and they keep appealing to it. Although their appeal to the social location of all claims to knowledge entails some risks, they nevertheless avoid the trap of thinking that their own understanding of something or other in the Bible is necessarily bound up with eternal truth just because that is what they understand the Bible to be saying.

Evangelizing Outsiders

One of the attractive features of the life-stories reported in chapter 1 is the interest in evangelizing people who are often overlooked by the church, or at very least largely untouched by the church's witness. For Spencer Burke, this meant artists;[6] for Dave Tomlinson, the people who feel most comfortable gathering in a London pub;[7] for Chris Seay, the arts district in Houston.[8]

This element is broader than the attempts of a few individuals within the movement. It is something inherent in the movement itself. The attempt to break out of what is perceived to be the holy huddle of traditional evangelicalism is driven, at least in part, by a concern for evangelism, in particular the evangelism of a new generation of people who are shaped by postmodern assumptions. Because of these postmodern assumptions, many of our

---

[5] This matter has been discussed at length in the literature. It is what Kevin Vanhoozer rather attractively calls a "Pentecostal plurality," *"which maintains that the one true interpretation is best approximated by a diversity of particular methods and contexts of reading.* The Word remains the interpretive norm, but no one culture or interpretive scheme is sufficient to exhaust its meaning, much less its significance" (*Is There a Meaning in This Text?* [Grand Rapids: Zondervan, 1998], 419, emphasis his).

[6] See pp. 14–19.

[7] See p. 25.

[8] See pp. 22–24.

contemporaries feel that the church culture of traditional evangelicalism is utterly alien to them, and these are the people whom the emerging church movement is particularly addressing.

This strength is easily documented. Dan Kimball, as we have seen, is concerned to explain biblical terms that would be opaque to many of our contemporaries; he is passionate about making the corporate worship meetings "authentic."[9] The church in the Chicago suburbs to which I referred offers a not-uncommon three-group profile of the population: the first group is Christian and therefore comfortable with the trappings of traditional Christian churches; the second group has had some exposure to Christianity so that even if it is not itself Christian it does not feel particularly alienated by traditional Christian trappings; and the third group is entirely biblically illiterate and therefore finds the traditional Christianity at best odd and at worst rather offensive. It is this third group that most needs to be evangelized. Brian McLaren has written a book to foster evangelism toward this group.[10]

In some ways this is reminiscent of the Jesus People movement in America in the late sixties and seventies. Very few traditional churches had much outreach into the tens of thousands of hippies who flocked to the cities, especially on the West Coast, and lived in communes that were simultaneously a protest against some of the trends in the majority culture and a slow-moving party of sex and drugs. Suddenly the Jesus People were seeing thousands of converts—preserving (at least initially) the communal living, but calling people to faith in Jesus, studying the Bible, and insisting on holiness and discipline. Inevitably the movement became diverse. Some of it was led by screwball self-promoters who did a lot of damage and then burned out. Some of it became cultic and eventually withered away. But a great deal of it was borne along by the Spirit. The conversions were real, and the Jesus People movement itself became the path through which people became, in time, more integrated with historic Christianity. Many a pastor who reads these lines was converted through the witness of the Jesus People.

Likewise, in some ways the emerging church movement is reminiscent of the early years of the seeker-sensitive movement, which attempted to reach

---

[9] See pp. 36–38.

[10] Brian D. McLaren, *More Ready Than You Realize: Evangelism as Dance in the Postmodern Matrix* (Grand Rapids: Zondervan, 2002).

out to suburbanites largely removed from traditional Christian interests, vocabulary, and ritual. Here, too, it is easy to list the debris: split churches, formulaic approaches, forms of idolatry in which the gospel perennially serves me and my perceived needs. But one can also find tens of thousands of men and women converted under the impact of the seeker-sensitive movement.

These mixed results must serve neither to permit any such movement to avoid penetrating evaluation nor to damn the entire movement to the lowest circle of Dante's hell. They remind us that movements are diverse, complex, and frequently (for better and for worse) called into being because the traditional churches are failing, or perceived to be failing, in some way. In each case the movement itself is on a journey, and the movement is difficult to evaluate if its trajectory is not taken into account. The Jesus People eventually died out as a movement, most of its genuine converts taken up in larger confessionalism. The seeker-sensitive movement is still in motion. Some of it has gone mainstream, even become "traditional"; parts of it are constantly trying to reinvent themselves; parts of it are even attracted to the emerging church movement, seeing in the latter a younger manifestation of itself.

The parallels with the emerging church movement are transparent. The protest against the older culture and the confidence that it is on the cutting edge may not always be its most attractive features, but even here it is not entirely wrong. More importantly, it is a movement with evangelistic concerns, even while it remains suspicious of a great deal of traditional evangelism. And since many of those whom the emerging church movement is reaching are often not reached by others, one cannot help but be grateful to God for genuine conversions and spiritual fruit.

Probing Links with the Tradition

Characterized as it is by protest, the emerging church movement obviously finds itself cutting links with many practices of more traditional churches. As we have seen, there are plenty of blunt dismissals of some suburban conservative ministry styles, such as hierarchical staff structures or parking lot ministries or the evident self-distancing from mainstream culture or the ugly absolutism seen as bound up with modernism. Some of the leaders of the movement raise questions about some traditional theological stances—regarding the Lord's Supper, for instance, or homosexuality.

By contrast, many of these same emerging churches are experimenting with candles, crosses, liturgical forms, drama, retreats in silence, and the like. In other words, while they are shedding some recent traditional forms, they are tending toward the adoption of some practices that belong to other traditions.

Transparently, then, the emerging church movement's attitude toward this strange thing called "tradition" is rather complex. While one may question the wisdom of some of the choices being made, there is something very refreshing, on the one hand, about not being bound by tradition—after all, isn't Scripture itself supposed to be our only *final* guide?—and, on the other, about wanting to be linked to historic Christianity and not merely the latest twenty years of Christianity.

●   ●   ●

I want to bring this chapter to a close by talking about one particular local church. Like any local church, it is not beyond reproach. But it is replete with many wholly admirable features.

This church began just over twenty years ago with a small group of Christians meeting in an apartment. They were committed to obedience to Christ and faith in him, and they deeply desired to be effective in reaching out to unconverted people in the major metropolitan area that was their home. The man who agreed to serve as their pastor not only enjoyed an excellent grasp of biblical theology, but was unusually astute in reading the metropolitan, largely postmodern culture around them. Many people who attended were deeply convinced that the Christianity lived out by these believers was authentic; the message rang true, the corporate worship (rather traditional in the morning and innovative in the evening) was full of vitality, integrity, and genuine expressions of contrition and praise.

Although these Christians were steeped in one particular theological tradition, they did not come across as arrogant, even when they were encouraging deep confessionalism. Their denomination was poorly represented in the demographics of their city, so the growth they experienced was not achieved by stealing sheep from sister churches of similar pedigree: it was mostly conversion growth. Penetrating the sealed apartment blocks and yuppie culture of a major city is never easy, but hundreds and eventually thousands were converted, generating a congregation where the mean age was late twenties or early thirties: it was the postmodern generation that was most powerfully affected. Across two decades this church planted numerous other congregations in their large metropolitan area and then reached out to help plant still other churches in other metropolitan areas.

The irony is that, while this sounds like an outstanding exemplar of the emerging church movement, this church—Redeemer Presbyterian Church in New York City—is thoroughly unlikely to identify itself as a candidate for emerging rolls. The reason I talk about this church should nevertheless be clear: *it displays all the strengths of the emerging church movement while avoiding most of its weaknesses.* In other words, the emerging church movement has numerous strengths, and we should be grateful for them—but they are not *exclusively* theirs. In fact, I could list a substantial number of local churches that share the strengths of the movement but would not want to be identified with it. This shows that the emerging movement is on to something. It means that more and more of the church senses a need for change in response to the culture, even if it isn't of one mind as to what that change should look like.

That sober reality suggests that, having looked at its strengths, we must also reflect on the weaknesses of the emerging church movement.

Chapter 3

EMERGING CHURCH
ANALYSIS OF
CONTEMPORARY CULTURE

In this chapter I shall outline some of the weaknesses I see in the emerging church's analysis of contemporary culture. At the risk of repeating myself, let me remind you of three things. *First*, this exercise is important because the emerging church leaders themselves ground their call to reformation in the cultural changes taking place all around us. *Second*, because the emerging movement is so diverse, my criticisms do not apply equally to all of its exponents. Here and there I shall try to make appropriate qualifications, but such qualifications easily become tedious, so at some junctures you must simply take this as a given. *Third*, this chapter focuses on the emerging movement's *analysis* of culture, not on the solutions they put forward. We shall examine their proposed solutions in the fifth and sixth chapters.

My argument will develop along four lines: the emerging church's tendency toward reductionism, its condemnation of confessional Christianity, some theological shallowness and intellectual incoherence, and a particularization of those three issues.

On the Evaluation of Modernism

For virtually all of the leaders in the emerging church movement, what is modern is the fruit of the Enlightenment. Modernism seeks rational certainty and therefore veers toward absolutism, because it has refused to recognize the essential perspectivalism in all human knowing. In other words, whether or not the term is used, modernism in emerging thought is tied up with certain approaches to epistemology (i.e., the study of how we know things, or think we know things). Epistemology must not be thought of as a narrow subject suitable only for advanced students in a philosophy of religion department. Because it is bound up with how people think and what they claim to know or not know, it necessarily touches relationships, emotions, social history, many elements in every culture, the role and capacities of different senses (e.g., the visual versus the aural), linear thinking versus the image and the metaphor and the associative leap, various analyses along the axis of certainty to probability to possibility, and much more of the same.[1]

Some emergents, as we saw in chapter 1, want to focus on economics and materialism, and certainly there are prophetic things that must be said along those lines. But by and large the focus of the emerging movement is on perceived shifts in epistemology, including the many implications of these shifts in social dynamics. For instance, when Brian McLaren talks about contemporary evangelism, he insists that because modernism is passé, many forms of evangelism have lost their usefulness. Gone is evangelism as sales pitch, as conquest, as warfare, as ultimatum, as threat, as proof, as argument, as entertainment, as show, as monologue, as something you do. Evangelism is disciple making and is bound up with conversation, friendship, influence, invitation, companionship, challenge, opportunity, dance, something you get to do.[2]

But all of these distinctions turn in substantial measure on how we think people learn or experience the gospel, how they come to put their full trust in Christ. We are in the domain of epistemology. Similarly, when he talks about the move from the "absolute" to the "authentic," Mike Yaconelli's antithesis is grounded in epistemological distinctions, whether or not he calls them that.[3] The same goes for virtually all of the antitheses

---

[1] Failure to recognize the comprehensiveness of epistemology lies at the heart of David Mills's strange discounting of the importance of the topic (see chap. 1, n. 97).

[2] See especially his book *More Ready Than You Realize: Evangelism as Dance in the Postmodern Matrix* (Grand Rapids: Zondervan, 2002).

[3] Note the subtitle: Mike Yaconelli, ed., *Stories of Emergence: Moving from Absolute to Authentic* (Grand Rapids: Zondervan, 2003).

that Robert Webber sets out:[4] for example, the ostensible move from propositionalism to narrative is tightly bound up with how one presents (and hears) the biblical material. To cite his chapter titles, "Apologetics: From Rationalism to Embodiment" is inescapably tied to questions of epistemology, as is "Educators: From Information to Formation."

This is not to say that there is nothing to these antitheses. But whether they are fair and wise turns, in the first instance, on the assessment of modernism and then, of course, on the assessment of postmodernism itself.

A Reductionistic and Wooden Understanding of Modernism

That brings me to my *first* criticism. The emerging church movement's understanding of modernism seems too reductionistic and wooden. The modern period is treated as if it were all of a piece, consistently devoted to the rational, the cerebral, the linear, the absolute, the objective. But history simply isn't that neat. Enfolded in the modern period is perhaps the most influential philosopher of them all, Immanuel Kant, who insisted that the mind imposes order and structure on the data that the senses take in. The result is a massive disjunction between the phenomenal world and the noumenal world and an implicit denial that human beings have any sort of direct access to objective knowledge.

Here stands, too, the nihilism of Friedrich Nietzsche, who conceived of truth as metaphor long before Jacques Derrida and Richard Rorty came on the scene. And what shall we make of the Romantic movement, not least the poets? As children at school, we memorized our share of Wordsworth and Shelley, being drawn into their vision that a passion for beauty and nature is the surest path to truth, since beauty and truth cannot finally be distinguished. Meanwhile, Arthur Schopenhauer was insisting that so-called "reality" is nothing but objectification of our drives, the fruit of our (frequently irrational) desires. While many orthodox believers were fighting over the correctness of various creedal statements, other thinkers, such as Friedrich Schleiermacher and Søren Kierkegaard, anticipated existentialism. At the

---

[4] Robert, E. Webber, *The Younger Evangelicals: Facing the Challenges of the New World* (Grand Rapids: Baker, 2002).

heart of the various forms of existentialism lay the conviction that we shape our existence by what we do, what we choose.

Even so, some useful contrasts can be drawn between "modernism" and "postmodernism." It might be argued, for instance, that whereas the luminaries I have just mentioned anticipated many of the stances of contemporary postmodernism, they tended to influence fellow scholars and academics, but never gained the popular approval that postmodernism has in many academic and media circles today (especially in America). So considered, postmodernism is nothing but the popularization of one strand of modernist thought, which itself was a reaction against other strands of modernist thought. In any case, I see the analysis of modernism itself within the emerging church movement so stylized and reductionistic as to represent a major historical distortion.

If we were simply talking about views of history with little bearing on what Christians think, the distortion might not matter a whole lot except in intellectually rigorous circles. But the distortion of modernism extends, in the case of some emerging church thinkers, to a distortion of confessional Christianity under modernism. In my reading of the emerging church literature, Christianity under modernism is rationalistic, cerebral rather than emotional, and given toward arrogance because of its absolutism. Exemplars of such sins can undoubtedly be found, but I remain little persuaded that the dominant cause is the kind of modernism that the emerging folk have in mind. For under modernism, one also finds Christianity that expresses itself in prayers such as these:

> Our hearts rejoice to hear the gladsome tiding that the Lord reigneth. Let His kingdom be established over the sons of men, for His kingdom must come, and of it there will be no end. Behold, we come to Thy throne this morning bearing about with us a body of sin and death, and consequently much of sin, and much of care, and it may be much of sorrow; but we would be unburdened at Thy mercy-seat now. As for our cares we are ashamed that we have them, seeing Thou carest for us. We have trusted Thee now for many years, and Thy faithfulness has never been under suspicion, nor Thy love a matter of question.
>
> We there leave every concern about our families or about ourselves, about our business, or about our souls, entirely with our God. And as for our sin, we bless Thee for a sight of the precious blood of Jesus: when Thou seest

it Thou dost pass over us. No angel of justice smites where once the blood is sprinkled. Oh, let us have a sight of the blood of Jesus, too, and rest because Thou hast for ever put away our sin, because we believe in Jesus.

Oh, let the masses of the people yet come to seek after Christ: by some means, by all means, by every means, may the ears of men be reached and then their hearts be touched. May they hear, that their souls may live; and may the Lord who in everlasting covenant sets forth His Son, glorify Him in the midst of the nations. Let all the nations know the Christ of God.

But, Lord, we have yet another burden—it is that we ourselves do not love Thee as we should, that oftentimes we grow lukewarm and chill, and doubt creeps over us, and unbelief mars our confidence, and we sin and forget our God. O Lord help us! Pardon is not enough, we want sanctification. We beseech Thee let the weeds that grow in the seed plot of our soul be cut up by the roots. We do want to serve Thee. We long that every thought we think, and word we say or write, should be all for Thee.

Most glorious Lord God, it is marvelous in our eyes that Thou shouldst become incarnate, that Thy Son should take our flesh upon Him. It surprises us greatly that the Lord of Life should condescend to die, and that the incorruptible One should be laid in the grave. We are full of loving gratitude, we are also full of adoring wonder. When we have stood at the sepulchre and looked into it and thought of Jesus having lain there, when we have seen it open and knew that it was empty, we bless Thy name that even He died and was buried, and magnify Thee that He is risen again from the dead.

These great facts concerning our divine Lord are the foundation of our confidence in Him. We bless Thee that they have been attested by such four-fold witness, and yet further that afterwards He appeared alive to so large a number of those who knew Him, that the fact of His rising from the dead might never be questioned again. We do not question it, our hearts devoutly believe the fact, but Lord, we want by Thy Holy Spirit to know the facts in their living power. We wish that we might have fellowship with our Lord, who is our Head, in all this. Oh, that we might know how to die with Him, and to live with Him in newness of life.

We lament that in the body of this death there is much that we abhor. We are tempted to indolence at times, and though busy in the world we become spiritually idle. Also, we are tempted to envy others because they excel us, and we mourn to confess the meanness of our spirit in this matter;

and also we have to lament our pride. We have nothing to be proud of; the lowest place is ours; but Lord, we often conceive ourselves to be something when we are nothing. We pray Thee forgive all these vices of our nature; but at the same time kill them, for we hate ourselves to think we should fall into such evils. Especially have mercy upon us for our unbelief. Thou hast given us proof of Thine existence, and of Thy love to us, and of Thy care over us: especially hast Thou given us Thine only begotten Son, best pledge of love. And yet we acknowledge that we do doubt. Unbelief comes into the soul. We are quite ashamed of this. We could lie in the very dust to think it should be so. Lord, have mercy upon us; but also help us to be strong in faith in the future, giving glory to God.

We now commit ourselves again to Thy keeping, O faithful Creator; to thy keeping, O Saviour of the pierced hand; to Thy keeping, O eternal Spirit, Thou who art able to keep us from falling and sanctify us fully that we may be made to stand among the saints in light. O God, we can trust Thee, and we do. Our faith has gathered strength by the lapse of years. Each following birthday, we trust, confirms us in the fact that to rely upon God is our happiness and our strength, and we will do so, though the earth be removed and the mountains be carried into the midst of the sea. We will not fear since God abideth fast for ever, and His covenant cannot fail.[5]

Obviously these prayers are dated. They spring from the last three decades of the nineteenth century and, as most pastors did in those days, were constructed in slightly updated Elizabethan English. Obviously, too, the pastor who is praying, C. H. Spurgeon, can speak of "facts" and "proof" — but as we shall see in chapter 7, the New Testament dares resort to such categories, too. And obviously, Spurgeon can make countless allusions to biblical passages and expect his hearers/readers to pick up on them, for on the whole Christians were a good deal more biblically literate in those days than they are today.

But what is most striking about these prayers is the wholeness of them. Here we find passion, joy, love, doubt, fear, hope, confidence — and above

---

[5] All of these quotations are drawn from C. H. Spurgeon, *The Pastor in Prayer* (Edinburgh: The Banner of Truth Trust, 2004 [1893]): pages 14, 17, 29–30, 41–42.

all a deep and multifaceted *relationship* between Christians and the Triune God. These prayers are a long way removed from the stereotypes of modernist Christianity constructed by the emerging church movement.

Fair enough, you may say, but this was Spurgeon—and surely Spurgeon wasn't typical. But although he was more gifted than most of his peers, and more quotable, Spurgeon represents a wide swath of evangelical confessionalism. A multitude of pastors, teachers, and simply ordinary Christians—known to me personally or crowding into my mind through the books I have read that cover the centuries this side of the Enlightenment and thus the modernist period—speaks the lie to the reductionism of the emerging church movement's depiction of Christianity associated with modernism. I recall a lunch I had with J. I. Packer a dozen years ago, in which I asked him how his book *Knowing God* was doing—one of the few books of the late twentieth century which, if the Lord tarries, will still be read a hundred years from now. He told me the figures and then quietly asked, "Do you know why it is still circulating so well?"

Then he answered his own question: "Because it is a book on spirituality."

Well, yes, a book on spirituality—though of course it is also a book on the doctrine of God. Once again, the nasty stereotypical antithesis does not fit: doctrine or spirituality, truth or relationships. It takes little thought to list more names, from many countries, from all recent centuries. Have any of the critics actually read the devotional writings of Benjamin Warfield or B. F. Westcott? True, many Christian thinkers in late modernism stressed the importance of truth. Yet this was not because they thought in epistemologically absolutist categories, but because they lived and served at a time when the truth of the gospel was progressively being denied by classic liberalism, which veered more and more toward the antisupernatural. Instead of condescendingly dismissing these leaders, even if in retrospect they did sometimes get the balance of things wrong, we should honor them for being faithful in their time. And in any case, the best of them tried pretty hard *not* to get the balance too wrong. It is still worth reading everything that J. Gresham Machen wrote. Even if one disagrees with this or that little snippet, there was a comprehensiveness to his thinking that might more often be emulated today than criticized. From his pen came numerous essays on Christianity and culture (including an essay on the Christian and human relationships!), another entitled "Mountains and Why We Love Them," and much more.[6]

An Almost Universal Condemnation of Confessional Christianity

This brings me to my *second* criticism. Not only are some emerging church leaders, at best, painfully reductionistic about modernism and the confessional Christianity that forged its way through the modernist period. They also, in failing to understand, almost universally give the impression of dismissing this Christianity. They could humbly offer critiques of modernist confessionalism at its best and gratefully acknowledge that many of us are Christians today because our forebears, sustained by grace, were faithful to the gospel. Instead, they tend to gravitate to the worst exemplars and seem to mock them.

Even when the better emergent writers project an attitude of balance, there is almost always a stinger in the presentation. For example, here is Neo (= Neil Oliver Edward) to Casey:

> According to the Bible, humans shall not live by systems and abstractions alone but also by stories and poetry and proverbs and mystery.
>
> That's not to say that we don't need theologians to work with words, but it is to say that believing as we do that the Word became flesh, the focus of our words should be the creation of communities that embody our good news.[7]

One cannot but be grateful for the "not only . . . but" form of argument. Nevertheless, Neo's emphasis is almost entirely on the stories and proverbs and mystery, and even where concessions might be made for the "system" and "abstractions," they are charged with three negative features.

---

6 These latter topics are most easily read in the recent collection, *J. Gresham Machen: Selected Shorter Writings*, ed. D. G. Hart (Phillipsburg, NJ: Presbyterian & Reformed, 2004). "Mountains and Why We Love Them" can be found on the Internet: http://www.opc.org/books/Mountains.html.

7 Brian D. McLaren, *A New Kind of Christian: A Tale of Two Friends on a Spiritual Journey* (San Francisco: Jossey Bass, 2001), 159, 163 respectively.

(1) What Neo emphasizes has positive overtones in our world: stories and poetry and proverbs and mystery. What Neo only concessively admits is cast negatively: human beings "shall not live by systems and abstractions alone." Whoever said they did? Why not say that human beings "shall not live by precious truth and revealed propositions alone," or something of that order? In other words, even where there is a show of balance, one cannot help but feel that truth and propositions are, at best, being damned with faint praise.

(2) The ostensible balance is always cast with the apparent concessions running only one way. One never stumbles across passages that say, in effect, that human beings shall not live by stories and poetry and proverbs and mystery alone, but also by revealed truths that are to be believed, trusted, understood, and obeyed—yet Scripture insists on this point count-less times. One might start by meditating on Psalm 119. Or again, while Neo concedes that we "need theologians to work with words," neverthe-less, "believing as we do that the Word became flesh, the focus of our words should be the creation of communities that embody our good news." This seems like a snide antithesis. While theologians do "work with words," the best of our theologians have also been preachers, teachers, and evangelists, and the "words" they work with are God's words, the embodied message of which focuses on Jesus Christ. In the Bible (as we shall see later in this book), "word" or "word of God" is tied far more frequently to the message, encoded in words, than to the incarnate Word. This is not to downplay the utterly crucial centrality of the incarnation, but in the emerging church lit-erature, the place of words or Scripture or propositions is *at best* conces-sively admitted, while almost all the emphasis is on Christ as the Word incarnate. Never does the argument run the other way. We are never told that although Christ is the Word incarnate and he is the very center and object of our faith, our access to him and our understanding of who he is and what he has done has been preserved for us first and foremost in words that God himself has disclosed.

(3) Despite the formal concessions, it is difficult to find a paragraph in any of the emergent writings that says anything positive and grateful about modernism or about the Christian churches that went around the world under modernism. I am not suggesting that there is nothing to criticize in modernism. I am merely saying that for the emergent writers, modernism is bad and postmodernism is either good or a glorious opportunity. In

short, I don't see in their writings the balance that the defenders of the emerging church movement claim to present.

Sometimes this slips out in amusing ways. In this respect, emergent writers are not unlike other contemporary writers who think in unrealistically antithetical categories. Here is John Stackhouse:

> [S]ince the Christian message is fundamentally an invitation extended to human beings—not just human brains—to encounter the person of Jesus Christ rather than to adopt a doctrinal system or ideology, it is only obvious then that establishing the credibility and plausibility of that message will depend upon more than intellectual argument. It will depend instead upon the Holy Spirit of God shining out through all the lamps of good works we can raise to the glory of our Father in heaven.[8]

Here again is that antithesis: the Christian message is an invitation "extended to human beings—not just human brains." I could happily live with this if he elsewhere said that the Christian message is an invitation to human beings—not just human emotions and aesthetics. As it stands, there is the implicit criticism of the modern, that in those days Christians were interested only in human brains. But has that ever been the case? When Francis Schaeffer kept stressing the importance of affirming biblical truth, did he not keep underlying the Bible's emphasis on Christian love as the distinctive mark of the Christian? When George Whitefield and John Wesley were evangelizing tens of thousands of people during the decades of the Great Awakening (called the Evangelical Awakening in the United Kingdom), did they not only preach the gospel, but do so passionately, often with tears, and insist on such moral reformation that part of the fruit of the movement was the abolition of slavery, the introduction of child labor laws, the invention of trade unions, care for the elderly, and prison reform?

Stackhouse's lines are troubling not only because his concession runs only one way, but also because he changes a "more" to an "instead." He rightly

---

[8] "From Architecture to Argument: Historic Resources for Christian Apologetics," in *Christian Apologetics in the Postmodern World*, ed. Timothy R. Phillips and Dennis L. Okholm (Downers Grove, IL: InterVarsity Press, 1995), 55.

asserts that the plausibility of the message will depend on *more* than intellectual argument (and probably no self-confessed modernist or self-confessed postmodernist would question this), but then says that such plausibility will depend *instead* on the Holy Spirit shining out through good works. Does he mean that the Holy Spirit does not shine out through the message preached?

To be sure, there is an element of validity in the criticism that the emerging church movement levels against the Christianity of the modern period. In the Western world, far more sermons were preached from didactic parts of Scripture than from narrative parts of Scripture. For instance, of the seventy or so books of published sermons preached by D. Martyn Lloyd-Jones, only one or two expound narrative texts. Still, even here one must be charitable. Lloyd-Jones used narrative portions of Scripture *within* his sermons and made constant appeal to proverbs, psalms, laments, apocalyptic, and all the rest. Moreover, Lloyd-Jones was addressing *his* generation. In retrospect, few of us, fifty years ago, were very gifted at handling narrative, and the improvement in that area has been a gain of the last two or three decades.

Yet, to put things in perspective, I have heard a fair number of African preachers handle narrative texts very ably, but can think of only three or four African preachers who can expound Romans very well. The narrative culture of many Africans (though that is now changing somewhat) produced certain limitations; the heritage of Western epistemology and culture produced another set of limitations. Only the best preachers readily transcend such limitations in their culture. So the obvious question that emerging leaders should be asking is, what limitations plague postmoderns? What parts of Scripture do we not handle well ourselves? What will our children and grandchildren say about our own blind spots? Will they treat us any more compassionately than we are treating those who passed on the gospel to us?

Moreover, the picture of modernist Christianity that some of the emerging people paint is nowhere near my own experience. My father was a church planter. Though he lived all his life in the West, he had to learn another language and culture to reach the people to whom he felt called. For the first four decades of his ministry, in a time and place where the gospel was simply not growing very fast anywhere, he seldom preached to crowds of more than forty, and often enough to ten or twelve (four of whom were his own family). He was so poor that he seldom had access to the commentaries, theologies, poetry, literature, science, and books on culture that I read today—but the books that he had, he knew well, and he kept poring over his Greek New Testament, and to some extent his Hebrew Old Testament, in the weeks before he died. But was he merely propositional? Did he understand nothing of the Holy Spirit shining through good works? The fact of the matter is that he was so generous with his limited resources that eventually Mum had to take over the family accounts, because we were going hungry as Dad gave everything away. Shall I tell you of his work for an orphanage? Shall I mention the odd time when, after a service when he had preached to thirty people, he withdrew to his study, got down on his knees, and wept in prayer for the people to whom he had preached?

In some ways, Dad was the most ordinary of pastors. If I ever edit and publish some of his papers, the title will be *Memoirs of an Ordinary Pastor*. I could tell you of a lot of ordinary pastors from that generation. Inevitably, in some measure they were creatures of their time—just as are Burke and Sweet and McLaren. But they were not given to condemning the previous generations.

A Condemnation That Is Often Theologically Shallow and Intellectually Incoherent

My *third* criticism can be stated briefly. The almost universal condemnation of modernism, and of Christianity under modernism, is not only historically skewed and ethically ungrateful, but is frequently theologically shallow and intellectually incoherent.

It is theologically shallow because it overlooks the basic fact that no worldview, no epistemological system developed by us in this fallen world, is entirely good or entirely bad. God's gracious "common grace" assures us that even systems that are deeply structurally flawed will preserve some insight in them somewhere; our sin ensures that even a system closely aligned with Scripture will be in some measure distorted. Thus thoughtful Christians should not identify themselves completely with either modernism or postmodernism, nor should they utterly damn either entity. The emerging church movement will have blossomed into some maturity when it becomes a little more even-handed, articulating the internal strengths of modernism and warning against the dangers of the latter.

It is intellectually incoherent because, in the spirit of postmodern toleration, most emergent publications go out of their way to find good things about every other "ism"—Buddhism, say, or Islam or the Aztec Indians or tribal animism. The one "ism" about which some appear to find it almost impossible to say anything positive, especially in the publications of emerging leaders, is modernism (as they understand it). Thus the intellectual stance they have adopted as part of gaining openness and less absolutism becomes quasi-absolutist in its condemnation of modernism.

This is tied to another complex historical development that I can only mention here, though I hope to publish a short book on the subject in due course. It used to be that tolerance was understood to be the virtue that permits, even encourages, those with whom we disagree to speak up and defend their point of view. One recalls Voltaire's famous dictum: "I may disagree with what you have to say, but I shall defend to the death your right to say it." In other words, one had to disagree with someone or something before one could tolerate it. But in our postmodern world, tolerance is increasingly understood to be the virtue that refuses to think that any opinion is bad or evil or stupid. One "tolerates" everything because nothing is beyond the pale—except the view that rejects this view of tolerance: for that, there is no tolerance at all.

Quite frankly, this is intellectually incoherent. A capitalist may tolerate a Marxist and vice versa; a Muslim may tolerate a Christian and vice versa. But is it coherent to say, "I cannot say that there is anything amiss in your stance, and I tolerate you"? One has to disagree before one tolerates.[9] But the only area where the postmodern voices of tolerance strongly disagree

---

[9] Failure to observe this elementary reality crops up well before the era of postmodernism. In an 1888 review of a book by Phillips Brooks entitled *Tolerance*, Benjamin B. Warfield wrote, "[T]he kind of tolerance which Dr. Brooks most admires, 'the tolerance which grows up in any man who is aware that truth is larger than his conception of it, and that what seem to be other men's errors must often be other parts of the truth of which he has only a portion,' appears to us no tolerance at all, but catholicity of spirit. We are not 'tolerant' of known or suspected truth; true tolerance comes into play only when we are confronted with what we recognize as error; and this is the reason why, as Dr. Brooks admirably argues, there can be no real tolerance in a mind which has not strong convictions and no firm grasp on truth" (*Presbyterian Review* 9 [1888], 161). I am grateful to Fred Zaspel for drawing my attention to this passage.

with anyone is in the arena of what they judge to be modernism: in this case, they think the "ism" is bad, and they have very little tolerance for it. If someone argues that another position, or another religion, is misconceived or erroneous or even evil at some point or other—e.g., child sacrifice among the Aztecs—they will reply that child sacrifice was probably very meaningful for the Aztecs and who are we to criticize?

Thus, where they disagree with no one, postmoderns claim to be tolerant (which is incoherent), and in the one primary arena where they strongly disagree with others (namely, with moderns) they themselves prove intolerant, not least by labeling their modernist opponents intolerant even though all that modernism opponents are asking for is the right to disagree civilly with stances they judge to be deeply mistaken—not for the right to shut them up. When we read some emerging leaders on all the other "isms" except modernism and admire their large-heartedness, and then turn to their treatment of what they understand modernism to be, don't we capture a whiff of intellectual incoherence?

One could argue that a considerable amount of so-called postmodern thought, including that found within the emerging church movement, succumbs to what Christopher Shannon calls "the tradition of conspicuous criticism," that is, to the "critical project of uprooting all received traditions." Insofar as that criticism is correct, postmodernism proves that at this juncture it has not escaped its modernist roots. The frequent appeal to tradition in postmodern thought, including the emerging church movement, is invariably an appeal to an older tradition or another tradition or an unfamiliar tradition or an eclectic tradition—anything but recent tradition, precisely because the agenda is the "critical uprooting of all received traditions."[10] I shall briefly return to one element of this point in the next chapter.

A Particularization of the First Three Criticisms

My *fourth* criticism is a particularization of the first three—not directed to everyone in the emerging church movement, but only to a few, who tend

---

[10] See Christopher Shannon, *Conspicuous Criticism: Tradition, the Individual, and Culture in American Social Thought, from Veblen to Mills* (Baltimore: Johns Hopkins University Press, 1996). See also Richard Stivers, *The Cult of Cynicism* (Oxford: Blackwell, 1994).

to be among the most capable. I mentioned that in his recent seminar,[11] Brian McLaren, working through the social history as he understands it, assigns the major blame for the litany of major evils during the past three centuries—Nazism, Communism, slavery, the slaughter of the Aztecs, colonialism, imperialism—to absolutism, and absolutism, he argues, is the fruit of the Enlightenment, the fruit of modernism's endless quest for certainty. Indeed, the end of World War II witnessed the thoughtful, even brilliant, reflections of a number of European (especially French) thinkers who were trying to understand what had gone wrong with the Enlightenment project. They came to recognize not only the terrible abuse and violence provoked by absolutism, but the intellectual instability of absolutism—and this contributed massively to postmodernism. Thus modernism has been at least a major contributor to most of the world's mega-ills of the past three centuries, and the answer is postmodernism.

Once again, we find broad-brush condemnation of modernism, and the solution is postmodernism. A detailed analysis would require a couple of books, and I will make some comments in the next chapter of this book. But let me give some critique here of this reading of modernism and its ills.

(1) Scholars have advanced rather different interpretations of the history of modernism, some with more plausibility than McLaren's. For instance, Richard Bauckham thinks that what is most characteristic of modernity from the Enlightenment to the present is the pursuit of freedom and the quest for human autonomy. Most of the early Enlightenment thinkers were theists, or at least deists, but as the modern period progressed, it increasingly marginalized God—and thus it became less and less clear what freedom means. The door was opened to the most arbitrary analyses or the most immediate pleasure-seeking self-assertion.[12] This reading of modernism will strike many of us as a stronger contender than absolutism itself.

(2) A serious problem with analyzing Western intellectual thought in terms of absolutism is that it is incapable of making necessary distinctions. It assumes that acts of power, engendered by absolutism, are all equally

---

[11] "Pluralism Revisited." See chap. 1, p. 30.

[12] See especially Richard Bauckham, *God and the Crisis of Freedom: Biblical and Contemporary Reflections* (Louisville: Westminster John Knox Press, 2002).

evil. That was very much the thesis of Michel Foucault, who argued that all utterance (including his own, he admitted) seeks, implicitly or explicitly, to convince and thus is guilty of "totalization." All claims to truth and right are masked exercises of power. Interestingly, long before Foucault was in fashion, Virginia Wolff famously remarked that Great Britain and Hitler's Germany were little different. And that was a pretty standard leftish line during the Cold War: morally speaking, it was argued, there was little difference between America and the USSR.

This sort of analysis is incapable of making distinctions that cry out to be made. I am not at all suggesting that the United Kingdom or America was always righteous. But the UK did not attempt to annihilate all gypsies and Jews; it did not deploy death camps; at the end of the war, the electorate dumped Winston Churchill, because the form of government was still a democracy (what electorate could have dumped Hitler?). Britain's greatest geopolitical moral failure immediately before the war was not brutally and violently annexing neighboring states, but blindly adopting an appeasement policy in the vain hope that determined evil can be stopped by good will and long conversations. In other words, it was the *failure* of Britain and France to stand up to Hitler when he annexed the Rhineland, the *failure* to be absolute, that constituted the greatest Allied contribution to the outbreak of World War II. Read a well-researched volume on Stalin,[13] and compare him with Franklin Roosevelt.

Nor do I overlook America's slaughter of its native peoples, sometimes in violence, sometimes because of diseases we introduced. Nor can we ever duck slavery and its legacy. Still, to blame all this on absolutism seems very reductionistic: what stopped the slave trade across the Atlantic, after all, was Britain's *absolutist* stance against the trade after Christians engineered abolition through the Parliament at Westminster, and British gunboats pretty much halted the slave trade across the Atlantic and in the Persian Gulf.

(3) We must compare the barbarities of the *premodern* world with the barbarities of the modern world. We have our Hitler and Stalin and Pol Pot; they have their Genghis Khan and Nero and Antiochus IV Epiphanes.

---

[13] Simon Sebag Montefiore, *Stalin: The Court of the Red Tsar* (New York: Knopf, 2004).

We could also make comparisons with another sort of world—the tribalism of Idi Amin, perhaps. Suddenly we recognize that outrageous cruelty and evil are not the unique products of modernism.

(4) We should also think about some of the good things that have emerged from modernism. As a start, modern medicine, hygiene, rapid transportation, rapid communication, greatly extended lifespan, and much greater knowledge of the physical world all come to mind. With these successes have come corresponding evils, of course, not because of the superlative evil of modernism, but because we human beings are rebels by nature and choice. We can corrupt *any* system; we can turn any epistemological structure to perverted ends; we can twist any ideology, we can invent evil uses out of any invention or discovery. This does not warrant tying to absolutism or modernism.

(5) Is absoluteness the problem? God declares, "You shall not commit adultery": that is an absolute. Is it evil? God is absolutely sovereign: is that intrinsically evil? Is the problem absoluteness, or human lust to become like God? But doesn't that lust exert itself under every worldview, every regime, every epistemology? This is not to say that therefore every system or epistemology or form of government is morally equivalent; it means that no system or epistemology or form of government can generate utopia, because we people are evil. Lord Acton is often cited: "Power tends to corrupt, and absolute power corrupts absolutely." That is true, of course, in a fallen and broken world; it is not a dictum that will make much sense in the new heaven and the new earth. So it is not the absoluteness of the power that is crucial, but who is wielding it. Indeed, sometimes evil springs up in part because of a *failure* to resist evil.[14]

Edmund Burke said that for evil to prevail, all that is necessary is for good people to do nothing. But granted, then, that in the fallen world all power corrupts, one can distinguish between forms of government according to how power is achieved, taken away, dispensed, checked, or removed. One achievement of the various forms of law-grounded, multi-party institutional

---

[14] That is why, under "just war" theory, when the conditions of a just war are met, it is a moral failure *not* to go to war, since it involves lack of love for neighbor, an unwillingness to sacrifice for the sake of others.

democracy in the world is that it provides a peaceful means for turfing rulers out every few years, without bloodshed. It may not be terribly efficient, but this in itself is surely better than the alternatives.[15] And democracy, too, is a fruit of the Enlightenment, arguably under the impact of Christian teaching about the distinction between church and state. But none of this comes across in McLaren's writing or in the earlier French voices of *déconstruction* to whom he refers. Instead, we read that modernism generates absolutism, absolutism is a primary cause of all our ills, and so modernism is the great Satan.

(6) Another dispiriting element in McLaren's writing is his willingness to lump all forms of Christianity together, without reflection on theology, vitality, biblical fidelity, or exceptions. Pizarro thus becomes prototypical. Even in the realm of missionary endeavor—far too much of which was confused with or at least accompanied by a colonial fervor—fairness and even-handedness require that we recall that William Carey was not wanted in India by the East India Company, who refused him transport and help and generally despised him and made things difficult for him, precisely because he was not there to exploit the people but to love them and evangelize them. Jonathan Edwards stood up against the authorities when they abused the Indians he tried to serve. J. Hudson Taylor insisted on dressing and eating and living like the Chinese to whom he was called. And almost a century before "contextualization" was heard of, Roland Allen was laying out the principles of establishing "indigenous" churches: they had to be self-governing, self-propagating, and self-supporting.[16] Between 1880 and 1910, about one third of all missionaries who went to Central Africa died within their first year. Some mission agencies advised missionaries to

---

[15] Winston Churchill said, "Democracy is the worst form of Government except for all those other forms that have been tried from time to time."

[16] Roland Allen, *Missionary Methods: St. Paul's or Ours?* 6th ed. (repr.: Grand Rapids: Eerdmans, 1962). Naturally, the work is seriously dated. From an emphasis on indigeneity, we have moved to contextualization, which adds (to self-governing, self-propagating, and self-supporting) the importance of fresh, context-based theologizing.

bring their own coffins; and still they went. In short, is it fair to write off the entire *modern* missionary movement? Was not the gospel so powerfully operative in many missionaries that they were, on many fronts, counter-cultural?

Moreover, as I travel around the world today and see different missionaries at work, the nation whose missionaries are most likely to demand that local converts conform in churchmanship, styles of spirituality, and culture to the patterns of the sending nation back home is South Korea. Many of their zealous and self-sacrificial missionaries have, I fear, learned all too little from the mistakes of the Western world. But make no mistake: in this case, the controlling pattern is not modernist epistemology, but an underlay of Confucianism (which many of these missionaries readily admit, at least in private!). Once again, the sweeping indictments advanced by some emerging church thinkers are at best reductionistic and frequently historically distorted.

So much, then, for these four points on the evaluation of modernism.

On the Evaluation of Postmodernism

As in the previous section, in which I attempted to evaluate the emerging church movement's understanding of modernism, so here: I am not now offering a critique of postmodernism, or of the emerging church's response to postmodernism (which is the concern of the next two chapters), but of the emerging church's understanding of what postmodernism is.

In many respects I agree with that understanding. Even though the roots of the movement go back a long way, the last few decades have witnessed a substantial shift in Western culture's approach to truth and our perceived ability to know truth. This has been accompanied by a decline in absolutism, an increase in perspectivalism (the view that all claims to truth are finally no more than different perspectives), a decreased confidence in reason and the possibility of knowing any objective reality, and an increased emphasis on other virtues such as relationships, affective responses, and the importance of community and therefore of tradition.

Whether these changes are best labeled "postmodernism" or "late modernism" or "ultramodernism" we may leave to the experts, but the changes themselves are hard to deny. If one focuses on how we arrived at this point, the lines of continuity become clearer, so labels such as "late modernism" and "ultramodernism" seem more appropriate. If we focus on the changes that these developments have brought into the culture, the expression "postmodernism" has some merit.

Despite this broad agreement, however, some of the emerging church's understanding of postmodernism strikes me as doubtful, short-sighted, and (predictably) absolutist. This is important, because what the movement is advocating by way of reformation and renewal turns in large measure on the accuracy of this construal. Since much of this construal is bound up with their response to postmodernism, it is best handled in the next two chapters, but I will make some observations here. I shall restrict myself to four points.

Appealing to a Buzz Word

First, American culture is very diverse, and within this diversity "postmodernism" has become a buzz word that some love and some repudiate. One of my colleagues recently argued in one of his classes that for all its strengths, there are some elements of postmodernism, in its strongest form, that appear to be incompatible with confessional Christianity. After the lecture he received an email from a student, who said, in effect, that as far as she could see, in her church postmodernism was the Lord's Prayer, more structured liturgy, and the Apostles' Creed. What's the matter with that? The answer, of course, is "nothing." However, churches that have used these components for centuries might be surprised that such habits constitute postmodernism. I think this student was merely expressing appreciation for being linked to some longer tradition, which is commendable. Yet such a use of "postmodernism" is not very penetrating. Worse, it may open the student up to some rather harmful elements in postmodernism simply because the word has a positive ring for her, if she doesn't have a real grasp of cultural developments.

There is a sense in which, for many people, being postmodern is being "with it"—even when that means merely reestablishing some sort of link to tradition. When an expression becomes a buzz word, the content that one thinker or movement puts into it is not necessarily what is being understood by someone else.

Some writers, of course, are fighting any form of epistemological postmodernism tooth and nail. Many of these are scientists who are convinced that, at least in their own domains, objective truth can in some measure be known—and some of them are fighting a bitter intellectual battle to expose the absurdities intrinsic to much that is labeled postmodern.[17] But there is also a segment of the younger generation that is getting sick and tired of postmodernism, and another segment that has become apathetic toward the discussion. Ten years ago, when leaders at a large training retreat of the InterVarsity Christian Fellowship warned the attendees that the forms of corporate worship would expand their comfort zones, they meant that some of the music would be harder rock than they had previously experienced in a Christian setting. Recently I attended another such meeting where exactly the same appeal was made—expanding the comfort zones of the participants—to introduce a selection of classic hymns, complete with "thees" and "thous." One reviewer of a book by McLaren[18] wrote,

> Postmodernism is something that we should give some thought to. All that said, I can't help but notice that we the Christians seem to be much more hot and bothered by the onset of postmodernism than are they the world. I mean, just take a look at all the apocalyptic Christian literature that has

---

[17] Perhaps the most striking example is the learned and humorous book by Paul R. Gross and Norman Levitt, *Higher Superstition: The Academic Left and Its Quarrels with Science* (Baltimore: Johns Hopkins University Press, 1994). Gross and Levitt are secular modernists with their own agendas, but they make some good points. I have observed that on many university campuses with strong churches around them, the ratio of Christian students and professors from a science/math/computers/business background to Christian students and professors from a fine arts/social science/psychology/literature background varies between about six-to-one and eighteen-to-one. I suspect that part of the reason for this is that the former disciplines still preserve categories for objective truth. Another part is that many of those involved in university evangelism are only slowly adapting to approaches that genuinely understand and respond to the epistemological structures of the latter disciplines.

[18] Brian D. McLaren, *The Church on the Other Side* (Grand Rapids: Zondervan, 2000).This book was previously published under the title *Reinventing Your Church* (Grand Rapids: Zondervan, 1998).

been put out about it; you'd think the antichrist had just been crowned. Frankly, I'm bored with it. This apocalypse has gotten old. I'm tired of the bombastic language; I'm tired of being told that we've never seen anything like this; I'm tired of all these excitable authors trying to one-up each other with their cataclysmic descriptions of how much the world has changed. ("We live in a time unlike any other time that any living person has known. It's not merely that things are changing. Change itself has changed." [21] Right.) On top of it all, I'm tired of being told that the church is on the edge of extinction if it doesn't have a complete overhaul to deal with these "tectonic" changes. I just don't believe it. And that's not because I'm an old codger who can't bring himself to embrace this brave new world. I'm 24 years old; I *live* this brave new world. Change is not a problem for me; I *love* it! I look forward to moving to a new city, meeting new people, seeing new cultures, learning new things. I relish the thought of casting off into the world and ministering to people who are not firmly grounded in, or even convinced of, truth. In that, Brian McLaren and I are on the same page. I like his chutzpah. But unlike McLaren, I'm also convinced that ministering to postmoderns does not mean diving head-first into their ocean of uncertainty. I don't want to commiserate with them; I want to offer them something different — something like Truth![19]

Of course, this is very much a minority report. In any case, part of the author's protest is against the emerging church movement's solutions (which is the subject of chapters 5 and 6 of this book). But part of it is against the overkill, sweeping claims, and exaggerations that time and sober reflection will eventually discard. Wise and measured warning are helpful, but divisive overstatement is not.

Lumping All Social Change under One Rubric

Second, a factor that ultimately reduces the credibility of the emerging church movement's analysis of postmodernism is its tendency to lump every social change under this rubric and somehow tie things together in

---

[19] The review is by Greg Gilbert and is published at http://www.9marks. org/cc/article/0,,ptid314526|chid598026|ciid1562286,00.html. The words Gilbert quotes from page 21 of McLaren's book are from a statement by William Easum quoted by McLaren.

causal relationships. It is as if one of the emerging leaders has just read the latest sociological analysis on something in Western culture, and the matter is then promptly written up in popularized and sometimes apocalyptic language and tied to postmodernism. The more that happens, the more postmodernism means nothing more than change in culture. All cultures change: there is nothing new in that. Sometimes the changes move along at the speed of a glacier; sometimes, as in the case of certain wars or major catastrophes, the changes are astonishingly rapid. Today the "regular" changes are rapid, owing in no small measure to the speed of our communications. But if every change is trumpeted as a crucial component of postmodernism, then postmodernism means nothing at all except change or speed of change.

It is better, I think, to distinguish postmodernism from what might be called the *correlatives* of postmodernism. In other words, it is more useful to define postmodernism fairly carefully, and then changes that fall outside that definition do not constitute postmodernism or serve as evidence of it or justify any particular thesis about postmodernism. The only alternative, as I have said, is so amorphous an approach that postmodern culture means nothing more than changing culture.

This is not to say that the cultural changes we observe taking place that are not part of a well-defined postmodernism have no relation to postmodernism whatsoever. Many of these cultural developments can be usefully thought of as *correlatives* of postmodernism—i.e., developments that may be spurred on by postmodernism or may themselves spur on postmodernism. For instance, many have taken note of the rising biblical illiteracy in Western culture. Postmodernism certainly cannot be said to be the sufficient cause of such illiteracy. However, once people come to think of all texts as essentially totalizing, or believe that all religions enjoy the same epistemological footing, or think that all religious claims are in principle nonauthoritative except for those who choose to walk in one particular tradition, it becomes less obvious why one should revere the Bible, let alone read it, unless one is also reading many other religious texts and assigning to all of them the same authority. Conversely, biblical illiteracy did not cause postmodernism. Nevertheless, it is clearly easier for large numbers of people to adopt postmodern epistemology once a deep knowledge of the Bible is no longer culture-wide.

Other correlatives abound. Many, for instance, have pointed to an emotional homelessness or loneliness,[20] often linked to the nature of urban life and some contemporary technologies. A few writers think these developments define postmodernism. But again, I find in this no clue as to what postmodernism really means. I suspect it is better to conclude that postmodern epistemology readily strengthens this tendency toward being disconnected from the human race, since so much is defined by the perspectives of a particular interpretative group—and, conversely, this sense of dislocation provides a kind of emotional support to postmodernism.

Thus, when we are told that in the postmodern world "we become postconquest, postmechanistic, postanalytical, postsecular, postobjective, postcritical, postorganizational, postindividualistic, post-Protestant, and postconsumerist,"[21] several fears spring to mind. Despite these best efforts at sophisticated definitions, several of the categories are little more than buzz words of disapprobation.[22] One or two of them are in direct conflict with the

---

[20] E.g., Brian J. Walsh, "Homemaking in Exile: Homelessness, Postmodernity and Theological Reflection," in *Renewing the Mind in Learning*, ed. Doug Blomberg and Ian Lambert (Sydney: Centre for the Study of Australian Christianity, 1998); Steven Bouma-Prediger, "Yearning for Home: The Christian Doctrine of Creation in a Postmodern Age," in *Postmodern Philosophy and Christian Thought*, ed. Merold Westphal (Bloomington: University of Indiana Press, 1999); Richard Stivers, *Shades of Loneliness: Pathologies of a Technological Society* (Lanham, MD: Rowman & Littlefield, 2004).

[21] Brian D. McLaren, *A New Kind of Christian: A Tale of Two Friends on a Spiritual Journey* (San Francisco: Jossey Bass, 2001), 19.

[22] Ibid., 16–19. For instance, is the postmodern world postconsumerist? Americans continue to rack up credit card debt, and younger Americans—those most likely to be postmodern in their epistemology—have been shown to be notoriously *less* generous than their parents and grandparents at the same time of life. Is the postmodern world postmechanical? If the age of the machine includes computers and the entire digital world, just watch postmoderns on their cell phones. Is the postmodern world postanalytic? All the emerging church leaders are busily analyzing modernism and postmodernism. All of McLaren's categories need serious qualification or, in some cases, overturning.

understanding of postmodernism adopted by others (e.g., see the comments of Andy Crouch in chapter 1),[23] and one or two, such as "post-Protestant," raise theological questions of enormous significance that must be faced (see chapter 5). But for now the thing to note is that unless postmodernism means nothing more than "a period of a lot of rapid cultural change," the multiplicity of tags adds little to careful thought about the nature of post-modern culture and proves rather more emotive than accurate.

In short, much of the emerging church's analysis of postmodernism would be more convincing if it were not such a grab bag of social changes. It is worth thinking about all of these changes, but the analysis cries out for more rigor than is usually applied. In all fairness, the emerging church movement is not alone in this failing.

Looking Passé

Third, although a lot of books are being churned out on the subject of post-modernism, including many by Christians, most of them are being published in America. Even here, in academic circles, the subject is beginning to look passé; in Europe, to which many analysts look as the source of the movement, it is hard to find serious thinkers who use the term very much anymore. In 2000, a special consultation was convened at the Sorbonne of about twenty of the world's leading intellectuals, tasked to reflect on the current cultural situation. In the book that emerged from that consultation, not one paper even used the word "postmodern."[24]

---

[23] Pp. 26–27.

[24] The book is *Christianisme: héritage et destins*, ed. Cyrille Michon (Paris: Librairie Générale française, 2001). Luminaries at the conference included Marie Balmary, René Girard, Julia Kristeva, Cardinal Ratzinger, George Steiner, and Charles Taylor among others. Interestingly, the conference boasted as its title "2000 ans après quoi? [2000 years after what?]" Henri Blocher concludes, "I grow more and more impatient, I confess, with the very word 'postmodern': as a tag, it is so convenient, it boosts your ego, and is favourable to book-selling [at least in America!] to have 'postmodern' in the title! Actually it is late modernism. I think all the serious writers are not using the language of 'postmodern'—the vast majority of them, at least." See the interview with him in *Themelios* 29/3 (2004), 37–42 (esp. p. 42).

In some ways this goes too far. The situation in Europe is not exactly the same as the situation in America. Yet one does fear, just a little, that once again a movement that was on the cusp of intellectual endeavor half a century ago, and popular in Europe four decades ago, and made popular on university campuses here a quarter of a century ago, is now the darling of popular evangelical writers trying to sound prophetic. I do not mind using "postmodern" and "postmodernism," at least while I am speaking in North America. But not only have the terms and ideas associated with them become unwieldy unless carefully defined; they have also been exploited to justify an entire movement that has been invested with apocalyptic overtones, at the very time when serious thinkers are beginning to question the stability of the movement.

In my view, the changes in practical epistemology that have been popularized during the last few decades in America are still with us, whether or not "postmodernism" continues to be the acceptable term in academia, so it is still worth investing serious thought and energy in trying to understand what has happened and trying to learn to communicate the gospel to new generations. But in some circles, epistemological apathy combined with a renewed lust for success and a determination to climb the organizational ladders probably constitute threats at least equal to that of postmodern epistemology,[25] and in other circles, various contemporary forms of pantheism and syncretism are surfacing. Postmodern epistemology can be tied to these developments, of course (correlatives?). But just as megachurch priorities now feel strangely dated in some contexts, so it is easy to predict that the priorities of the contemporary emerging church movement will, unless they change, seem strangely dated in twenty years.

Proclaiming Authenticity

Fourth, some of the emerging church writers talk about postmodernism as if the age of authentic Christianity has arrived. What came before was nasty

---

[25] See especially the penetrating essay of David Brooks, "The Organization Kid," *Atlantic Monthly* 287/4 (April 2001), 40–54, which arose out of Brooks's indepth interviews with many undergraduates at Princeton University. This new generation, he asserts, is *more* likely to accept authority.

in that it was absolutist. And if there was something of value in the older period, it has been captured *within* postmodernism (recall McLaren's attempt to make postmodern enfold the modern, as described in chapter 1). Although McLaren can admit, "Postmodernism is the latest in a long series of absurdities,"[26] it is less than clear why he wants so much of our approach to accommodate the absurdity. In any case, in much of the emerging literature what is missing is evenhanded evaluation, like that of Michael Horton: "That much has changed since the storming of the Bastille and the invention of television, I do not doubt—some for the better and some for the worse. But the cheerleading for the idea that we have entered a radically new era, a utopia of unprecedented opportunity, fails to move me . . . because I just don't believe this hype. I think that every period has its pluses and minuses and that typecasting periods leads to demonizing or equally impulsive lionizing."[27] But this brings us to the subject of the next chapter.

On the Social Attractiveness of Particular "isms"

Obviously there are significant variations in level and approach among the leaders and writers of the emerging church movement. At one end, one worries when Dan Kimball says that in the light of current biblical illiteracy we need to "deconstruct" and "redefine" biblical terms such as "Armageddon" and "gospel."[28] If all he means is that we need to explain terms in the Bible that are likely to be misunderstood by today's biblical illiterates, then of course he is right, and all who evangelize biblical illiterates know it, whether they think of themselves as moderns or postmoderns or something else. I will happily give Kimball the benefit of the doubt, hoping that is what he means. But he should be careful when he uses words like "redefine" and "deconstruct." To "redefine" a word is not to determine its customary meaning in given contexts by careful study; it is to give it a new meaning so as to

---

[26] *The Church on the Other Side*, 165.

[27] Michael Horton, "Better Homes and Gardens," in *The Church in Emerging Culture: Five Perspectives*, ed. Leonard Sweet (El Cajon, CA: emergentYS / Grand Rapids: Zondervan, 2003), 107.

[28] Cf. chap. 1, p. 37.

make a passage mean something novel—a perfectly legitimate procedure in some postmodern literary exercises, following the well-known practice of Humpty Dumpty.[29] Probably Kimball uses "deconstruct" to mean "unpack" or something of that order—but no one in the field of postmodern studies uses it that way. It has to do with a literary approach, under the hermeneutics of suspicion, that hunts down tensions and inconsistencies in a text (those who deploy deconstruction insist that all texts have them) in order to set them at odds with each other and thus *deconstruct* the text, to generate new insights that might actually contradict what a text ostensibly says.

It appears that Kimball is completely unfamiliar with any serious discussion of postmodernism, despite his ardor for explaining what it is and what we ought to do about it. David Mills thinks this sort of criticism is unfair, since, he argues, most Christians could not define "deconstruction" accurately.[30] True enough—but most Christians are not trying to define postmodernism or tell us how we should change because of it. At very least, Kimball should tone down his rhetoric.

Some discussion within the emerging movement is more sophisticated and introduces a few of the contemporary strategic thinkers in the broader marketplace of ideas. But apart from occasional concessions, the rhetoric of these discussions is almost always over the top: the church must adapt to the postmodern world or it will die; unless we get on board with the direction of the emerging church movement, we are probably out-of-date modernists and absolutists to boot—all set forth in absolutist terms.

That, perhaps, is the wry irony that lies at the heart of this movement, or "conversation." In its tone and approach, it tends to see the world in very black-and-white categories. Of all the Christian writers who explore

---

[29]   "'When *I* use a word,' Humpty Dumpty said, in rather a scornful tone, 'it means just what I choose it to mean—neither more nor less.'"
        "'The question is,' said Alice, 'whether you can make words mean so many different things'" (Lewis Carroll, *Alice's Adventures in Wonderland* and *Through the Looking Glass* [New York: Modern Library Paperback, 2002], 185).

[30]   David M. Mills, "The Emergent Church—Another Perspective: A Critical Response to D. A. Carson's Staley Lectures," at http://kevincole.blogspot.com/2004_04_01_kevincole_archive.html.

postmodernism, none is quite so modernist—so absolutist—as the emerging church movement leaders in their defense of postmodern approaches.

It is easy to understand why. Most theological aberrations appeal to particular segments of Christendom in general, or of evangelicalism in particular. For instance, theologians who espouse open theology make almost no inroads into the Reformed community; for obvious reasons, their appeal is almost entirely among Arminians. The "new perspective on Paul" appeals to a wider range of Christian readers, but not surprisingly, its most enthusiastic defenders are those in the Reformed tradition who have adopted a fairly static view of theological structure (more systematic theology than biblical theology) and have given some serious thought to the connections between justification and self-identity, and justification and holiness. The appeal of the Disciples of Christ and their insistence that baptism is as necessary to salvation as faith is likely to make more inroads among those with little or no theology of baptism than among those who are well-informed in their tradition. Theonomists make inroads into the Reformed churches; their appeal among Arminians is virtually nil. These sorts of tendencies are not absolute, of course, but they are so common they can scarcely be overlooked.

And the emerging church movement? One of the striking commonalities among its leaders is the high number of them who come from intensely conservative or even fundamentalist backgrounds.[31] When they describe the kinds of churches from which they spring, a very high percentage of them have emerged from a tradition that is substantially separated from the culture. These churches often lay considerable emphasis on getting certain doctrine, often cast in fundamentalist mode, nicely constructed and confessed. The passage of time has moved these churches farther and farther from the very different directions being pursued by the broader culture, and sensitive and concerned individuals within such traditions finally make a break, not least for the gospel's sake. It becomes a mark of freedom to have a glass of wine and watch some movies that our

---

[31] This is not to say that *all* emerging leaders come from this background, for that is as patently false as saying that *all* theonomists come from Reformed backgrounds. But the alignments are both demonstrable and noteworthy.

former ecclesiastical friends wouldn't approve. Understandably, the pendulum may continue to swing quite a long way.

None of this background is meant to determine whether the emerging church movement is right or wrong, biblically faithful or otherwise. Rather, it shows that a fair amount of its heat and overgeneralizing seems to spring from the mistaken assumption that most of traditional evangelicalism is just like the conservative churches from which they came. That betrays the narrowness of many of their backgrounds and helps to explain why their rhetoric and appeals to postmodern sensitivity sound so absolutist: this is the language and rhetoric on which they were weaned.[32]

None of this criticism is meant to set aside the positive assessments of the emerging church movement I offered in chapter 2. Granted the nature and focus of the movement, however, one must not only try to evaluate how accurate its understanding of contemporary culture is, but how wise and biblically faithful are its proposals for the way ahead. And that takes us to the next three chapters.

---

[32] Two or three have objected, sometimes sharply, that by saying these things I seem to be imagining that I myself am entirely neutral, above the fray. But that entirely misses the point of my argument. I would be the first to insist, that none of us, myself included, ever escapes the limitations intrinsic to our finitude and cultural locatedness: see the next chapter. But does that condemn us all to the worst forms of perspectivalism? If so, there is no hope for the preservation of the gospel; if not, then there are lessons to be learned by reading history more broadly, by becoming intimately familiar with Christians in other languages and cultures, by enlarging the frames of reference in which we can comfortably move. We are then far more likely to become self-critical.

Chapter 4

PERSONAL REFLECTIONS
ON POSTMODERNISM'S
CONTRIBUTION AND
CHALLENGES

Before venturing criticism of the emerging church movement's approach to postmodernism, it may be helpful to outline my own approach to these matters. In large part this is because I concur that postmodernism, however difficult to define and however disputed the prognostications as to its future, must be taken seriously. I want to state clearly that my quarrel with Emergent is not that it is trying to read the times or that it thinks that postmodernism, properly defined, introduces serious challenges that need to be addressed; rather, its response is not as penetrating and biblically faithful as it needs to be. To act fairly, I should not only say where I think Emergent has gone wrong, but also outline my own approach to these matters. That way I can avoid becoming the proverbial armchair critic.[1]

So in this chapter I lay out, in a survey fashion, what postmodernism looks like in the North American context, and something of my own response. Then in the next chapter I shall make clear where both the analysis and the response of the emerging church movement strike me as regrettably weak and sometimes misguided.

---

[1] This chapter is a simplification and updating of a couple chapters of my book *The Gagging of God: Christianity Confronts Pluralism* (Grand Rapids: Zondervan, 1996).

Historical Reflections

Many people find it helpful to distinguish premodern epistemology, modern epistemology, and postmodern epistemology.

Premodern Epistemology

Premodern epistemology is a notoriously loose catchall category for what is common in Judeo-Christian epistemology before the Enlightenment. The important fact is that most people presupposed that God exists and knows everything. That means that all human knowing is necessarily an infinitesimally small subset of God's knowledge. Otherwise put, our knowledge depends on revelation—i.e., on God disclosing some part of what he knows, however that revelation is accomplished. On this point, a great medieval theologian like Thomas Aquinas and a great Reformer like John Calvin were agreed. This means that for the premoderns, epistemology does not begin with the self, with me: it begins with God.

To say that premoderns began with God does not mean that they thought he must know things *before* we do. Rather, it means that when premodern people thought about how they came to know things, they realized that the knowledge they were talking about was a small subset of what God already knew (since most of them assumed the existence of an omniscient God). They could not think about how they came to know something without first recognizing that, if the knowledge being considered is genuine knowledge (i.e., it conforms to what is in fact the case), God must know it first. Thus *how* they came to know things could not be separated from God's omniscience. Indeed, it could not be separated from God's omnipotence, and thus from his providential ordering of their lives; it could not be separated from revelation, and thus from his gracious willingness to disclose truth; it could not be separated from God's truthfulness, and thus from the reliability of whatever God chose to disclose. Human epistemology revolved around the "given" of God's existence, attributes, and character.

One must not think that in premodern epistemology God was so much the presupposition, the "given," that no one ever thought to advance "proofs" for the existence of God. Many Christian theologians and philosophers did exactly this. The so-called "ontological argument" for the existence of God has many forms, and some of them go back to the earliest centuries of the Christian church. After all, there were atheists in those days as well, even if their number was not great,[2] and in any case Christian theologians have always been interested in working out how to conceptualize the givens of biblical revelation into coherent systems.

Initially one might think that this is a wonderfully faithful approach to thinking about epistemology. What Christian will want to criticize a stance that begins with God? Yet in practice there were plenty of places in premodern epistemology where a wheel could come off. Just because most people in the surrounding culture believe in God does not mean that everyone does: witness Servetus the atheist, burned at the stake in Calvin's Geneva. More importantly for our issues, premodern epistemology was usually tied to a fairly "open" universe:[3] the connection between the universe and what God does is so "open" that a firm, evidence-based, coherent, and predictive science of the physical world remains largely alien.

This becomes clearer if we think about the strongest alternative—viz., a "closed" universe in which everything proceeds by cause and effect within the universe itself, without outside intervention by any God. In a closed universe the only acceptable explanations are those that deal with matter, energy, space, and time. God is an unnecessary hypothesis or, at best, some kind of figure that keeps the closed order going or stands behind it in some way. But he does not directly and continuously intervene in the world. In an open universe, however, the interventions may be so continuous and so unconstrained by the kinds of "cause and effect" sequences we take for granted today that a large space is opened up for superstition, magic, and fear. In other words, from an historical perspective the world of premodern epistemology had its own problems.

By the late premodern period, however (for convenience, the end of the sixteenth century), in intellectual circles another sort of universe was

---

[2] One thinks, for instance of Lucretius. In fact, not a few of the Epicureans were only a whisker from atheism.

[3] I am not using the word "open" the way it is used in contemporary "openness of God" theologies, in which God cannot know the future where that future depends on the free decision of sentient beings, but the way it was sometimes used in older philosophical discussion relating to the nature of cause-and-effect in a material universe.

envisaged, neither "open" nor "closed." We might call it "controlled." In a controlled universe, the sovereign God does things in regular ways so that science as we know it becomes possible, indeed inevitable: science (then called "natural philosophy") is part of finding out about God and how he does things. Thus, by careful observation of the physical universe, by experiments under controlled conditions, by trial and error, we find out more about the universe and therefore about how God habitually does things. Nevertheless, this leaves place for God to do things in extraordinary and highly irregular ways. Call such ways miracles. That leaves room for such things as the resurrection of Jesus.

Once again, of course, it was possible to distort this insight into a controlled universe. One large wing thought of God as setting up the entire universe and then letting it run, like a giant watch, while he himself is so big and so distant that he pays little or no attention to the details. This form of monotheism became known as Deism. By contrast, the more orthodox heritage pointed out that the biblical writers knew of such regularity in the world as the water cycle (Ecclesiastes 1:7 knows of water that falls from the heavens, flows into streams and rivers and ultimately into the sea, and is then evaporated back into the heavens to begin the cycle afresh), but they preferred to speak of God *sending* the rain. Of course plants provide food for the herbivores, and the carnivores eat other animals (including the herbivores), but the Bible speaks of God *feeding* all these creatures (e.g., Psalm 104:21; 136:25; 145:15; 147:9; Matthew 6:26). In other words, thoughtful Christians wanted to think of a controlled universe without succumbing to Deism.

The move toward modernism at the beginning of the seventeenth century added a crucial development that we will turn to in a moment. First, however, it is worth remembering what the church had to confront during its first few centuries. One might have thought that the world of polytheistic paganism would have had no trouble adding one more religion, this religion that came to be called Christianity. But Christianity proved impossible for paganism to swallow, precisely because Christianity was absolutist.[4]

---

[4] See especially the discussion by Robert L. Wilken, *Remembering the Christian Past* (Grand Rapids: Eerdmans, 1995), esp. the chapter "Religious Pluralism and Early Christian Thought," pp. 25–46.

It insisted that salvation came exclusively through faith in Jesus Christ, and this struck pagans as narrow-minded and, well, absolutist. Without exception, all of Christianity's earliest pagan critics insisted that there is no one way to the divine, including such important figures as Symmachus, Celsus (whose committed multiculturalism was answered by Origen), and Porphyry. The latter contended, "No teaching has yet been established which offers a universal way for the liberation of the soul."[5] In other words, Christianity provided a frame of reference that began with God and his revelation, and thus to a particular history of a particular people, and ultimately of one individual, yet claimed universal exclusiveness. The issue was not whether God in his common grace had given others some insight into this or that; the issue, rather, was how a human being could be saved, could enjoy the forgiveness of sins, could be reconciled to God the sovereign Creator and final Judge. Christians claimed *knowledge* of these matters—exclusive knowledge—and demonstrated it by how they lived and how they died.

That brings us to a rather obvious observation that can be introduced here, even if it must be developed further as we go along. Some forms of absolutism are not bad; they may even be heroic. When all the world is appealing to the finality (!) of religious pluralism, the insistence that there is only one way of salvation may be the mark of faithful witness, not least when those who bear the witness are willing to suffer and die for their confession of the truth. So it was during the first three centuries. With the Constantinian settlement (beginning of the fourth century), for the first time Christianity gained political power. How well or how badly this was handled over the centuries varied enormously, but there is no escaping the evil effects of, say, the Inquisition, where absolutism was married not to confessionalism willing to be martyred before a polytheistic pagan pluralism, but to a state determined to wield the sword to force compliance to the church's authority.

It appears, then, that "absolutism" in itself is the wrong target. Everything depends on the context. Hitler demanded absolute allegiance, and all who read these pages, I imagine, will concur that such absolutism was bad. Christ demands absolute allegiance, and most who read these pages, I imagine, will concur that such absolutism is good—even if some readers will try to soften

---

[5] Cited by Augustine, *City of God* 10.32.

this absolutism by various postmodern appeals that I have yet to confront. My point, at this juncture, is that absolutism is not quite the issue. If in formally acknowledging the absolute authority of King Jesus, Christians actually disown many fundamental things that King Jesus says—such things as the importance of meekness, the distinction between the roles of the church and the roles of the state, the deceitfulness of the human heart in its perennial lust for power—the problem is not absolutism, but selective absolutism.

So much, then, for a few preliminary observations on premodern epistemology.

The Six Elements of Modern Epistemology

Modern epistemology is a label commonly applied to the epistemology of the Western world from about the beginning of the seventeenth century until a few decades ago. Historical movements are invariably messy. The entire culture does not carefully walk along one circumscribed path. But at the risk of oversimplification, the onset of modern epistemology is often, for convenience, connected with the thought of René Descartes.

Descartes (1596–1650) observed that an increasing number of his intellectual friends no longer bought into premodern epistemology. In fact, some of them were closet atheists. As a devout Roman Catholic, Descartes wanted to be able to convince them of the truth of Catholicism, but found the common "givens" were too few to make significant progress in discussions with them. So he set himself the task of doubting everything, not because he himself actually did doubt everything, but because he was trying to find a bedrock, a foundation, that he and his intellectual friends could share. He settled on the formula for which he is famous: in Latin, *Cogito, ergo sum* (I think, therefore I am).[6] This stance Descartes

---

[6] It is often pointed out that more than a millennium earlier, Augustine had said something rather similar: *Si fallor, sum* (If I err, I am). But Augustine never attempted to develop an entire epistemological structure out of this observation and never treated it as an axiomatic foundation. It is even possible that Descartes vaguely recalled Augustine (since every learned person in those days read Augustine) and unwittingly developed his thought along lines never envisaged by the great patristic thinker.

judged to be self-evident, a sure foundation. Nestled into a fairly complex philosophical structure (which we need not explore here, since virtually no one accepts that structure as credible), this ostensible axiom became the foundation of Cartesian thought (as the thought of Descartes is often called).

Cartesian thought, Enlightenment thought, modern epistemology—popular writers often view these as synonymous expressions. That is not quite fair, not least because Descartes's axiom was only one small part of his thought, and because of other complexities, some of which are mentioned in the first chapter. But if we can risk generalization, we may lump these three together and argue that over time modern epistemology was characterized by six elements:

1. Instead of beginning with God, as premodern epistemology did, modern epistemology began with the finite "I." In Descartes's expression: *I* think, therefore *I* am. This means that for the modernist thinker, God is not the "given," but at best the conclusion of the argument. How human beings come to know something *may* still be a matter of revelation, of finding out (by whatever means) some small subset of what God already knows perfectly and exhaustively, but it no longer has to be. We are no longer dependent on God for all our knowing. *We* must learn things, *we* must come to know things, out of the limitations of our own finitude, by tools and approaches to which finite beings like us have access.

2. Modern epistemology was profoundly foundationalist. Descartes was looking for a *foundation* that he could share with his atheistic friends, on which they could together build a common structure. He thought he had discovered it in his famous *Cogito, ergo sum*. This foundation, he was convinced, plus his detailed philosophical structure would surely drive every right-thinking and logically coherent person to become a Christian, indeed a Catholic like himself. This search for foundations became endemic to the fundamental thought of most disciplines. Some things, it is argued, are axiomatic—i.e., they are self-evident and thus suitable as foundations on which to build other things by appropriate logic and appeals to various kinds of evidence.

One must not think that modernism invented foundations. The geometry of Euclid, for instance, worked out several carefully formulated axioms centuries before Christ, and from these axioms developed propositions that it set out to prove and that in turn could become the foundation for another layer of propositions. But the appeal to well-defined foundations as the base of all human knowing was a distinctive development in modernism, made necessary by the fact that God was no longer the foundation.

3. Modern epistemology was constrained by rigorous method. The idea is that one began with appropriate and convincing foundations, added carefully controlled methods, and then turned the crank to generate truth. The methods might include how to gather and organize data, well-defined tools whose capacities and limitations were understood (whether the tools were physical or literary-critical), procedures, observation, measurements, testing of various kinds, and much more. The importance of methodological rigor can still be seen in many Western Ph.D. dissertations. In most disciplines, in addition to making a contribution, a doctoral dissertation must make its foundations and its methods clear and then rigorously work itself out within the stipulated methods, or it will not be accepted.

4. Modern epistemology rarely doubted that epistemological certainty is desirable and attainable. This stance was in continuity with premodern thought. That does not mean, of course, that the best thinkers were confident that their knowledge, or what they claimed to be knowledge, was exhaustively right. But few doubted that human beings could know things truly (objective knowledge was attainable) and that this was a good thing (such knowledge was desirable). After all, as the centuries of the modernist period wore on, scholarship disclosed more and more things about more and more things. Scholars could extrapolate and imagine a time when all their questions about this or that subject could be satisfied. Even if they sometimes discovered that what they previously thought they knew was mistaken, they were encouraged to recognize the progress that had led them to such a correction. Few doubted that more progress would and could be made and that, in principle, certainty about many things would be achieved.

5. Modernist epistemology embraced an understanding of truth that ascribed to it what some have called "ahistorical universality." In other words, what is true is *universally* true. The truth of what is true is not jeopardized by moving from one historical period to another, from one culture to another, or from one language to another: if it is true, its truth is *ahistorical*. If it is true that a water molecule is made up of two atoms of hydro-

gen and one atom of oxygen, this truth must be true in Patagonia and in Patavia, in Leicester and in Lima, in Jerusalem and in Japan—whether in the twenty-first century or during the Ming Dynasty. Another way of saying this is that truth was understood to be *objectively* true.

6. Although the earliest major figures of the Enlightenment were theists (like Descartes himself) or Deists, over the centuries a rising number of modern thinkers adopted philosophical naturalism—the view that matter, energy, time, and space are all that is. This development took time and has never been universal. Probably the biggest impetus along these lines occurred in the nineteenth century when Darwinian evolution made atheism respectable. This stance makes a closed universe inescapable, and ostensible knowledge about a personal-transcendent God outside or beyond the universe nothing but childish myth.

Postmodern Epistemology's Challenges to Modernism

Postmodern epistemology modifies or challenges or overthrows every one of these six characteristics of modern epistemology. I shall briefly go through them in the same order.

1. Postmoderns, no less than moderns, begin with the finite "I," but the inferences they draw are quite different. Each "I" is different from every other "I," so the point of view expressed is bound to be different. Alternatively, one may lay less emphasis on the individual and more on the cultural group: after all, each individual "I" is a member of a defined culture with a particular set of assumptions, values, structures of thought, linguistic usages, and the like. Each group, culture, or identifiable unit of people will invariably look at things a little differently from the way people in other cultures look at things. I cannot help but observe things out of the reality of being a Canadian, white, middle-aged, male, with certain kinds of education and exposure to the world and a set of experiences that contribute to making me who I am, not to mention the contribution of my genes. I do not look at the world out of the eyes of a semi-literate child prostitute on the streets of Bangkok, or out of the eyes of a black president of an African state, or out of the eyes of a professional football player.

The reasons why postmoderns have drawn very different inferences from the finite "I" with which they begin their reflections on human knowing, as compared with those drawn by modernists, are many and complex and have long roots in history.[7] What is striking, however, is the simple fact that both moderns and postmoderns begin the epistemological quest with that finite "I," even though they then come up with such radically different structures of thought. In fact, as far as I can see, it is this continuity of the focus on the finite self as the starting-place in epistemology that constitutes the chief reason why some thinkers prefer to treat postmodernism as a form of late modernism or even of ultramodernism. If the primary point of analysis is this starting point in the "I," in the finite self, they are surely right. Postmodernism sees the implications of modernism's move to the finite "I" more clearly than did the early modernists themselves. From one perspective, postmodernism is merely modernism gone to seed; from another, postmodernism teases out the implications of modernism's first premise, however uncomfortable that makes the modernists feel.

At the same time, because the directions taken by the postmoderns are sufficiently different from those of the moderns and can be nicely identified and evaluated, something is to be said for preserving the word "postmodern." In other words, it is helpful to see how the changes bring us to a form of epistemology that no longer has the profile of modernism: it is *post*modern, even if crucial points of continuity must not be overlooked.

2. Postmodern epistemology is profoundly suspicious of all foundationalism; one could even say it is passionately anti-foundationalist. It argues that all the "foundations" are not secure, because they are "self-

---

[7] They include developments in hermeneutics in Germany, literary-critical developments in France (largely post-structuralist studies, initially tied very tightly to Marxist dissatisfaction with the state of affairs in Western Europe), the turn to the subject within many disciplines in the Anglo-Saxon world, the indirect influence of the Romantics, the enormous influence of Immanuel Kant and the belated influence of Friedrich Nietzsche, the challenges of Feuerbach and Schleiermacher, and more recently, the impact of the various forms of existentialism and of (largely American) sociological approaches to knowledge. Even this is far from being an exhaustive list. This is not the place to unpack each of these developments, of course, not least because there are now many studies that establish the links. But it is worth mentioning them because from time to time various writers in the emerging church movement tend to stumble across one or another of these contributory streams and give it a popular exposure that assigns it more credit than it is due.

evident" only within given cultures. In other words, the foundations are themselves products of finite human beings, so everything that is built on them is no more stable than the foundations themselves. There is no ultimate fulcrum on which the levers of knowledge can rest.

"But surely," you might protest, "there *are* some universal axioms. Can we not rest at least some weight on Descartes's 'I think, therefore I am'?" But do you not sometimes "think" you are something when you are dreaming, a something that has no real connection with any external reality?

3. Postmodernism accepts that there are methods, of course, but insists that there are *many* methods, all of which produce distinguishable results and none of which is any more or less "true" than the results pursued by other methods. This is not only because the foundations on which the methods rest are not secure, but also because the methods themselves are human creations, creations by human beings in particular cultures. The medical methods of traditional Chinese medicine are rather different from those of most Western medicine. How can one possibly adjudicate which are the "true" methods? We can strive for consistency in the use of the chosen methods and the chosen assumptions, but this does not give us the right to assert that the outcome is "objective" knowledge.

4. Postmodernism therefore insists that objective knowledge is neither attainable nor desirable. At this point it finds itself in absolute opposition to modernism. It argues that knowledge is not attainable for the reasons already given, but neither is it desirable. Far from thinking that this loss in epistemological certainty is tragic, postmodernism glories in the diversity of outcomes. It says epistemological certainty is undesirable because, apart from being intrinsically monofocal and therefore boring, it breeds absolutism that manipulates people and controls them, trampling on the splendid diversity of creeds and cultures and races that constitute humankind. Let the diversity flourish—but let none of the disparate voices claim to be "true." Or better yet, let them all claim to be true, but none in an exclusive or objective sense.

5. It follows, then, that truth under the regime of postmodern epistemology cannot partake of "ahistorical universality." All truth claims are merely true for some people, even if not for all people at all times and places.

6. Although philosophical materialism continues to be a dominant force in many Western intellectual circles, postmodernism has fostered its

decline in at least some quarters. Because postmodern epistemology does not rely so strongly on the kind of rigorous method inherent in modernism but encourages many presuppositions and methods and approaches, it turns out to be more open to mystical appeals, assorted religious appeals (provided they make no exclusive claims, and especially if they are Eastern religions rooted in some form of pantheism), or superstition (as modernists would have considered it).

In short, when we compare the profile of postmodern epistemology suggested by these six characterizations, with the similar profile of modern epistemology, the differences are sufficiently substantial that one can nicely distinguish between the two structures. *Post*modernism still seems like a useful term, even if at the level of the focus on the finite self as the beginning point in the epistemology there is plenty of continuity between modernism and postmodernism.

Correlatives and Entailments

In the previous chapter I suggested that many elements in Western culture that are sometimes lumped together under the rubric of "postmodernism" could more usefully be considered the correlatives of postmodernism. This is partly because these elements can live and flourish in very different environments. They are not *necessary* components of the epistemology that lies at the heart of what postmodernism is. On the other hand, the postmodernism I have described tends to strengthen these elements. Conversely, these elements, when they have come into being for other reasons, in turn tend to strengthen postmodernism.

Five Correlatives

I shall briefly mention only five of these correlatives.

1. Syncretism: The more that people try to pick and choose elements of fundamentally disparate religions in order to construct some sort of syncretistic concoction, the more vindicated is the postmodern penchant for disallowing the link between any person's claims to knowledge and reality itself. Conversely, the more such links are disallowed, the easier it is to sanction syncretism. Indeed, failure to be syncretistic may appear old-fashioned, narrow, and epistemologically straitjacketed.

2. Secularization: As I have already mentioned, most sociologists do not think of the processes of secularization as abolishing religion, but as squeezing religion to the periphery of life. In the Western world, most religious expressions were, until recent times, cast in terms of competing claims that needed to be thought through, evaluated, and accepted or rejected. If these religions are marginalized, then their truth claims do not matter that much for most real-life issues anyway, and other cultural pressures enjoy a freer hand. Conversely, if postmodernism succeeds in encouraging many people to conclude that the truth claims of religion are no more than personal or communal choices rather than the truth of reality, of God himself, it is much easier to relegate religion to the margins.

3. Biblical illiteracy: In a culture where many people read and substantially know the Bible, the Bible's absolute claims regarding God, salvation, many forms of right and wrong, and the like will discourage the rapid spread of postmodern relativism. Where biblical illiteracy abounds, one of the barriers is taken away.[8] Correspondingly, when postmodernism

---

[8] One can hardly overestimate the importance of widespread Bible reading among Christians during the first centuries of the Christian church. At a time of decaying education, the church insisted on deep and constant reading of Scripture, across all ranks and classes, across genders and age ranges, and this as much as anything else left the church in the sole position to preserve the best of Graeco-Roman civilization when the Roman Empire itself collapsed. Later, when Bible reading was progressively shut away from ordinary Christians, when illiteracy abounded to the point that the great Charlemagne was considered something of a scholar because he could at least barely read, the theological, moral, and educational life of the church—indeed, of Western culture—fell into desperate decline despite the existence of exceptional lights. It is not for nothing that the Reformation coincided with Bible translation, printed Bibles, and above all, widespread reading of Scripture. This, of course, can lead in turn to reckless individualism, but it has the potential to check the tide of the current fads. On these matters, at a popular level it is still worth reading Benjamin B. Warfield, "The Bible the Book of Mankind," first delivered as a lecture at the World's Bible Congress in 1915 and now available in *Selected Shorter Writings of Benjamin B. Warfield*, 2 vols., ed. John E. Meeter (Nutley, NJ: Presbyterian and Reformed Publishing, 1970), 1:3–22.

flourishes, there will be less inclination to read the Bible constantly, at least as the authoritative revelation of God himself. At that juncture the Bible reading that takes place will likely invoke post-critical theory, so that the Bible itself becomes domesticated. A small percentage of the population will delight to read the Bible that way and find it a liberating experience, but the large-scale and still growing biblical illiteracy in the population at large will certainly not be reversed.

4. Ill-defined Spirituality: Ill-defined contemporary notions of "spirituality," shaped in part by the popularity of assorted New Age religions, inevitably serve to support a postmodern outlook (whether they intend to or not) and are in turn supported by it. Religions that speak of being right or wrong on certain matters or that support any form of exclusive claim or that uphold rigorous standards of personal and public morality will be dismissed as "intolerant," even if they vigorously support the right of all religions to defend their own patch and seek new converts.

5. Globalization: This slippery concept is handled so variously in the treatments of different writers that it is difficult to say something pointed in few words. For many, the word has primarily economic overtones: multinational corporations make the entire world a global village, with both good and bad results. No less important, instant communication with almost every part of the globe simultaneously fosters a recognition of global smallness and oneness and, paradoxically, forces us to become aware of how different we are and how separated by diverse cultures. Let this diversity sink in, and it becomes harder to accept everything about one's own culture unthinkingly. That sort of experience can easily vindicate postmodern theory. Conversely, postmodern epistemology can easily lend itself to this particular reading of globalization.

Some people use "postmodernism" to include these and other correlatives, while others use the expression more narrowly than I do. My earlier observations on the decline of the term in Europe (especially France)[9] reflects in part, I think, the French penchant for connecting postmodernism explicitly to the critical theories of Jacques Derrida, François

---

[9] See chap. 3, p. 81–82.

Lyotard, Michel Foucault, Paul De Man, Jacques Lacan, and others. As their critical theories have largely fallen out of vogue in France (even in America, where they are still popular in many academic series, they are no longer in the ascendancy), so "postmodernism" has fallen into disuse. But I am far from convinced that the turn to the subject, the various forms of perspectivalism, the denial of our capacity to know "objective" truth, have all run their course. If one identifies it with this essentially epistemological shift, postmodernism does not seem to me to have died away, even in France, though the term is no longer helpful there in serious discussion.

In America, we find a converse danger. Although here, as in Europe, some academics connect postmodernism with certain critical theory and are therefore inclined to drop the term as the theories are gradually eclipsing their "sell by " date, far more use the term with respect to epistemology and related matters. In the popular arena, many in America use the term to refer to every cultural change that comes along, which of course tends to turn "postmodernism" into a rhetorical battering ram while making clear thought about these cultural changes more difficult.

Five Entailments

If we allow, even for the sake of argument, that postmodernism and its correlatives are in some measure as I have described them, even if in some academic quarters they are under attack, what are some of the entailments?

· A very partial list might include the following.

1. Notions of objective morality are among the first things to be questioned. Under postmodernism, personal morality easily becomes a social construction. Certainly, in university evangelism today it is far harder to get across something of what the Bible says about sin (whatever vocabulary is used) than it is to explain the doctrine of the Trinity or the importance of the resurrection.

2. Similarly, evangelism, understood to be proselytization, is often viewed in the broad culture as intrinsically obnoxious, because no matter how gently it is done, it cannot avoid giving the impression that Christians think they have something superior. Otherwise, what would be the point of trying to win others to their camp? If Christianity is presented as something superior—or something true!—it is necessarily saying that what it proposes to displace is inferior. In fact, proselytization may be viewed as

intrinsically intolerant (under the new definitions of tolerance and intolerance).[10] By way of response, some Christians refuse to engage in any overt evangelism, except the demonstration of a Christian life, in the hope that others will simply ask them what makes them tick—which then gives them opportunity to share their life-story and talk about Jesus Christ. If someone then opts to become a Christian oneself, that's fair enough: no one is telling them that their own way is inferior or that they are lost, rather they have simply decided to try this new Christian way. The reason for doing so is not that this Christian way is objectively true, but that it seems attractive to at least some people—i.e., that it is true for them.

3. People are likely to be helped into adopting a new position by something other than, or at least more than, careful argument. Feeling, aesthetics, personal relationships, mysticism, unexplained leaps, coincidences, and a panoply of other subjective perceptions are commonly viewed as being as determinative for what a person believes, what people think they "know," as the structures of foundations and methods.

4. Postmoderns are likely to be happy with personal narratives—i.e., with individuals telling their own stories and explaining how they view things. They are likely to be suspicious of metanarrative—i.e., of a big story that claims to explain all of life, or that claims to be true for everyone.

5. Even the hard sciences do not escape postmodern analysis. In the domain of science it is possible to distinguish between "hard" and "soft" postmodernism. (I'll come back to the distinction.) But postmodernism in all its serious forms, while admitting that there are some individual scientific "facts" (e.g., the earth rotates on its axis, water boils at 100 degrees C at sea level), insists that the grand theories that make science what it is are, in very substantial measure, socially determined constructions. The same "facts" could have been constructed in quite different ways.

Having outlined what I think "postmodernism" is (especially in the North American context) and how the term can be deployed most usefully, I must lay out some of its strengths and weaknesses.

---

[10] See the earlier discussion, pp. 68–70.

Strengths of Postmodern Epistemology

Postmodern epistemology shows several strengths for which to be grateful.

1. It has been very effective at exposing the weaknesses and pretensions of many strands of modernism. Enlightenment thought has often succumbed not only to a cheerful and sometimes unwarranted optimism, but to an unfettered arrogance. Postmodernism has powerfully exposed the Achilles' heel of modern epistemology: the finiteness of the "I" means that the path to certainty about almost everything is far more difficult than many Enlightenment thinkers have supposed. The belatedly acknowledged mistakes have played some part in arriving at this conclusion. After all, many things have been labeled "scientific" that time and distance have proved were not: phrenology, Marxism, Aryan superiority, phlogiston, and much more. The roles of reason and of methodological control in human understanding in the modern world have sometimes been seriously overstated. Above all, the line from a finite knower's perceptions to a grasp of objective reality is certainly murkier and more difficult than was frequently presupposed under modernism (though I shall shortly argue that the line is not as impossible as postmodernism frequently avers).

2. Postmodernism has been open to thinking about nonlinear and methodologically unrigorous factors in human knowing. It has worked harder than its predecessor at the intuitive leaps of imagination that sometimes play a huge role even in science. It has encouraged us to think a little more about the role of metaphor, the countless ways personal experience shape our judgment, the impress of culture on our thought forms, and the way these and other factors interact with one another.

3. Postmodernism has been sensitive to the diversity of cultures in the world. If it has been too quick to argue that all cultures are as intrinsically "right" or "good" as all other cultures—(Is a culture that practices child sacrifice as good, in this respect, as one that abominates the practice? Is a more racist culture as good, in this respect, as a less racist culture?)—it has at least been quick to reject the easy assumption that "my" culture or "our" culture is necessarily superior to all others—a common assumption behind colonialism. Insofar as postmodernism fosters more humble listening and more respectful efforts to understand, even if one finally disagrees, it has surely been a good thing.

4. Above all, postmodernism has insistently demanded that the implications of finitude in all claims of human knowing be recognized. I shall argue in due course that postmodernism has not always sorted out these implications very well, but at least it has recognized that there are unavoidable things that flow from the fact that all human knowing is necessarily the knowing of *finite* knowers. Indeed, at one level Christians might well argue that at this juncture postmodernism does not go far enough. Christians assert not only human finiteness, but human depravity. We get things wrong not only because we are not omniscient, but also because we are corrupt, morally blind, painfully selfish, and given to excuses and self-justification.

The question to ask, then, is this: Once we have acknowledged the unavoidable finiteness of all human knowers, the cultural diversity of the human race, the diversity of factors that go into human knowing, and even the evil that lurks in the human breast and easily perverts claims of knowledge into totalitarian control and lust for power—once we have acknowledged these things, is there any way left for us to talk about knowing what is true or objectively real? Hard postmodernists insist there is not. And that's the problem.

Weaknesses of Postmodern Epistemology

For all its insights, postmodern epistemology displays severe weaknesses on several fronts, weaknesses that must be confronted and addressed. I shall list four.

1. Many postmoderns channel the discussion into a manipulative antithesis. The antithesis is this: *Either* we human beings can know something absolutely, perfectly, exhaustively—one might say omnisciently—*or* we human beings can at best glimpse some small perspective on something or other without any mechanism for discovering whether our perspective is an important part of the whole, a distorted view of the whole, or a skewed view of the whole, and so forth—precisely because we have no way of knowing what the whole is. The antithesis is designed to drive everyone to a postmodern approach to truth. Since it can easily be shown that no human being or group of human beings ever gains a perfect and exhaustive knowledge of anything, then the antithesis declares that only one alternative remains: Our knowledge is not only partial, but we have no means of test-

ing to see how close what we think we know actually corresponds with the whole, with reality. The antithesis demands that we be committed perspectivalists—i.e., those who say that human "knowledge" is never more than the perspective of some finite individual or group, without any means of grasping any perspective's relative importance, since none of us can compare our perspective with ultimate reality. After all, other human beings look at the same thing from another perspective: Who is to say which perspective is closer to the reality of the whole, if no one has access to a vision of the whole?

In short, if the antithesis is correct and that is all there is to be said, we are driven toward postmodern epistemology. This antithesis is rarely argued in the literature, but it is almost everywhere assumed by postmodern writers. Yet buried within it are some unacknowledged problems that are crying out to be addressed. The most important of these is that it sets up a standard that is impossibly strict. In effect, the antithesis demands that we be God, with all of God's omniscience, or else be forever condemned to knowing nothing objective for sure. If the sole possible standard for knowing anything objective with certainty is being omniscient, then of course the antithesis works: we human beings are not omniscient.

But may there not be legitimate ways of talking about *finite* beings actually knowing something objective? In other words, as measured by the standard of omniscience, certainly all human knowing is perspectival. Yet does it follow that the intrinsic limitations of being finite rule out any possibility of knowing something truly? Can one move from admitted perspectivalism to true knowledge of what is objective?

I shall shortly probe these questions a little further. For the moment, it is enough to recognize that scholars who think of themselves as belonging in some sense to the postmodern camp tend, at this point, to divide into two camps (though the line between the two camps is not always a very clear one). On the one side are those who take the antithesis very seriously and conclude that we human beings cannot have objective knowledge about anything. All we can ever sensibly mean by "truth" is what is "true" for some individual or group. Let us call this position *hard* or *strong* postmodernism. On the other side are those who admit that although human knowledge is necessarily perspectival (after all, that is part of what makes them postmodern), we human beings can in measure approach the truth in some objective sense. How they reach this conclusion we shall think about in a moment. Let us call this position *soft* or *weak* postmodernism.

In short, hard postmodernism leans on the antithesis I have just described and concludes that all human knowing cannot be knowledge of what is objectively true, because it never has a sure, omniscient vantage point. Soft postmodernism leans on the antithesis in order to affirm that all human knowledge is necessarily perspectival (after all, we cannot escape our finitude), but probes a little farther to suggest ways in which human beings can know some true things, even if nothing exhaustively. It is the use of this antithesis in the hands of the hard postmodernists that is terribly manipulative.

2. The second weakness of postmodern discussion, especially among the strong postmoderns, is that however great the difficulties in knowing things and in communicating things with other human beings, a great deal of knowing and effective communication do take place. If the standard is *perfect* communication—absolutely everything of the source thought and feelings, in its exact proportions, overtones, and historical and cultural context, being grasped with 100 percent accuracy by the one receiving or listening to or reading the communication—then once again it is easy to show that no communication is perfect. But if the standard is less than this, then we can know some of what Aristotle thought, some of what Paul thought, some of what Aquinas thought, some of what our next-door neighbor thinks.

A look at the current debate among philosophers of science may be helpful here. In the past, philosophers of science have laid special emphasis on different elements that contribute to the body of knowledge we call science. Some have focused on the important role of reason (rationalism); others have emphasized the place of experimentation under controlled conditions (empiricism). Some combine these and other elements to try to account for the fitful, trial-and-error, nonlinear development of science, in which theories are advanced and tested, competing theories are defended until disproved, awkward data are collected until some reigning theory cries out to be displaced. All sides acknowledge that defining the "scientific method" is no easy task.

Now, however, under the influence of postmodern epistemology, another approach to science has become fashionable in some quarters, often labeled "constructionism." These social constructivists argue that the conclusions of science are not so much the result of reason working its way through evidence as the result of social forces.

The reasons for adopting this line are many. Some appeal to the influential work of Thomas Kuhn.[11] Kuhn argued that scientists do not simply add one hard fact to another or make logical changes to existing theories demanded by advancing accumulations of data. Rather, scientists suddenly come up with some new paradigm, some new model that views the world in a different way. These creative bursts are "paradigm shifts." If they seem to be compelling to enough people, the relevant scientific community is won over by the new theory and begins to operate within the new paradigm. Some go further than that. They argue that even controlled experiments cannot test a theory in any final way. After all, the very theoretical prediction that is being tested depends on the reigning paradigm, on various theories and assumptions that support or challenge that paradigm, on observations that were themselves framed by assumptions about reality that have not been finally tested.[12] The paradigm itself then shapes the world—indeed, constitutes the world—of the scientists who operate within it. At this juncture it appears that scientific knowledge is nothing more than a respected body of traditions defended by a particular community of thinkers, viz., the scientists who are engaged in research in that discipline. It is nothing more than the belief system of that group of scientists at that point in history.

An example may help. Those who are strongly committed to this postmodern way of looking at scientific knowledge regularly demand sociological explanations for questions not only about why a particular scientist was interested in a certain scientific problem and chose to address it in such-and-such a way, but also about the content of the scientific theories themselves.[13] In the first decade and a half after World War I, many German thinkers turned

---

[11] Thomas S. Kuhn, *The Structure of Scientific Revolutions*, 2nd ed. (Chicago: University of Chicago Press, 1970).

[12] See, for instance, from a voluminous literature, H. M. Collins, "The Meaning of Experiment: Replication and Reasonableness," in *Dismantling Truth: Reality in the Post-Modern World*, ed. Hilary Lawson and Lisa Appignanesi (New York: St. Martin's Press, 1989), 88.

[13] See, for instance, Barry Barnes, David Bloor, and John Henry, *Scientific Knowledge: A Sociological Analysis* (London: Athlone Press, 1996).

away from a mechanical worldview and toward mysticism. Hence physicists were viewed with increasing suspicion. That is why, it is argued, physicists themselves developed the nondeterministic, noncausal—one might almost say mystical—theory of quantum mechanics: it enabled them to win back the high social standing they had lost. Thus quantum mechanics, at least in the German tradition, was not generated by data that compelled its development nor by reason playing on this data, but by social ambition.

This approach to scientific thought is commonly associated with the hard postmoderns. After all, almost everyone today is a soft postmodern in the sense that all of us recognize that personal and social dimensions play their part in how and why scientists approach certain questions the way they do. Moreover, just as the English language is a cultural phenomenon, so the subset of English used by English-speaking scientists is a cultural phenomenon.

Nevertheless, very commonly this hard postmodern analysis of scientific knowledge upsets actual scientists, who commonly point out that virtually none of the hard postmoderns are scientists or know much about what they are talking about. In particular:

a. Observe, again, the subtle importing of the ugly absolute antithesis to which I've already drawn attention. We are assured that experiments cannot test a theory in any *final* way. True enough, if "final" smuggles in the absolute connection with reality that only omniscience can guarantee. But are we then forced to the conclusion that all scientific (and other) knowledge is nothing more than social construction?

b. Thomas Kuhn is regularly misrepresented by the postmoderns—or more precisely, extrapolations have been drawn from his theory of paradigm shifts that he himself would probably not have accepted. In any case, there has been a great deal of important work seriously modifying the Kuhnian proposal or, better, integrating it into more comprehensive visions of what goes into the scientific search for knowledge.[14] That paradigm shifts take place, no one doubts. But they are often triggered by the

---

[14] Among the best of the early discussions triggered by Kuhn's work are Frederic Suppe, ed., *The Structure of Scientific Theories*, 2nd ed. (Urbana: University of Illinois Press, 1977), and Gary Gutting, ed., *Paradigms and Revolutions: Applications and Appraisals of Thomas Kuhn's Philosophy of Science* (Notre Dame, IN: University of Notre Dame Press, 1980).

genuine advance of collection of new data that forces recognition that the old explanatory theory has defects. When the damning data are sufficiently telling, the old theory is waiting to be replaced by a better theory that can explain the more recent and comprehensive data. In other words, data usually have some driving force in the generation of the new theory, even if some part of the creation of the new theory involves an intuitive leap. The reason many scientists adopt the new theory so quickly (in other words, the reason for the "paradigm shift") is the explanatory power of the new theory. And in at least some cases, the old theory is not so much proved wrong as inadequate—i.e., it is still entirely justified in limited cases. Einsteinian relativity did not so much overthrow Newtonian physics as provide a more comprehensive theory. Newtonian equations still work, so long as we are not dealing with speeds approaching the speed of light or with the peculiar properties of subatomic particles.

c. The hard postmoderns, the strongest constructivists, are deeply inconsistent. They keep insisting that all scientific knowledge (and all other knowledge too, for that matter) is the product of social construction, but apparently they exclude their own knowledge of this analysis from a similar charge. In other words, they are convinced that their sociological analysis is the truth. If in fact, however, their sociological analysis of scientific epistemology is itself a social construction that may or may not correspond to reality, then it may be that scientific knowledge is *not* in reality nothing more than social construction. In the case of the German physicists after World War I, it may be that the constructivists' insistence that Germans turned from mechanism to mysticism is *not* the truth, but merely the construction of social scientists who for various cultural reasons want it to be the truth. Or it may be part of the truth, along with some hard data that drove physicists to propound a more comprehensive theory.[15]

d. The constructivist argument does not meet the exigencies of the actual science. The older quantum theory of Niels Bohr was known by physicists to have some flaws; it could not account for some of the data. The revision advanced by physicist Werner Heisenberg better accounted for

---

[15] For this example I am indebted to James Robert Brown, *Who Rules in Science? An Opinionated Guide to the Wars* (Cambridge, MA: Harvard University Press, 2001), 256.

the anomalous data, especially the "Zeeman effect," so physicists accepted the new quantum theory. But that means there is a crucial dependence on data and reason, regardless of social ambition. To put the matter differently, the newer theory explains more of the data than the old theory and turns out to have stronger predictive power. It is therefore judged to be closer to the *truth*—i.e., to what the universe is actually like. But these sorts of *scientific* factors that play into the adoption of a new theory are skirted or not even evaluated in the work of the strong postmoderns. In other words, the strong constructivists simply do not include enough data.

It is obvious to most people that scientific knowledge has advanced. Yet it is not exhaustive and not omniscient. Some theories are still being revised. Many physicists think, for instance, that there will have to be a substantial revision in relativity theory or quantum theory or both, or perhaps a more comprehensive paradigm, to generate the holy grail of the "unified field theory"—the convincing demonstration that all four fundamental forces are related to one another. But compare the current state of affairs with what was known in the domain of physics one hundred years ago or half a millennium ago. Track similar progress (and "progress" is in this case the right word) in the domains of biology or chemistry or entomology or astronomy. We know far more about the physical realities of our world and our universe than our forbears did five hundred years ago. It is *not* just a matter of now enjoying a different socially constructed theory, with neither theory being any closer to the actual reality of the universe than the other. We know more about fluid dynamics—which is why we can construct planes that fly so reliably. We know more about subatomic structure—which is why magnetic resonance scanners enable doctors to scan our bodies. We know more about genetics and microbiology and metal alloys and meteorology.

I am surprised that strong postmoderns are so reluctant to acknowledge the place of "critical realism." Critical realists hold that meaning can be *adequately* determined, over against both naive realists, who are inclined to think that meaning can be exhaustively determined, and non-realists, who hold that the objective meaning cannot be determined. Otherwise put, in the realm of science, critical realists insist that scientific theories do in fact approximate the natural world that exists apart from any scientific descriptions of it (that is why they speak of "realism") but are constantly probed, critiqued, improved, revised, replaced, and evaluated (hence the adjective "critical"). But when the strong postmoderns refer to critical realism, their comments are almost always rather dismissive.[16]

We could have lengthy discussions on various domains besides science, but let's choose history as another example. True, we can never be *absolutely* certain that something or other in the past took place, or grasp its full significance, if the standard of "absolute certainty" demands omniscient knowledge. I cannot prove beyond all possible doubt that last year I was in the Czech Republic. I suppose that some clever investigator could check what the computers say about my airline flights, talk to witnesses who saw me there, interview the pastors and others who heard me speak, and note how my name was registered in this or that center. But computer records can be doctored, witnesses can be bribed, and perhaps someone else took my name and told the pastors he was Don Carson when in fact the real Don Carson went hiking in the Rockies. Yet in the normal conversation of ordinary people, who do not expect the standards of infallible omniscience,

---

[16] For instance, Stanley J. Grenz, *Renewing the Center: Evangelical Theology in a Post-Theological Era* (Grand Rapids: Baker, 2000), 242, acknowledges that critical realists "do have a point." That point, he writes, is that there is a universe that predates the existence of scientists, of observers. Grenz does not concede anything about the scientists' actual knowledge of this universe. In fact, he adds, "To assume that this observation [that a universe exists and predates the scientists themselves] is sufficient to relegate all the talk of social construction to the trash heap, however, is to miss the point." Then he launches into further defense of constructivism, largely by insisting, again, that culture is a "*signifying system* through which necessarily . . . a social order is communicated, reproduced, experienced, and explored" (p. 243, at that point quoting the words of Raymond Williams). But I contend that Grenz is the one who misses the point. The issue is not whether a universe exists and predates the scientists, but whether scientists may come to know anything true about that universe even though their knowledge is finite. Very few scientists argue that there is *no* personal or social influence on their scientific decisions. Soft postmoderns happily acknowledge such influence. But they also insist that the roles of observed data, concrete measurements, repeated experiments, and reason playing out on these data drive us to falsify bad theory and, in time, bring us closer to an understanding of the universe as it is.

it can be established as a fact that I spent a bit of time in the Czech Republic last year.

Exactly the same sorts of methods apply to ascertaining what actually happened in earlier times, except that we must make allowance for the fact that the witnesses are dead and cannot be interviewed. In some instances the records are so poor, so late, so disparate, or so contradictory that it is virtually impossible to determine what happened. But in other instances the records are substantial, the witnesses multiple, the documentation early, and the reasons valid for concluding that such-and-such *did* take place: that is the historical truth. This truth is not *all* the truth about that event, but it is the truth. And we can *know* it the way human beings know anything—with a knowledge that is real and substantial, though without being omniscient. Indeed, as we shall see in chapter 7, that is a fundamental element of how Christians *know* that the resurrection of Jesus Christ is a fact of history: they depend on witnesses who left records (1 Corinthians 15).

But the sad contemporary situation is that many postmoderns, especially strong postmoderns, have a great deal of difficulty acknowledging these realities. Many undergraduates I have met who have been influenced by personable postmodern thinkers are extremely uncomfortable when it comes to talking about truth if there is any hint that this truth is universal. They are reluctant to say that anything is *true*, and they are reluctant to claim that they can truly describe some element of reality, partly because their standard is that of omniscience (in other words, they have succumbed to the wretched antithesis I described a few pages back), and partly because they think that *any* acceptance of perspectivalism rules descriptions of reality out of court. At this juncture one wants to cry out that postmodern epistemological theory is not only inconsistent (since it thinks that its theory is true), but is blind to fairly transparent phenomena.

3. The third weakness in much postmodern theory is its handling of moral issues. The strongest postmoderns argue that all distinctions between right and wrong have no absolute status, but rather are social constructions. Thus the literature abounds with people who argue that even something as ghastly as the Holocaust can be thought of as evil only from a certain perspective. It is not evil from other perspectives—e.g., those of the Aryan supremacists.

But although this stance is still defended in some quarters, every passing day makes it look less plausible, for several reasons:

a. In the face of so much evil in the world, the stance is soon seen, by most sensitive souls, to be bankrupt and offensive.

b. Experience shows that no one can live very long by it anyway. The French existentialists insisted that there is no ultimate distinction between right and wrong, and then Jean Paul Sartre signed the Algerian Manifesto because he was convinced that the actions of the French government were *wrong*. Most of the social-literary criticism that underlies the French roots of postmodernism were promulgated by thinkers who were deeply committed to a quasi-Marxist view of what is "good" and "bad" in any society. And my exposure to current postmodern thinkers, both in person and through the literature, confirms that they are as full of opinions about what is right and what is wrong as the next person. Simply raise questions about, say, President Bush's policy in Iraq, the rights of homosexuals, genocide in Darfur, and the meaning of economic justice, and postmoderns are no more reluctant than their modern counterparts to voice what they think are the rights and wrongs of the situation. They almost always invest their own opinions with more than personal value.

c. A modicum of exposure to American university campuses during the last half-century demonstrates that in the hands of the young, these strong postmodern approaches to ethical matters rapidly become intellectual justification for each individual's personal pursuit of immediate pleasure.[17]

---

[17] One thinks of the penetrating book by Richard Bauckham, *God and the Crisis of Freedom: Biblical and Contemporary Reflections* (Louisville: Westminster John Knox Press, 2002). Bauckham argues that in the Bible freedom is understood to be liberation from slavery to serve the living God, whether the paradigm is the Exodus or the freedom from sin and its entailments as promised by Jesus. But under the Enlightenment, the pursuit of freedom became the quest for human autonomy. And we could add that under the Enlightenment's bastard child, postmodernism, it becomes easier still to cast off the remaining constraints, because these constraints have no final absolute significance. After a while it becomes clear that "freedom" means nothing more than the most avid forms of pleasure-seeking self-assertion at the expense of others—which thus generate new forms of domination.

d. Once again the theory shows itself to be absurdist. Postmodern theory has to be preserved as *right* in order to obliterate any final difference between *right* and *wrong*. We wouldn't want a little matter like morality to stand in the way of a good theory, would we? But eventually it is just too much. After a while, strong postmodern theory begins to unravel, simply because it cannot responsibly address the toughest moral questions of our time.

So although there are still many articulate postmodern thinkers, especially in America, writing books and defending their epistemology, a rising number of scholars are taking them to task—and these scholars can no longer be ignored. The detailed theory of the postmoderns is proving less convincing than it used to be, prompting one influential critic, Terry Eagleton, to title his most recent book *After Theory*.[18] Eagleton is a Marxist, and I find some of his arguments less than convincing. Nevertheless, his critique of the strongest forms of perspectivalism, liberal postmodernism, and mere tribalism is both witty and penetrating. He argues, for instance, that in proper usage the predicate "is true" commonly attributes universality to the claims to which the predicate is attached. Eagleton says that if the proposition "racism is evil" is true, then it is true not only for me and for my tribe, but for everyone everywhere, even those who deny it (which makes their denial evil). Moreover, to know the truth belongs to our dignity as moderately rational beings. None of this vitiates the fact that our knowledge of this truth is framed within a specific culture, or the fact that we cannot possibly know all there is to know about racism and its evil. It is to say that even in the moral realm it is possible to know some things truly, even if nothing omnisciently—or better put, perhaps, it is possible to know some true things even if we do not and cannot know everything about them or grasp them in all their detail and proportion.

4. The fourth weakness of postmodern theory is its strange combination of absurdism and arrogance. The absurdism we have already noted. The more that strong postmodern theory forges its way forward, the less plausible it becomes. That is because the more it insists that all theoretical stances are social constructions and that no theoretical construction bears

---

[18] Terry Eagleton, *After Theory* (New York: Basic Books, 2003).

any necessary relation to objective truth, the more it undermines the truth-fulness of its own construction. The wisest strong postmoderns recognize this absurdity, of course, but they do not retreat because of it: they simply say that this is the way it is, and there is no escaping the entailments of the irrefutable facts of our finitude and social location.

At this juncture, the arrogance kicks in. Postmodernism, which has proved so effective in exposing the pretensions of modernism, suddenly displays its own pretensions. The movement that mocked the arrogance of the heritage of the Enlightenment displays its own arrogance. If modernism boasts of how much of reality it understands, postmodernism boasts that it understands nothing of reality. Neither the absurdity of its dogmatic epistemology nor the implications of genuine advances in knowledge will compel the strong postmoderns to modify their position.

These four weaknesses—and there are others—are all bound up with postmodernism's relationship to truth claims.

A Measured Response

The discussion in this chapter so far has already included some response to the various forms of postmodernism. Postmodernism has been a useful antidote to modernism, not least because modernism is part of its own pedigree. It has shown, more clearly than modernism, how many and diverse are the personal and social factors that go into all human knowing. In its insistence on the inescapable entailments of human finitude, it has done a reasonable job of destroying foundationalism. In consequence it has emphasized the importance of relationships and aesthetics. In the assortment of collateral movements that postmodernism has reinforced (and from which it has benefited), it has exposed the painful and odious side of absolutism.

On the other hand, strong postmodernism is awash in moral relativism and is in its own structure of thought embarrassingly absurd. It tries to control the argument by deploying a manipulative and finally foolish antithesis, in either demanding the kind of absolute and exhaustive knowledge that only Omniscience enjoys, or relinquishing all claims to objective knowledge.

Yet, although this antithesis goes too far, postmodernism reminds us, again and again, that all of us see things from our own perspectives. In that sense we are all perspectivalists. I recall Carl F. H. Henry's shrewd remark about presuppositionalism: "There are two kinds of presuppositionalists: those who admit it and those who don't." Similarly, we may happily aver that there are two kinds of perspectivalists: those who admit it and those who don't.

What I discuss next takes the discussion forward in two respects. Before I do that, however, I must offer some justification for the soft postmodernist. Granted postmodernism's insights, how can it affirm that there are truths, universal truths, that can in some measure be known and taught? How does one escape the drift toward relativism intrinsic to hard postmodernism? To put the matter another way, what warrant is there for rejecting the absolute antithesis by which postmoderns so often seek to control the discussion? What alternative is there to this absolute antithesis?

Models to Help Us Think

I hold that it is possible and reasonable to speak of finite human beings knowing some things truly, even if nothing exhaustively or omnisciently.[19] It is worth reviewing some of the models that have been put forward to help us think about these things:

The fusion of horizons of understanding. Suppose we liken a person's entire outlook—their worldview, including presuppositions, preferences, cultural baggage, belief systems—to their "horizon"—i.e., what they see when they look out to the horizon. Clearly, no two people have *exactly* the same horizons. On the other hand, two people from very similar cultures and families would have similar horizons; two people from very different backgrounds would have different horizons. We could say that this horizon—or "horizon of understanding," as it is sometimes called—in Paul about the time he writes Romans will be very different from the horizon of a twenty-first-century secretary living in Manhattan who has never read

---

[19] This position is common enough in the literature and perhaps received its clearest exposition, in recent times, in the voluminous writings of Michael Polanyi. Some (e.g., Lesslie Newbigin) have drawn relativizing inferences from Polanyi's thought; others (e.g., John Frame, Esther Meeks) have not.

any part of the Bible and does not know a word of the languages Paul knows. How can the secretary be expected to understand what Paul says in his letter to the church in Rome?

Yet it *is* possible, in measure, for the secularist to understand Paul. A first reading of Romans might find it pretty obscure. But suppose the secretary is unusually determined, reads the Bible right through, learns Greek, joins some Bible studies, begins to read some books about culture and word use in the first century, and studies all of Paul's writings. The process is twofold: "distanciation," as the secretary tries to distance himself or herself from twenty-first-century beliefs and givens, and "fusion of horizons," as an attempt is made to look at things from Paul's perspective, to read what Paul read, to understand how he used words, to learn something of the historical setting in which Paul found himself. Naturally, the secretary can never see things *exactly* as Paul saw them; the fusion of understandings is *never* perfect. But experience shows that it is possible to get much closer to Paul's thinking by repeated re-reading, by cycles of distanciation and fusion of horizons, than would be the case if there were no effort along such lines.

This does not mean that everyone must become a Pauline scholar, of course. Sometimes those who study the most will simplify and popularize their findings, so that the speed of their dissemination is much more rapid than the speed of learning them in the first place. Moreover, Pauline scholars sometimes disagree with one another. Some readers are simply not as good as other readers (just as some runners are not as good as other runners). But the most egregious interpretations of Paul's writings, or of any other ancient piece of literature, are in due course taken down by other scholars, who expose the inconsistencies and inaccuracies. Some new paradigm for interpreting Paul comes along, and it may take two or three decades to evaluate it thoroughly and then qualify it or overthrow it: research in the humanities is never a fast process. But over time, it is surprising how much agreement can be reached by readers from very different backgrounds as to what the apostle Paul actually says in his letter to the Romans.

Strong postmoderns keep focusing on the differences in order to drive us to the conclusion that we are not really finding Paul's meaning at all, but merely the interpreter's meaning. This is really one more example of that manipulative antithesis: unless you can understand Paul's letter to the Romans omnisciently, you cannot really understand it all, except in the subjective sense that your understanding of it is a function of your social setting, nothing more. Yet there *is* improvement in understanding Paul, given time and re-reading. Some elements of Paul's thought we *can* know, even if we know none of them perfectly.

I would add that fusing one's horizon of understanding with someone else (whether it be Paul or, for that matter, the postmoderns who are trying to get us to understand and adopt *their* thoughts) is never *exclusively* a cerebral matter. In the case of Paul, whether we come to *like* what we find there may play into the question of how much we understand, for when we thoroughly dislike another's position, the temptation is very strong to caricature it in some way and thus distort it. In the realm of morality, often obedience is as foundational to understanding as is exegesis. And so far I have said nothing about the work of the Spirit of God. My only point at the moment is that the model of "fusion of horizons of understanding" offers us a window on how it is possible to understand another person's thought, even if not perfectly.

The hermeneutical spiral. Hermeneutics is the art and science of interpretation and understanding, and its history is very complicated. The rubric "hermeneutical spiral" was coined after scholars (especially in Germany) had been talking for a while about the "hermeneutical circle." Talk of the hermeneutical circle was part of an attempt to overthrow earlier, modernist models, in which it was thought that the interpreter need only ask the *right* questions of the object being studied, then what was being studied would spit back the right answer. But instead of this direct and simple approach, many pointed out that we interpreters do not bring accurate and entirely neutral questions. Our questions are necessarily a function of who we are, so the answers we hear back, shaped as they are by our bias-driven questions and the cultural limitations of our own ears, are not neutral and objective and accurate. Moreover, when those answers come back to us, they subtly reshape us, so that when we ask the *next* round of questions, we have been in some measure shaped by the text. Here we are, trying to interpret the text, and in some ways the text has "interpreted" us—not so much understood us, as shaped us, just as our attempts at "understanding" the text find us actually reshaping the text as a reflection of who *we* are. So instead of going right in with the right question and coming back out with the truth, we find ourselves in a hermeneutical circle, going round and round and round.

But wait a minute. Let us grant that all of our questions and all of our methods for studying the text are never entirely neutral, and we do not get "straight" answers back by simply deploying methodological care and turning the crank: is it fair to give the impression that in our hermeneutical circle we always remain at the same distance from the text? Does the hermeneutical circle always have the same radius? Would it not be truer to our experience to say that the radius of the circle gets a little shorter with time—i.e., that we start to spiral into the text? The spiral is never entirely smooth, of course, but with time we learn more about statistics than when we first started studying it, we learn more of the Greek language than we knew before we started studying it, we learn more of Paul's Romans than before we started studying it. We will never know all there is to know about statistics, Greek, or Romans, but we do spiral in closer than we once were.

The asymptotic approach. This mathematical model was developed by Karl Popper to explain knowledge acquisition in the field of science, but it has been applied elsewhere. An asymptote is a curved line that gets closer and closer to a straight line without ever touching it. Consider the following graph, using the epistle to the Romans as an example:

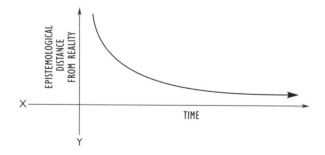

If the x-axis measures time and the y-axis measures epistemological distance from reality (i.e., how far one's understanding of something is removed from the reality of the thing itself), then the graph suggests that with time the knower gets closer and closer to the reality, though without ever touching the line that would mark perfect knowledge: we will never be omniscient. Thus a child in a Christian home learns a little about Romans from family Bible reading and Sunday school, but when he is, say, eleven years old (still not very far out on the x-axis), the graph of his knowledge of Romans shows that he is still a long way away from reality. But eventually he is called to the ministry, studies the ancient languages, works hard at studying the entire Bible including Romans, and eventually writes a doctoral dissertation on that epistle: now his understanding of Romans is much closer to the x-axis. But even fifty billion years into eternity, the asymptote will never touch the line: he will never enjoy an omniscient knowledge of Romans (or of anything else). Omniscience is exclusively an attribute of God.

Of course, this curve is rarely smooth. Human understanding can go up and down, in the individual life and in any human culture and in the race at large. But the graph fruitfully portrays that growth in understanding and in knowing something, and improvement in getting closer in knowledge to what a thing actually is, is possible.

Other approaches. In my book *The Gagging of God* I provide some of the documentation for the three models of human knowing I have outlined here, but there are many other writers with still subtler approaches.

1. During the last four decades, Paul Ricoeur has been among the most productive thinkers in wrestling not only with how language (and especially metaphor) works, but with the justification of claims to knowledge. Ricoeur is perhaps the premier figure in simultaneously recognizing the limitations of the finite knower, yet refusing to relativize all knowledge.[20] For instance, it is all very well to say that we all carry our presuppositions with us, or to acknowledge that because we are finite we are all perspecti-

---

[20] Ricoeur's writings are voluminous. Perhaps the most helpful evaluation is now that of Dan R. Stiver, *Theology after Ricoeur: New Directions in Hermeneutical Theology* (Louisville: Westminster John Knox Press, 2001). Not everyone will be convinced by all of Ricoeur's work. For instance, when pressed as to whether he thinks the resurrection of Jesus is an actual historical event, he demurs, preferring to think of it as a metaphor for the rise of the early church: see his *Critique and Conviction: Conversations with François Azouvi and Marc de Launay* (New York: Columbia University Press, 1998), 152–53. I am indebted to Kevin Vanhoozer for this latter reference.

valists whether we admit it or not—but which perspectives are finally warranted? Is the perspective of apartheid warranted—if not, why not?

Other scholars have developed speech-act theory to allow much more interplay than in the past between what a text *means* and what it *does,* and they can emerge from the discussion with a chastened version of authorial intent still intact.[21]

Some sociologists have also weighed in with helpful distinctions. As early as the 1960s, Robert Merton introduced us to "middle-range social theory." At that time the field of sociology tended toward either (1) abstract grand theories that tried to explain everything but which were tied to very little empirical research, or (2) what might be called local theories—i.e., theories tied to particular social phenomena as measured by controlled empirical research, but which could not yield much by way of general principle or integrating theory. Merton found neither option attractive and proposed the new category of "middle-range social theories"—i.e., theories substantially tied to empirical research yet sufficiently detached from particular social phenomena to generate generalizing and even transferable results. The application to other fields of learning is transparent.

In short, my first "measured response" to postmodernism is to say that there are many helpful models out there to enable us to think through how finite human beings can know some objectively true things. Hard postmoderns are simply wrong, and their position is logically absurd. The best of the soft postmoderns preserve what is best in postmodernism—including the implications of our finitude, the complexities surrounding how we learn

---

[21] Kevin J. Vanhoozer, *Is There a Meaning in This Text? The Bible, the Reader, and the Morality of Literary Knowledge* (Grand Rapids: Zondervan, 1998). At its best, speech-act theory responds helpfully to Karl Barth's wish to safeguard God's freedom and transcendence. "Speech-acts allow us to transcend the debilitating dichotomy between revelation as 'God saying' and 'God doing'—for saying too is a kind of doing" (Kevin J. Vanhoozer, *First Theology: God, Scripture and Hermeneutics* [Downers Grove, IL: InterVarsity Press, 2002], 130). In other words, this responds to the fairly constant categorization of some emerging church writers that an emphasis on the truthfulness of Scripture makes for a "static" revelation, domesticated, and "freeze-dried" (to use McLaren's oft-repeated expression).

and know, and a useful critique of modernism—while preserving the possibility of knowing some things truly, even if nothing omnisciently. In other words, they preserve a place for truth, objective truth.

2. My second response has to do with the fact that for all its innovations, postmodernism remains the bastard child of modernism and shares its fundamental weakness: it begins with the "I," the finite self. In this sense, postmodernism, like the modernism that spawned it, is *methodologically* atheistic—or more generously put, it takes no account of God at the beginning of its deliberations. For Descartes, this was a tactical choice so that he could find common ground with atheists; for many later modernists, it was the conclusion to which their naturalistic philosophy drove them. In much of late modernism, God is at best the conclusion, not the premise. Postmoderns vary enormously on what they mean by "God," but none of them begins by thinking about how the existence and omniscience of a personal God might have some definitive bearing on human epistemology. In this regard, moderns and postmoderns are both very different (as we have seen) from the premoderns in the same way.

But there is something to learn from the premoderns. Yes, their reliance on reason *at the expense* of experimentation and observation made their approach to "natural philosophy" (what we now call science) less than fruitful, and this, combined with too "open" a universe, left them awash in more than a few superstitions. But at least they recognized the rightness of beginning with God.

Suppose there had never been a Fall. Such a supposition requires that we push our imaginations to the limit, but it is not too difficult to see that our fixed point, our orienting point in epistemology as in everything else, would be God himself. We would see that all of human knowing is indeed a subset of God's knowing, and it is our immense privilege, as creatures made in God's image, to share some small part of that knowledge. We would recognize our finitude, of course, and happily acknowledge that each human being looks at things slightly differently, but the ultimate test of true knowing, the ultimate resolution of all perspectives, would be in God himself, who alone enjoys the perspective of omniscience.

But fallen as we are, we will twist every epistemological structure we construct. The peculiar conceit of modernism was to think that by beginning with the finite "I" we could nevertheless arrive at certain knowledge and finally make assertions about God's existence: yes, God exists, and here are the proofs; or no, God does not exist, and here are the reasons. It's not that there is no evidence or no reasons; it's that by beginning with "I," the foundation is so unstable. Postmodernism shares the same beginning point, of course, but seeks to empty modernism of its certainty. And God? Especially in hard postmodernism, he is no more than the belief structure of a particular social group. He has no more reality or truth than the belief structure of some other group. Every religious view is as right or wrong as every other religious view. If there is a real God out there, we finite beings have no means of knowing it or him with genuine certainty. To claim anything more would be to abandon postmodernism — and, equally bad, it would mean being intolerant. So let your religious life be personal, your own story, and make sure you use it to do good (even though the definition of "good" is now notoriously plastic).

Even if one opts for some kind of soft postmodernism, however, the problem of beginning with the finite "I" simply will not go away. The result is that even when soft postmoderns, rather begrudgingly, leave some place for truth, they are often still uncomfortable with it. Christian postmoderns will acknowledge, in general terms, that they believe the Bible and want to espouse the doctrinal verities of historic confessionalism, but whenever a preacher or teacher lays the same stress on truth that the Bible does, or the same stress on the exclusiveness of Jesus Christ that the New Testament does, they are instantly nervous. For they are still operating with the fundamental axiom shared by both modernism and postmodernism: it is appropriate to begin with the finite "I."

This is profoundly mistaken. An omniscient, talking God changes everything. It does *not* change the fact that I will always be finite and that my knowledge of him and about him will always be partial. But once I know that he exists, that he is the Creator and my Savior and Judge, it is improper, even idolatrous, to try to think of my knowing things without reference to him. All of my knowledge, if it is true knowledge, is necessarily a subset of his. Whether I came to know him (as far as I can tell) through observing the good works of those who believe in him, or by reading texts he has given us, or by studying (greatest wonder of all!) his self-disclosure in a human being, or by the secret work of his Spirit in showing me my sin and rebellion and drawing me to his grace and forgiveness — whatever the means, in every instance I have come to know him by his self-disclosure. I am a dependent being, and my knowledge is dependent knowledge. For all the methodological rigor of modernism, for all the useful recognition of the entailments of finitude in postmodernism, the fundamental starting point of these systems is disastrously mistaken.[22]

---

[22] Those who study the history of apologetics will recognize that I am now meddling in old debates. The battle lines drawn between evidentialism and presuppositionalism were generated by the move to the "I" in modern thought. One of the unintended by-products of postmodernism is that those debates now appear in new guises. Evidentialist approaches seem remarkably unconvincing to postmoderns, partly because they are suspicious of truth claims anyway, and partly because all the structures of the evidences are necessarily the product of finite human experience, which is so terribly insecure from an epistemological perspective. But the presuppositionalists fare no better. In one sense, every postmodern is a committed presuppositionalist. The question is what authorizes you to assert that your presuppositions are better or more truthful or more convincing than anyone else's. Even to begin to probe these sorts of questions here would demand another book. But it is worth mentioning in passing that a committed presuppositionalist such as John M. Frame can see the place for adducing evidences, provided it is not at the expense of abandoning the Christian "givens" (i.e., the Christian presuppositions) of God, his revelation, the authority of Scripture, and so forth: see his *Apologetics to the Glory of God* (Phillipsburg, NJ: Presbyterian and Reformed, 1994). And over the last three decades, Alvin Plantinga has convincingly argued that beginning with God is an entirely credible approach to epistemology (a kind of non-foundationalist foundationalism, though Plantinga would reject this label). Most of his writing constitutes a better defense of theism than of Christian theism. Of his numerous books, perhaps the most important is *Warranted Christian Belief* (Oxford: Oxford University Press, 2000). In fact, a small but very bright circle of former anti-foundationalists is now mounting impressive arguments in favor of a chastened foundationalism: e.g., Laurence Bonjour, *In Defense of Pure Reason* (Cambridge: Cambridge University Press, 1998), passim. Bonjour started writing along these lines in a series of critical essays beginning in 1978. Cf. the penetrating essay by J. Andrew Kirk, "The Confusion of Epistemology in the West and Christian Mission," *Tyndale Bulletin* 55 (2004): 131–56.

Chapter 5

EMERGING CHURCH CRITIQUE OF POSTMODERNISM

Because the emerging church movement is extraordinarily diverse, evaluations of it are especially difficult. Just as warm commendation may be particularly appropriate with respect to one section of the movement but not another, so also penetrating criticism may be more than warranted with respect to one section of the movement but not another. With appropriate caveats, I have indicated some areas where I think the emerging movement is helpful (chapter 2). I have also argued that its historical and analytic assessments of both modernism and postmodernism, though not entirely mistaken, are overly polarized, rather reductionistic, and somewhat outdated (chapter 3). To level such charges requires that I lay my own cards on the table and outline how in my view postmodernism should be understood (chapter 4).

That brings us to the central problem with the emerging church's response to postmodernism. Apart from occasional asides, emerging writers and preachers are so busy telling us how culture has changed that their response has offered very little critique of the changes. It vehemently denounces modernism, but offers nothing very penetrating when it comes to postmodernism. In particular, it has wrestled unconvincingly with the related matters of truth, certainty, historical witness, and even with the nature of the gospel itself.

These are serious charges. My argument will now proceed in two steps. In this chapter and the next I shall interact with various aspects of the emerging church movement's handling of truth. Then in chapter 7 I shall summarize some of the biblical evidence that I believe emerging writers downplay or overlook.

It may prove helpful to break down the emerging church movement's handling of truth-related issues into five overlapping discussions that I shall cover in this chapter.

Failure to Come to Terms with the Importance of Non-Omniscient Truth-Claims

Although some writers in the emergent movement continue to praise post-modernism and denigrate modernism in absolute terms, the movement's better thinkers occasionally warn against absolutizing postmodernism. Thus Leonard Sweet, for example, rightly warns his readers not to embrace postmodernism,[1] while most of his argument urges Christian living and preaching characterized by the anagram EPIC—we must focus on the experiential, the participatory, the image-driven, the connected.

Some of this is very helpful. But it is disquieting that he fails to say *why* we are not to embrace postmodernism. Is it not, at least in part, because strong postmodernism sacrifices the category of objective truth, a category (as we shall see) that both historic Christianity and the Bible itself have always insisted on? So where is the counsel that tells us not only how to respond to what is good and useful or at least neutral in postmodernism, but also how to correct and refute what is dangerous and sloppy in post-modernism? To what extent are the EPIC categories, *if they become the central touchstones of Christianity under postmodernism*, likely to sacrifice too much? Yes, postmoderns are more open to nonlinear thinking than moderns, and they probably appreciate imagery and metaphor more than the preceding generation. As a result, I have found it very useful on occasion to preach evangelistically in university settings from the Apocalypse. Its colorful imagery, far from being off-putting, can actually open windows and be very appealing to twenty-first-century students. But there are plenty of dangers with "image-driven" witness. While it can fire the imagination, it may prove so subjective that it leads people astray from what the text

---

[1] Leonard Sweet, *Postmodern Pilgrims: First Century Passion for the 21st Century World* (Nashville: Broadman & Holman, 2000), xvii.

actually says.[2] So where are the substantive warnings about *how* to respond to postmodern errors?

Similarly, Brian McLaren can write, "Postmodernism is the latest in a long series of absurdities."[3] By this he seems to mean that the omni-tolerance of what I have called hard postmodernism is ultimately self-refuting. A Christian must see this, of course, or stop being a Christian. Unfortunately, however, McLaren does not unpack this or explain in what ways Christianity must therefore expose or confront or contradict postmodernism because of its absurdism. All of the concrete advice in the book is built on the assumption that postmodernism has effected such a gigantic and irreversible shift in people's thought patterns[4] that the church is faced with a fundamental choice: adapt so as to respond better to postmodernism, or be relegated to

---

[2] Obviously, I here assume that *in measure* one can determine what a text "actually says": see the discussion in chap. 4. If one cannot admit that much, then Christianity is (at the risk of an image-driven statement) frankly sold for a mess of postmodern pottage.

[3] Brian D. McLaren, *The Church on the Other Side* (Grand Rapids: Zondervan, 2003), 165.

[4] This is standard rhetoric among emerging writers and others who push a postmodern agenda. Even while recognizing that many changes have indeed taken place, we have to keep in mind that the more one insists on this point as a dogmatic depiction of reality, the less convincing it becomes. Consider this example from Justo L. González, *The Changing Shape of Church History* (St. Louis: Chalice, 2002), 74: "The reason that entire sections of the church today ignore the challenge of true catholicity is that the modern intellectual map makes it difficult to be truly catholic. By insisting on objectivity, the modern map makes no allowance for the importance of perspective in all knowledge—including theological and religious knowledge. By insisting on universality, it invites each particular perspective to impose itself on the rest—in other words, it invites every theology and every tradition to become sectarian.... But if there is the Scylla of syncretism, there is also the Charybdis of sectarianism—a danger against which many in the Western church have not been sufficiently vigilant." There is some wisdom here, of course, but is this an objective description of what is going on in the church? Is it true that the dangers of universalizing the local are peculiarly Western? Not in my experience of Christians around the world!

irrelevance. All of the strategies he offers are in support of this thesis; none respond to the absurdism in postmodernism.

McLaren offers twelve strategies in the book:

1. "Maximize discontinuity"—i.e., we need to make some big changes, not just little ones.
2. "Redefine your mission"—by living in missional communities.
3. "Practice systems thinking," because the church is more organic than linear.
4. "Trade up your traditions for tradition." In other words, don't fret so much about denominational distinctives. Embrace the entire Christian tradition as your own.
5. "Resurrect theology as art and science," because theology is not so much a matter of learning answers as "a quest for beauty and truth."
6. "Design a new apologetic"—i.e., we must find new ways to communicate the gospel.
7. "Learn a new rhetoric"—i.e., listen carefully to how people talk today and find appropriate modes of conversation with them.
8. "Abandon structures as they are outgrown."
9. "Save the leaders"—i.e., help Christian leaders who are in the front lines of mission, since "there's no shame in being injured on the front lines."
10. "Subsume missions in mission."
11. "Look ahead, farther ahead."
12. "Enter the postmodern world"—i.e., understand it, engage it, and get ready for revolution.[5]

There is some good advice here, but there is nothing to help us refute the absurdism in postmodernism, largely because, under the influence of his understanding of postmodernism, McLaren is remarkably averse to trading in the coinage of truth. We all look at the world from our own perspective, so inevitably we are left with difference, change, uncertainty, mystery. Instead of being afraid of this, we should embrace it.

---

[5] McLaren, *The Church on the Other Side,* 120. The strategies listed are chapter headings in the book.

When we "do theology," we are clay pots pondering the potter, kids pondering their father, ants discussing the elephant. At some level of profundity and accuracy, we are bound to be inadequate or incomplete all the time, in almost anything we say or think, considering our human limitations, including language, and God's infinite greatness.[6]

Our words will seek to be servants of mystery, not removers of it as they were in the old world. They will convey a message that is clear yet mysterious, simple yet mysterious, substantial yet mysterious. My faith developed in the old world of many words, in a naive confidence in the power of many words, as if the mysteries of faith could be captured like fine-print conditions in a legal document and reduced to safe equations. Mysteries, however, cannot be captured so precisely. Freeze-dried coffee, butterflies on pins, and frogs in formaldehyde all lose something in our attempts at capturing, defining, preserving, and rendering them less jumpy, flighty, or fluid. In the new world, we will understand this a little better.[7]

Here it is again: the absolute antithesis. Either we can know God exhaustively, or we are restricted to the mysterious. Of course it is always true that we cannot know God exhaustively: we are not omniscient. God is infinitely greater than we are. Moreover, the best of the modernist theologians were among the most adamant on this point. It did not take postmodernism to discover that God is infinitely greater than we and in that sense forever remains mysterious. But although the comparison of elephant and ants is helpful at one level, it overlooks the fact that in this case the ants have been made in the image of the elephant, and this elephant has not only communicated with the ants in ant-language, but has also, in the person of his Son, become an "ant" while remaining an "elephant." If the ants were left on their own to figure out what the elephant knows and thinks and feels, "mystery" would be too weak a word. Yet in the case of the revealing elephant with whom we have to do, he has told us ants what he is like, what he thinks, what he feels, what he has done, and what he is going to do—not exhaustively, of course, but truly.

True, we must never think we have domesticated God, making him a specimen, a frog in a bottle of formaldehyde. But which of the great modern

---

6 Ibid., 65.
7 Ibid., 89.

theologians *ever* thought of God in those terms? On the other hand, if this God has disclosed a great deal about himself, is it not appropriate to talk about and think and write and sing about the attributes that he himself has chosen to disclose in the language of the ants? Is this reducing God to a frog in formaldehyde? Surely not: it is merely the mark of faithfulness to the self-disclosure of this gracious God. Because we are small and sinful, we will sometimes misunderstand and distort what he has disclosed. Sadly, we will sometimes be tempted to pretend that we know more about him than we actually do. But when he has disclosed so much, it scarcely honors him to say, "Ah! He is so big, everything is so mysterious, that I cannot say a single true thing about him." Only if "true" demands *omniscient* truth (that antithesis again!) is that a responsible position. Otherwise, it is merely a new idolatry: we refuse to take God at his word and prefer to worship the dogmatic not-knowing of hard postmodernism.

Or consider this example from Stanley Grenz. At one point he asks himself the questions, "Can Christian theology make any claim to speak 'objective truth' in a context in which various communities offer diverse paradigms, each of which is ultimately theological?... Does the move to nonfoundationalism entail a final and total break with metaphysical realism?"[8] That is exactly the question we must ask. A hard postmodernist would answer no to the first question and yes to the second; a soft postmodernist would be much more careful, insisting that we may indeed know some objective truth, but never exhaustively or omnisciently, and that we can never make a final break with realism if we hold that there is a God "out there" who has made himself known to us in history.

---

[8] Stanley J. Grenz, *Renewing the Center: Evangelical Theology in a Post-Theological Era* (Grand Rapids: Baker, 2000), 245. I should add that I have used this example before in a lengthy review essay of the book, first published on the web (Alliance of Confessing Evangelicals) and then elsewhere. Dr. Grenz afforded me the courtesy of an extensive response. I have revised the review article to respond to his points, and it appears in a chapter titled "Domesticating the Gospel: A Review of Grenz's *Renewing the Center*," in Millard J. Erickson, Paul Helseth, and Justin Taylor, eds., *Reclaiming the Center* (Wheaton, IL: Crossway, 2004).

How then does Grenz answer his own questions? He asserts that such questions are "both improper and ultimately unhelpful."[9] It would be better to ask, "How can a postfoundationalist theological method lead to statements about a world beyond our formulations?"[10] This in turn leads him to his Pannenberg-inspired references to the eschatological world, the ultimate world that does not pass away. This eschatological world can ground our epistemology.

But wait a minute! Why are the initial questions either improper or unhelpful? Grenz has simply ducked them by substituting another question, one he prefers. In any case, how can he make *any* true statements "about a world beyond our formulations"? If the expression "world beyond our formulations" is taken absolutely, we cannot say anything about it, so we may as well stop trying. But if the expression assumes some limitations that are not absolute, then in this case we are obligated to say what we can say. And if we can do that for the eschatological world, why cannot we do it for this world? After all, what we know about the eschatological world is disclosed in Scripture, which also, of course, discloses some things about this world. If, on the other hand, Grenz thinks that we will not be able to make any true statements about the eschatological world until the eschaton, then (a) it is hard to see how such confidence gives us any epistemological base here and now; (b) it is hard to see how we can *now* know that we *shall have* such confidence in the future, unless we can know certain things now; and in any case, (c) since even in the eschaton we shall remain finite beings, it is difficult to see that we shall overcome the postmodernists' objections even there.[11]

In short, emergent writers do not handle the truth claims of Christianity very well. While formally repudiating the hard forms of postmodernism, when it comes to their actual arguments they either cave in to these hard forms or, to say the least, never provide any hint of how Christians informed

---

[9] Grenz, *Renewing the Center*, 245.

[10] Ibid.

[11] One reviewer rather acidly comments on this eschatological appeal, "While it appears to be a concession to placate the postmodernist, it is unlikely to succeed even here since postmodernists revile eschatological metanarratives as much as any other" (Randal Rauser, in *Studies in Religion / Sciences Religieuses* 31 [2002]: 436).

by postmodern insights can speak about truth in the ways that Scripture does (on which see the next chapter).

Failure to Face the Tough Questions, Especially If They Are Truth-Related

The ablest of the emerging thinkers are not unaware of these problems, of course, so it is important to try to understand how they suggest we forge ahead.

Probably the best way to get at this question is by observing how some emergent writers handle world religions. After all, the emerging church movement is pretty strongly evangelistic—i.e., it is committed to outreach of one sort or another. The question then becomes, "On what basis do emerging church leaders commend the gospel and invite others to join them if at most levels they are more than a little reluctant to say that Christianity is *true*?"

The answers vary from writer to writer. Great stress (rightly so) is laid on the quality of Christian living and discipleship. Christians commend Christ to others by acting like Christ. That is certainly one part of a response that is faithful to Scripture. But what about the larger claims of world religions?

Let us return to Grenz for a moment. He tells us we must not ask the question, "Which religion is true?" Rather, we must ask, "What end is most ultimate, even if many are real?"[12]

> The communitarian reminder that the goal of all social traditions is to construct a well-ordered society (although the various communities might well differ from each other as to what that society entails) suggests that the truth question is better formulated: Which theologizing community articulates an interpretive framework that is able to provide the transcendent vision for the construction of the kind of world that the particular community itself is in fact seeking? Hence, rather than settling for the promotion of some vague concept of community, the communitarian insight leads to the question, Which religious vision carries within itself the foundation for the community-building role of a transcendent religious vision? Which vision provides the basis for community in the truest [*sic!*] sense?[13]

---

[12] Grenz, *Renewing the Center*, 280–81.
[13] Ibid., 281.

This is a shocking response. How are we to decide which "religious vision" provides the basis for the best community—especially if what is judged best is simply "the kind of world that *the particular community itself* [emphasis added] is in fact seeking?" We now face not only the respective claims of each subgroup—say, Christians and Muslims—each thinking that their own respective religious visions offer the best basis for the kinds of community they envisage, but each subgroup enjoying the same prerogative—say, Anabaptist versus Dutch Reformed, Shi'ite versus Sunni, and so forth. Why not First Baptists and Second Baptists in a particular town? There is no hint of any truth claim that must be adjudicated, despite Scripture's manifold witness to the contrary (as we shall see).

Or consider Brian McLaren's approach. In several of his books he rejects both absolutism and relativism. What, then, is the way ahead? He does not want to be thought of as a pluralistic relativist; equally, he refuses to trade in the coinage of absolute truth.[14] What then is the way ahead? Somehow he wants to work *through* pluralism to something on the other side. He thinks that all religions of the world are under threat—whether from fundamentalist Islam or from the "McDonaldization" of the world, and rather more from forces emanating from New York and Hollywood than from Arabia and Afghanistan. So the Christian faith, McLaren proposes,

> should become (in the name of Jesus Christ) a welcome friend to other religions of the world, not a threat. We should be seen as a protector of their heritages, a defender against common enemies, *not* one of the enemies. Just as Jesus came originally not to destroy the law but to fulfill it, not to condemn people but to save them, I believe he comes today not to destroy or condemn anything (anything but evil) but to redeem and save everything that can be redeemed or saved.[15]

---

[14] For his latest statements along these lines, see Brian D. McLaren, *A Generous Orthodoxy* (El Cajon, CA: emergentYS / Grand Rapids: Zondervan, 2004), esp. chap. 19. See also, for instance, *A New Kind of Christian* (San Francisco: Jossey-Bass, 2001), 65–66.

[15] *A Generous Orthodoxy,* 254. This is McLaren at his frustrating best. Seldom have I read a paragraph I simultaneously agree with as much and disagree with as much.

But isn't there a lot of evil *in* other religions? Yes, of course, McLaren acknowledges, but there is so much evil in ours, too. Besides, isn't there *good* in other religions? Here McLaren wants to be careful *not* to give the impression that he is falling into the old "all religions say the same thing" trap. Sometimes they talk about rather different things. For instance,

> Zen Buddhism ... says little about cosmic history and purpose as do Judaism and Christianity (and Theravada Buddhism). Western Christianity has (for the last few centuries anyway) said relatively little about mindfulness and meditative practices, about which Zen Buddhism has said much. To talk about different things is not to contradict one another; it is, rather, to have much to offer one another, on occasion at least.[16]

At this juncture McLaren returns to the influence David J. Bosch had on him (discussed in chapter 1, above) and proposes "eight emerging obligations of a generous orthodoxy,"[17] which are adaptations of Bosch's eight points. Elsewhere, McLaren elaborates, "The church must present the Christian faith not as one religious army at war against all other religious armies but as one of many religious armies fighting against evil, falsehood, destruction, darkness, and injustice."[18] But if our mission, along with the missions of other religions, is to get people to fight against evil, it is still fair to ask which mission people should join. "Of course, in a pluralistic world, there are many choices"—but this does not mean that each religion is as good as any other. Just when McLaren is on the brink of relativism, he steps back: "Contrary to relativism's implications, it does matter which mission one joins."[19]

But *why* does it matter? If religions are not of equal worth, as MacLaren rightly affirms, what makes a religion better or worse? Here McLaren does not say that one is closer to the truth than others, or anything of that sort. Rather: "The religion that sees the pride in Pharisees 'in here' and the devotion in prostitutes 'out there,' the religion that hears Satan whispering in the top disciple and that sees love exemplified in a Samaritan wayfarer—that religion will inspire their allegiance."[20] But as one reviewer puts it, "Is Christian-

---

[16] Ibid., 255.

[17] Ibid., 256.

[18] McLaren, *The Church on the Other Side*, 83.

[19] Ibid., 84.

[20] Ibid.

ity more desirable than other religions simply because we have more cool paradoxes to capture people's hearts?"[21] Elsewhere McLaren quotes Bosch with approval: "We cannot point to any other way of salvation than Jesus Christ; at the same time, we cannot set limits to the saving power of God.... We appreciate this tension, and do not attempt to resolve it."[22] McLaren adds, "This means that anathemas and damnation can be invoked rarely if at all."[23] I certainly do not want to invoke anathemas and damnation any more frequently than Scripture does, and then always with tears, just as Jesus wept over Jerusalem. But I wonder how faithful I am to what God has said if I adopt McLaren's "rarely if at all." How far removed is McLaren's stance from Paul's assessment of the idolatrous religions of his own day, "In the past God overlooked such ignorance, but now he commands all people everywhere to repent" (Acts 17:30)? And where, in either the Old Testament or the New, does the revealed religion of Scripture align itself with other religions as one army among many armies to fight evil? Is it not much more typical in the Bible to think of other religions as various forms of idolatry?

Sadly, I find just about every step of McLaren's argumentation at this point either factually questionable or frankly manipulative.

1. Is it true that all religions of the world are under threat? Perhaps, but there is a great deal of published research that argues that there is a *resurgence* of religions around the world, even if the resurgence is uneven.[24]

2. This slogan-wielding condemnation (the McDonaldization of the world) scores points with some people, I suppose, but is rarely even-handed. Yes, McDonald's is all over the world. So also are Thai restaurants, Indian restaurants, Greek restaurants, French restaurants, Korean restaurants, Chinese restaurants, Arab restaurants, Japanese restaurants, Italian restaurants, and on and on. I find the whole lot in just about every major city I visit, on six continents. This is the result of transportation, migration, flowing capital,

---

[21] Review by Greg Gilbert, published at http://www.christianity.com/partner/Article_Display_Page/0,,PTID314526|CHID598014|CIID1562286,00.html, second-to-last paragraph.

[22] McLaren, *A Generous Orthodoxy*, 262.

[23] Ibid.

[24] For instance, see Alister McGrath, *The Twilight of Atheism: The Rise and Fall of Disbelief in the Modern World* (New York: Doubleday, 2004). McGrath's view is a bit roseate while McLaren's is quite dour.

and much more. Is it all bad? Isn't exposure to other ways of life, other languages and smells and food, a good thing? Yes, I know, like most things in the world, globalization has some good elements and some bad. In 1970, 11 percent of the world's poor were in Africa; 76 percent were in Asia. By 1998, 66 percent of the world's poor were in Africa, and only 15 percent were in Asia.[25] Asia accomplished this by stimulating economic growth, including world trade, in contrast to the socialism and anti-capitalism that still pervades much of Africa. Still, isn't it a good thing to see the reduction of poverty somewhere, through capitalism, even though we also well recognize the dangers of wealth and materialism?

3. McLaren repeatedly states that Christianity has committed its own share of evils, so how can it pronounce on the evils of other religions?[26] There is important insight, though I do find his standards of comparison quite skewed (as I will mention below). My point here is simply that Christians claim that the revelation given them in Scripture, and supremely in the person and work of Christ, is wholly good. That Christians do not live up to this revelation is terribly shameful, something for which we must constantly ask forgiveness and which we should be constantly striving to overcome, even as we long for the consummation of the kingdom. But insofar as other religions actually contradict the revelation of God, we claim that these religions are not true revelations at all. In other words, quite apart from whether any religion's adherents do or do not live up to their own traditions, there is the question of whether or not

---

[25] See Jagdish Bhagwati, *In Defense of Globalization* (New York: Oxford University Press, 2004).

[26] In addition to the passage quoted, see, for instance, Neo's comment in *A New Kind of Christian*, 66: "Look, my understanding of the gospel tells me that religion is always a mixed bag, whether it's Judaism, Christianity, Islam, or Buddhism. Some of it reflects people's sincere attempts to find the truth, and some of it represents people's attempts to evade the truth through hypocrisy. Some of it reflects glimpses of God that people get through nature, through experience, through the fingerprint of God in their own design and the design of the universe—like Paul talked about in Romans 1 or in Acts 19. And some of it represents our own ego, our own pride, as we try to suppress the truth and look holy while we do it."

the authoritative documents of those religions tell the truth. If they are encouraging the worship of a god or of gods who in whole or in part are distanced from or contradictory to the God who is there (to use the famous Schaefferism), is that not to be of concern to Christians who long to be faithful to revelation? McLaren ducks this issue by talking about how all sides have sinned. True—but are all the putative revelations equally true, equally right, equally good? If so, we have retreated into philosophical pluralism; if not, why not? When will we admit that truth claims cannot be ducked, even if they are not the claims to *omniscient* knowledge of *absolute* truth?

4. When he does talk about differences between religions, McLaren sometimes wants the differences to be additive: Some religions talk more about cosmic history, and others (such as Zen Buddhism) talk more about meditation; let's learn from all of them, for they all make a contribution to genuine spirituality. But quite apart from the failure to address what we must do when the religions contradict one another, this merely additive approach carries a hidden set of problems. In this instance, meditation in Zen Buddhism is not conceived of as mere technique. It is integrally related to Zen's understanding of the divine, which is fundamentally alien to that of the Bible. Meanwhile, the Bible does speak of meditation from time to time (reflect on Psalm 1:2; 119). Does the Bible have anything pertinent to say in our evaluations of the different trajectories of meditation that have developed in Christianity—say, in the Puritans or in Julian of Norwich? And if the Bible calls us to account over the way meditation has been practiced in Christendom, may it not also have something to say about how it is practiced in Zen Buddhism, where it is irrefragably tied to an entirely different conception of the divine?

5. In any case, some adherents to other world religions would find McLaren's approach insulting, because they hold that their own religious understandings are *true* and can be addressed respectively only by adjudicating truth claims. I shall not soon forget the Native American woman who was listening to her college professor ramble on about postmodernism. She became more and more agitated and finally exploded with the comment, "First you took away our land, then you took away our language, then you took away the rest of our culture, and now you want to take away our religion!"

Regretfully, I cannot resist the conclusion that McLaren keeps ducking all the hard questions while claiming he has found a better way. I do not see how he has wrestled with the question of how abominable idolatry is to the God of the Bible. I have not found him coherent and convincing, precisely because he will not deal with the claims of truth.[27] Nor does he wrestle with the way the church in both New Testament times and the patristic period had to find its way in a world of many competing religious voices, all of them asserting that Christianity was arrogant for insisting that there is only one way of salvation.[28]

---

[27] It would be easy to list other approaches with similar problems. Robert C. Greer, *Mapping Postmodernism: A Survey of Christian Options* (Downers Grove, IL: InterVarsity Press, 2003), includes a lot of useful survey material. But his own solution is deeply problematic. In brief, he proposes what he calls "post-postmodernism." He wants the Scripture to be seen as God's Word, but in its representation of the one (and therefore universal) Christ-event, it leaves open the possibility of multiple paradigms springing from this Christ-event, multiple paradigms that are actually taught by the Spirit. So (for instance) paedobaptists and credo-baptists are both right in their own paradigms, Calvinists and Arminians are both right in their own paradigms, conservatives and liberals are both right in their own paradigms and so on—or, to cover himself, Greer says that they *may* all be right. "In post-postmodernism, different religious traditions with diverse ways of ordering truth are recognized as legitimate within the body of Christ. This is because the Holy Spirit is given the freedom to shape truth differently for various believers without violating the essential integrity of the Word of God" (p. 201). Greer's book cries out for detailed evaluation but because it does not appear to be used directly by the emerging church movement, I had better refrain from doing so here. Moreover, by itself this presentation does not work out the challenges of world religions. I cannot restrain myself, however, from observing how often Greer deploys surprisingly muddled theological categories to further his argument (e.g., his subsuming of the Lordship controversy under the imputation/infusion debate).

[28] We have returned, by another route, to our earlier discussion of contemporary notions of "tolerance," in which it is "intolerant"

Failure to Use Scripture as the Norming Norm over against an Eclectic Appeal to Tradition

As we have noted in the earlier chapters of this book, many emerging church thinkers characteristically want to call into question many local traditions and appeal to Tradition, the whole tradition. This seems to work out in the literature in one of three ways.

First, at a sloppy level, this entitles various proponents to pick and choose: we'll have icons, or journaling, or candles, or robes, or incense, because all of these things are part of the Tradition.

Second, at a more rigorous level, the emerging leaders, taught by postmodernism, recognize that all of us think out of a tradition. We are not utterly autonomous knowers. At very least this means that we have a much bigger heritage than many Christians acknowledge, so we ought to think and work and live out of this massive tradition—Catholic, Eastern Orthodox, evangelical, liberal, and so on.

Third, McLaren draws attention to the splendidly influential book of Alasdair MacIntyre, *After Virtue*,[29] briefly discussed in the first chapter. MacIntyre rejects modern individualism, whether in the liberal or the Marxist strain, claiming that our lives are fragmented by the piecemeal approaches to knowledge characteristic of late modernism. His solution is to appeal to

---

if one says that anyone else is wrong. I do not think it is possible to maintain the earlier definition of tolerance, which alone is coherent and avoids moral bankruptcy (see pp. 68–70), without preserving a significant place for truth claims. Similarly, modern notions of "pluralism" are sometimes remarkably nonpluralistic: all the voices agree in saying that all the voices are equally right—or, if one is superior (which is what McLaren wants to say about Christianity), it cannot be because there is a nonnegotiable truth claim. One recalls the observation of George M. Marsden about "tolerance" and "pluralism" on American campuses: "Pluralism remains a basis for imposing uniformity" (*The Soul of the American University: From Protestant Establishment to Established Nonbelief* [New York: Oxford University Press, 1994], 436). His entire discussion makes for salutary reading.

[29] *After Virtue: A Study in Moral Theory*, 2nd ed. (Notre Dame, IN: University of Notre Dame Press, 1984).

the Aristotelian tradition of the virtues, without which, he argues, no stable virtues are finally possible. One must return to the thought of Aristotle and develop it afresh in our time, or face the withering demolition of Nietzsche, who at least understood the inadequacy of modern thought, even if his own solution was no better. McLaren then points to a little book by Jonathan Wilson,[30] who, building on MacIntyre, offers five practical lessons for Christians living under postmodernism, lessons culled either from MacIntyre or from a slightly revised MacIntyre. Those five lessons are

a. If we are to live faithfully, the church must live with its history. In our context, that means we must distinguish among church, kingdom, and world as we tell our story to the world.

b. We must fight the fragmentation that we scarcely recognize. To live faithfully means more than doing little faithful bits. Everything must be directed to the right end.

c. We must recognize the failure of the Enlightenment project so that we will squarely face the many failures and instances of unfaithfulness in the church.

d. Although MacIntyre sought to recover Aristotelian tradition, Wilson wants to recover tradition in the light of Christ. This includes deep reflection on what the *telos* (the goal or end) of human life is. In particular, we need to work things out within the heritage of the Tradition, deeply embodied in our lives, our values, our practices, and our community.

e. We must establish a new monasticism—not quite the kind of monasticism that MacIntyre advocates, but a kind of retreat from such engagement in the fragmented life of the culture that we are morally compromised at every turn.

McLaren's three appeals to Tradition differ quite a bit from one another. Nevertheless, several observations seem called for, which may apply to one or more of these appeals.

1. It is ironic that some emerging leaders speak constantly of the importance of Tradition, yet fail to live in any long-standing living tradition. By constantly appealing to the "capital T" Tradition, and then in effect pick-

---

[30] Jonathan R. Wilson, *Living Faithfully in a Fragmented World: Lessons for the Church from MacIntyre's* After Virtue (Harrisburg, PA: Trinity Press International, 1997).

ing and choosing from its offerings, they do not succeed in living out any of the traditions that flow from the Tradition, but create their own eclectic, ad hoc churchmanship. If this were genuinely controlled by Scripture, a good case could be made for it. But in fact, protestations notwithstanding, it is not shaped by Scripture. It is controlled by what these emerging thinkers judge to be appropriate in the postmodern world—and this results, rather ironically, in one of the most self-serving appeals to tradition I have ever seen. As long as you can pick and choose from something as vast as the great Tradition, you are really not bound by the discipline of any tradition. While thinking yourself most virtuous, your choices become most idiosyncratic.[31]

2. As for those who argue, instead, that the various traditions are all equally valid, there are two insuperable difficulties. The first is that sometimes these traditions of Christendom contradict one another in fundamental ways. Vague thoughts about the Spirit interpreting the text differently in different communities simply do not handle the tough cases of unambiguous mutual contradiction. The second is that Scripture is not permitted to adjudicate. Where Scripture is unclear on some matter, differences may flourish without much loss. But where Scripture is adequately clear,[32] Scripture must adjudicate, as long as we hold Scripture to be above the creeds.

Most (though not all) emergent leaders want to affirm Scripture's supremacy. McLaren's "generous orthodoxy," for instance,

> upholds and affirms the Apostles' and Nicene Creeds. It also acknowledges (rather perversely) that a number of items many hold as vital for orthodoxy are found nowhere in those seminal creeds and adds (somewhat sheepishly) that the creeds should never be used as a club to batter into submission people with honest questions and doubts. It also affirms (this is so Protestant) that Scripture itself remains above creeds and that

---

[31] Emerging leaders are not all on the same page on this matter. Robert Greer, as already mentioned, runs in the opposite direction: all of the separate traditions are equally valid reflections of the Tradition (see note 27 above).

[32] I use this expression to avoid giving any impression that we can ever enjoy the kind of clarity that belongs exclusively to omniscience.

the Holy Spirit may use Scripture to tweak our creedal understandings and emphases from time to time.[33]

Actually, the affirmation of the unique role of Scripture is not merely "Protestant," but also Patristic.[34] But *why* is Scripture given this unique status? Is it simply because more Christians acknowledge the authority of Scripture than the authority of this or that creed? Why cannot I hear any emerging leader saying that Scripture is more authoritative *precisely because it is God-revealed and true,* and that creeds must be tested (and, if necessary, revised) by Scripture, and not vice versa, *for precisely this reason*?

3. That brings us to the MacIntyre/Wilson proposal. The appeal to a holistic tradition out of which to think, to what many would call a worldview, is immensely important and speaks volumes against the fragmentation of our age. But MacIntyre's work was not cast so much against denials of truth as against narrow thinking that was deeply flawed by the academic commitments to hermetically sealed disciplines. In the hands of Wilson and McLaren, however, MacIntyre becomes a voice in defense of a postmodern agenda. That is, Christians self-consciously choose to work things out within the heritage of the Tradition. These are *our* convictions; they constitute *our* frame of reference.

Well said; very important. But are the traditions true? Are they true even for, say, educated and thoughtful Hindus who disbelieve them? Or are they our convictions just because they are our convictions?

There is a similar debate among post-liberals. George Lindbeck, carefully followed by Grenz, insists that doctrines are not intended to say anything true, but constitute the belief mosaic of the believing community.[35] I agree that they constitute the belief mosaic of the believing com-

---

[33] McLaren, *A Generous Orthodoxy,* 28.

[34] See, for instance, the evidence well assembled by John D. Woodbridge, *Biblical Authority: A Critique of the Rogers/McKim Proposal* (Grand Rapids: Zondervan, 1982).

[35] Cf. the extended discussion in my review article, "Domesticating the Gospel: A Review of Stanley J. Grenz's *Renewing the Center,*" *Southern Baptist Journal of Theology* (Winter 2002), 82ff. As an example of Lindbeck's thought, one might select, from his voluminous writings, *The Nature of Doctrine: Religion and Theology in a Postliberal Age* (Louisville: Westminster John Knox Press, 1984).

munity—but is what the community believes *true*? In other words, does what the community believes conform, in substantial measure, to what actually is? After all, we are not saved by *ideas* about God, Jesus, the cross, his resurrection, the role of the Spirit, regeneration, and so forth. Rather, we are saved by God himself, by Jesus himself, by what he accomplished on the cross, by his resurrection that really did take place in history, and so forth. We are not saved by the ideas in the text, but by those things to which the text bears witness. The text has "extra-textual referentiality"—i.e., it refers to things outside the world of the text itself—and those extra-textual realities are what save us. Post-liberals are very eager to affirm the importance of the Christian Bible as conveyer of Christian ideas; they are extraordinarily reluctant to affirm that those ideas, when they talk about extra-textual realities, are *true*.[36] True, the Bible conveys a "canonical-linguistic world," but when that canonical-linguistic world speaks of extra-canonical realities, is it speaking the truth?

Like McLaren, John R. Franke, who wrote the foreword to *A Generous Orthodoxy,* appeals to the important work of Hans Frei.[37] Frei argues that whereas earlier Christians simply lived in the narrative of the biblical text, by the eighteenth century liberals under the influence of modern thought began to question what *really* happened. Conservatives, replying to the liberal skepticism, tried to show that what *really* happened was more or less what the text says. So suddenly *both* sides were far more interested in the minutiae of what "really" happened and were no longer living in the narrative text of Scripture. Both sides had been snookered by modernism.

---

[36] Grenz has responded to me on this point by saying that I charge him with buying into Lindbeck uncritically, whereas in fact he wants to go beyond Lindbeck to affirm "the extra-linguistic referential character of Christian doctrine." I am glad to hear it, but at no point in his book does he go beyond Lindbeck in this way. He goes beyond Lindbeck by insisting on the prescriptive force of Christian traditions *for Christians*, not because they are objectively true. See the detailed discussion in n. 13 of "Domesticating the Gospel" and the discussion below, in the next chapter, on 1 Corinthians 15.

[37] *The Eclipse of Biblical Narrative: A Study of Eighteenth and Nineteenth Century Hermeneutics* (New Haven: Yale University Press, 1974).

But this analysis is grossly unfair. The reason why earlier Christians lived so comfortably in the narrative of the biblical text is that they believed that the biblical narrative is *true*. When liberals began to doubt that it is true, conservatives replied in similar detail that it is. Of course, in itself such discussion does not constitute living joyously within the narrative. But the suggestion of Frei, and of Lindbeck and others who followed him, that we must simply return to living within the narrative, *while refusing to consider, once these doubts have been raised, whether this narrative is telling the truth*, is myopic counsel. It is the counsel of those who think we are transformed *by ideas about God* and what God does in history, not *by God* and what he does in history. It is a merely intellectualist approach.

The issues are complicated. For Lindbeck, the Christian religion is like a culture with its own language. This language shapes who we are and what we think even before we reflect on our experience and thought. This means that doctrine, which thus becomes second-order grammar, actually "sets the rules for proper, culturally literate first-order religious speech."[38] Lindbeck's frequently cited example pictures a Crusader crying "Christus est Dominus" ("Christ is Lord") while cleaving an infidel's skull. The question, then, is whether this claim is true or false. Lindbeck insists it is neither: it is nothing more than a grammatical ryule, akin to "subjects and verbs must agree in number." "As religious speech, the statement would be assessed for its fit with life in the Christian culture (*intrasystematic* truth); then we would ask the true-or-false question of Christianity as a whole religion (*ontological* truth)."[39]

But surely the Crusader example is open to a quite different analysis. The statement "Christ is Lord" is in fact true, objectively true, insofar as it

---

[38] Daniel J. Treier, " Canonical Unity and Commensurable Language: On Divine Action and Doctrine," in Evangelicals and Scripture: Tradition, Authority and Hermeneutics, ed. Vincent Bacote, Laura C. Miguélez, and Dennis L. Okholm (Downers Grove, IL: InterVarsity Press, 2004), 212.

[39] Treier himself refers to David K. Clark, "Relativism, Fideism and the Promise of Postliberalism," in The Nature of Confession: Evangelicals and Postliberals in Conversation, ed. Timothy R. Phillips and Dennis J. Ockholm (Downers Grove, IL: InterVarsity Press, 1996), 113.

refers to the extra-textual realities: the (objective) Christ is Lord of the universe, its Maker and final Judge, regardless of whether he is confessed as such or not or, as in this instance, confessed as such while an action is being undertaken by the confessor that flies in the face of what it means truly and faithfully to confess Christ as Lord. To make matters still more complicated, the Crusader may have uttered the confession with a clear conscience, truly meaning every word, but having a false understanding (false from the perspective of New Testament teaching) of what it means for a Christian to confess Christ as Lord. In the light of the New Testament, then, the Crusader is not living up to his own confession. Further, granted also that the lordship of Christ works out not only in "good" things perfectly in line with his teaching, but also in the mystery of providence (for he must reign until he has put the last enemy under his feet), then even in the evil that is being done, Christ remains the Lord. The statement, in other words, is objectively true, once its extra-textual reference is understood in the light of New Testament teaching. The reason Lindbeck (and his followers) have a hard time seeing this is that he has a hard time allowing texts to have extra-textual referentiality.[40]

In other words, the tough questions about truth simply will not go away. Yes, we must live within the biblical narrative; yes, we fall into various Christian traditions; yes, we must learn to think holistically. But we hold that the biblical narrative is telling us the truth about what happened in history, and about God and his character and action, and about ourselves and our need, and so forth—even if it is not, and never can be, the whole truth, which is known only to the Omniscient. The Christian traditions are attempts to work out a biblical understanding, but at the end of the day they must themselves be revisable in the light of Scripture, which is what God himself has given. On none of these matters is the emerging church movement very clear. So loathe seem its members to talk at length about truth (even though Scripture, as we shall see, shares none of these inhibitions) that the appeals like Wilson's to live out a tradition keep ducking the tough question: *Why* should we live out this tradition? Because we

---

[40] It is disappointing that neither Clark nor Treier (see previous note) explores this point.

were born into it? Because we find it more coherent than others? Because
the notion of self-sacrifice is attractive? Or will we allow space for the apostolic insistence on *truth*?[41]

Failure to Handle "Becoming" and "Belonging" Tensions in a Biblically Faithful Way

In the first chapter I noted how the emerging movement pretty consistently
puts "belonging" before "becoming." Repelled by those who are so exclusive that they do not allow others to get close—i.e., you have to "become"
a Christian before you can "belong" to the Christian club—the emerging
folk have reversed the order. Invite people to belong, welcome them aboard,
take them into your story (your individual story, and the story of your local
Christian community), and the "becoming" may well follow. Attracted by
what they experience as in some measure they begin to belong to this Christian community, these erstwhile outsiders eventually become Christians
themselves. Thus we saw that Spencer Burke glories in TheOoze because
this website allows people to voice their opinions and interact with each
other without anyone being "up" or "down," or "right" or "wrong." Some

---

41 There are other problems with Wilson's "take" on MacIntyre that
would lead us outside the purpose of this book. I briefly mention
one of them. Even though Wilson revises MacIntyre's appeal to a
"new monasticism," the resulting picture is of a separatist
community, a sort of updated Anabaptist community. Speaking of
tradition, that is only one of several possible models that appeal to
Scripture to justify a set of relations between the church and the
broader culture. Doubtless the best-known typology is the fivefold
scheme of H. Richard Niebuhr, *Christ and Culture* (New York: Harper
& Row, 1956). Wilson's adoption of one of those patterns without
wrestling with whether or not any of the other four might have equal
or better claim to biblical warrant is doubtless prompted by the fact
that, as he himself attests, he first learned to read MacIntyre under
the tutelage of Stanley Hauerwas. For myself, I am inclined to think
that all five patterns in the Niebuhr typology are found in Scripture
but that each is tied to peculiar historical circumstances. I defend
this view in a forthcoming publication.

argue that nonbelievers should be permitted at the Lord's Table, since they may actually meet Christ there for the first time. Over against the typical "Believers Church Tradition" to which they are normally thought to belong, some Baptists are now openly advocating belonging before becoming.[42] One of the attractions of Neo[43] is his warmly embracing way of interacting with people who are not yet Christians.

Once again, there is more than a little insight here. Especially if one has emerged (that word again) from a very conservative twig (in McLaren's clever metaphor) where Christians have almost no meaningful contact with the broad sweep of humanity, it is extraordinarily important to put into place priorities that maintain and develop such contact. That should be so simply because we are human beings; it should be all the more so because we are Christians entrusted with the Great Commission and charged with being salt and light in a decaying and dark world. I have a lot of sympathy for those who are concerned about the wrong kind of withdrawal from society.[44]

Yet five observations must temper any wholesale shift to the belonging/becoming paradigm.

1. The New Testament provides abundant evidence that in some ways Christians *do* constitute a new and distinctive community.

---

[42] The references are all in chapter 1.

[43] The primary protagonist of two books by Brian McLaren, *A New Kind of Christian: A Tale of Two Friends on a Spiritual Journey* (San Francisco: Jossey-Bass, 2001) and *The Story We Find Ourselves In: Further Adventures of a New Kind of Christian* (San Francisco: Jossey-Bass, 2003).

[44] I know urban pastors, for instance, who are conducting thoughtful Bible studies with homosexuals even though the homosexuals in question know full well that these pastors do not think that homosexual practice is a legitimate option. Every year I look for those M.Div. graduates at Trinity Evangelical Divinity School who can talk with anyone—any race, any religious background, any economic level, any sexual orientation. I want these graduates to serve in our cities, in our most multi-cultural, multi-ethnic centers. Some pastors will serve well only in North Dakota or in Arkansas or in southern California, but for our cities I constantly search for those who can talk evenhandedly and nondefensively with anyone.

> Do not be deceived: Neither the sexually immoral nor idolaters nor adulterers nor male prostitutes nor practicing homosexuals nor thieves nor the greedy nor drunkards nor slanderers nor swindlers will inherit the kingdom of God. And that is what some of you *were*. But you were washed, you were sanctified, you were justified in the name of the Lord Jesus Christ and by the Spirit of God (1 Corinthians 6:9–11, emphasis added).

Formerly we were dead in our transgressions and sins, and like the rest of humankind, "we were by nature deserving of wrath" (Ephesians 2:1–3). But all of this has been gloriously changed: we are no longer foreigners and strangers, "but fellow citizens with God's people and members of God's household, built on the foundation of the apostles and prophets" (vv. 19–20). On the last day, there will be a massive divide between those who inherit the consummated kingdom and those who do not (Revelation 21:6–8). These passages are only a small sampling on the subject.

Moreover, the New Testament handling of church discipline presupposes that "in" and "out" are meaningful categories, or else excommunication, the highest sanction,[45] would be meaningless. Such church discipline can be traced back to Jesus himself (Matthew 18), but surfaces in various parts of the New Testament (e.g., 1 Corinthians 5; 2 Corinthians 10–13). Christians are called to make distinctions on both doctrinal (e.g., 1 John 2:22) and ethical grounds (1 John 3:14–15; Matthew 7:15–20). Indeed, it can even be argued that on rare occasions when the presence and power of God are most dramatically displayed, while the crowds of nonbelievers may well press in for healing, none of them will dare to join the believers themselves (Acts 5:1–16).

2. The handling of some New Testament passages in this debate is troubling. Burke, as we have seen,[46] gives the appearance of mocking those who take the warning of 1 Corinthians 11:29 to refer to unbelievers: "For those who eat and drink without discerning the body of Christ eat and drink judgment on themselves." If they are already damned, he says, what threat is there in that? Can they be damned twice? So why not permit them to participate in the Lord's Supper? Why could the Supper not become a means of grace to them?

---

[45] A sanction restricted, as far as I can see, to only three categories of sin in the New Testament. But that is another subject.

[46] Chap. 1, pp. 16–17.

Granted the seriousness of the warning, Burke would be wiser to tell us what he thinks the passage *does* mean rather than what it does *not* mean. I agree that the warning is not aimed at unbelievers. The context shows that the warning is directed primarily against Christians who approach the Lord's Table while nurturing sin. They ought to examine themselves before eating the bread and drinking the cup (1 Corinthians 11:28).[47] But if the warning is against thoughtless Christians, does this mean that there is no reason why non-Christians should be excluded from the Table? Burke does not discuss the most central reason: the Lord's Table was given to believers, to Christians, as a *commemorative* rite. Whatever the precise force of "remembrance," the words "Do this in remembrance of me" presuppose that there is something to remember. Add to this the overtones of fellowship bound up with eating in the first century and the transparent parallels with the Passover (another rite bound up with the community of the redeemed), and the suggestion that unbelievers should be admitted to the Table becomes very hard to justify.

3. The New Testament lays an enormous amount of emphasis on teaching. This teaching includes both conduct and doctrine—i.e., both how to behave and what to believe. The gospel of John, which clearly articulates the love command (John 13:34–35), also provides a number of propositions that people must *believe* if they are to be followers of Christ.[48] The tendency of some emerging writers, whenever a truth question comes up, is to move away from the content of Scripture and to Jesus as the *personal* Word of God (John 1:1), as the *personal* truth of God (John 14:6). This is right in what it affirms, but wrong in the antithesis. The presentation of Jesus as the truth incarnate, as the Word of God, is critically important, and certainly something to rejoice over—but it is a relatively rare theme compared with the biblical emphasis on the truthfulness of God's words when he speaks.[49] Hebrews 5:11–6:4 presupposes that the indoctrination (I use the term advisedly) of ordinary Christians in the first century was, ideally, very comprehensive, including a firm

---

[47] This is true regardless of what "without discerning the body of Christ" means in verse 29.

[48] E.g., John 11:27, 42; 14:10.

[49] See the careful documentation of Wayne Grudem, "Scripture's Self-Attestation and the Problem of Formulating a Doctrine of Scripture," in *Scripture and Truth*, ed. D. A. Carson and John D. Woodbridge (Grand Rapids: Zondervan, 1983), 15–59, 359–68.

grasp about how the new covenant related to the old, how Melchizedek (mentioned in only three passages) fits into the Bible's story line, and much more of the same.

The place of propositional content in the lives of the first generation of believers can be set in a very broad first-century context. It is common knowledge today that Judaism and Christianity, unlike the surrounding paganism of the time, tightly tied together religion and ethics. But specialists also know that early Christianity's emphasis on belief and truth was a major departure from the surrounding religions. Christianity's focus on preaching and teaching and discussion, on words and hearing and persuasion, was viewed as so extraordinary by outsiders that in their view Christianity was more a philosophical movement than a traditional religion.[50] This is also why creeds became so important in the early church.

We need to think a bit more about creeds. Christian creeds are affirmations of what Christians believe to be *true*. But it is important to recognize that, *without exception*, creeds came into being, in very large measure, in the cauldron of controversy. As Gerald Bray states, "Almost every phrase in the creeds came into being because somebody had questioned some aspect of the Christian faith which then had to be reaffirmed for the benefit of the church as a whole."[51] This is important, because most emerging leaders, as far as I can see, affirm at least the Apostles' Creed and the Nicene Creed. Thus they are affirming truths born out of controversy, where some people were judged right in the light of Scripture and others wrong in the light of Scripture. Questions of truth, of faithfulness to Scripture, of being right and wrong intersect in the creeds.[52]

---

[50] The literature is nicely summarized by Peter Bolt, *The Cross from a Distance: Atonement in Mark's Gospel*, NSBT (Leicester, UK/Downers Grove, IL: InterVarsity Press, 2004/2005), chap. 1.

[51] Gerald Bray, "I Believe: The Value of Creeds in the Christian Life," *The Briefing* 310 (July 2004): 8. The entire article is worth perusing. See also Luke Timothy Johnson, *The Creed: What Christians Believe and Why It Matters* (London: Darton, Longman & Todd, 2003).

[52] Since this is true of *all* creeds, it is hard to see why so many of the emerging church leaders are so suspicious of Reformation creeds. These, too, were born in controversy. If they are to be questioned, it cannot be because they say certain things are right and others are

Some writers who are very impressed by postmodern realities clearly lead us astray on these matters. How should we preach today? One reviewer accurately summarizes the approach of one such writer:

> The thesis of this book is that in the postmodern world, in which contingency replaces certainty, foundations dissolve into what is fleeting, and the eternal seems transient, the Christian preacher should learn to abandon false certainties and live by faith alone. Sermons should be shaped by the Christian practice of confessing faith in Jesus Christ, a practice exemplified in the Scriptures.[53]

But wait a minute. If the "certainty" that is so despised belongs to omniscience, no certainty is possible. In that case, a "confession" cannot be the confession of something we think to be true, but merely of something we prefer: this is the position of hard postmodernism, and as we have seen, it is self-refuting. But if the "certainty" is the appropriate kind that belongs to finite knowers, it is hard to see why we cannot have it—and those who claim the creeds as theirs are among them.[54] But worse: to argue that the abandonment of certainty is part of what it means to "live by faith alone" is to misunderstand, massively, what "faith" is in the New Testament. In contemporary parlance, "faith" is often no more than private, personal, religious preference. But in the New Testament (as we shall see in

---

wrong (and therefore offend the sensibilities of hard postmoderns), because the same charge could be leveled against the Apostles' Creed and the Nicene Creed. The only appropriate response, for those with a higher view of the authority of Scripture than of the creeds, is to try to evaluate, as humbly and accurately and attentively as we can, how faithfully any creed reflects Scripture. This argument will not convince those who think that the early creeds are inerrant (so Keith A. Mathison, *The Shape of Sola Scriptura* [Moscow, ID: Canon Press, 2001], 339, following and slightly modifying his mentor, Heiko Oberman), but that would open up another discussion, one that does not seem to be an issue for the emerging writers.

[53] Philip Crowe, in *Theology* 107 (2004): 234, in a review of David J. Lose, *Confessing Jesus Christ: Preaching in a Post-Modern World* (Grand Rapids: Eerdmans, 2003).

[54] Unless, of course, the creeds have no extra-textual referentiality.

chapter 7 of this book), faith's validity is tied to the truthfulness of its object. Once again we return to truth-claims and teaching, and we find ourselves distinguishing between those who adhere to truth and those who do not—and thus to questions of who really is a Christian.

4. How, then, shall we tie together the biblically mandated responsibility of Christians to interact warmly with those who are not believers, and the biblically mandated responsibility of Christians to distinguish, on doctrinal, experiential, and ethical grounds, between those who are Christians and those who are not? Or, to put the matter in terms of the current debate, what is an appropriate relationship between belonging and becoming?

What must *not* be done is to overthrow either priority. There are churches that are mightily concerned to preserve their own comfort zones, to preserve all their prized traditions (whether they are genuinely mandated by Scripture or not). Christians in these churches are likely to evangelize only those people who are already churched or who in some sense belong to a churchy culture. Of course, in the sheer grace of God, some biblical illiterate may come in off the street and be converted—but this will owe very little to the church's commitment to spread the gospel among those who have never heard. They will insist that people *become* Christians before they can actually *belong* to them. Sadly, however, these believers may find it almost impossible to explain the gospel to people whose subculture is far removed from their own.

On the other hand, to praise the openness of discussion found in an Internet chat room as if it were an end in itself is no less misguided—it is simply at the other end of the spectrum. Emergent writers commonly so prioritize *belonging* that it is difficult to see how one can honor the precious responsibilities and privileges of those who have actually *become* Christians. The biblical evidence I have already briefly canvassed is skirted.

What we should strive for, surely, is a church that is full of teaching (doctrinal, ethical, historical, spiritual), rigorous in its discipleship, and patently faithful in its exercise of godly discipline—*and at the same time* a church in which believers know how to communicate with nonbelievers, a church whose public meetings, however full of teaching and discipline they may be, are authentic in all they do, welcoming and warm to strangers, and careful to apply the Scriptures to all of life, with contemporary probings that are simultaneously faithful to Scripture and culturally penetrating. At one level, that church will be saying that you have to *become* a Christian to *belong*; at another level, that church will be so authentic in its communication, so warm in its acceptance of people as people, so genuine in its belief and conduct, that outsiders will be attracted. And that church may have many forms of ministry—Bible studies for biblically illiterate outsiders, for instance, run on a gentle, inductive basis—in which nonbelievers will feel comfortable. They may not belong to the church, but they may belong to this study group, or to the group of people who engage in Habitat for Humanity projects, or countless similar ventures. Christians in such a church will gradually learn, out of sheer love for people, to try to get across, with winsome gentleness, what the Bible says, while refusing to soft-pedal the Bible in any way.[55]

Actually, this sort of tension between belonging and becoming may prove to be *more* evangelistically fruitful than churches that slide toward one of the two extremes. The pastor of a Baptist church I know in a metropolitan area—a church with strong teaching and wise discipline but also a strong commitment to evangelism both within its building and in the surrounding community—recently told me of one of their more interesting conversions, a recently retired professor from Harvard University. Musing on his conversion some months later, the professor said that a year previously he could not have imagined becoming a Christian, and still less belonging to a staunchly evangelical church. But what drew him, he said, was that these Christians knew him more thoroughly and transparently than his lifelong friends and colleagues. These Christians knew his name, of course, and his likes and dislikes and went out of their way to get to know him, but more importantly, they knew him *deeply*—they genuinely understood what made him tick, what made him a human being, what moved him, and what he cherished, even though they made a clear distinction

---

[55] A very helpful recent book in this regard is that of Randy Newman, *Questioning Evangelism: Engaging People's Hearts the Way Jesus Did* (Grand Rapids: Kregel, 2004). See also his forthcoming *Corner Conversations* (from the same publisher). These books were born out of two decades of fruitful ministry in some of the toughest universities on the East Coast and represent forms of discussion that are far less biblically compromised than what Neo has to offer.

between who was a Christian and who wasn't.[56] In one sense, then, the man felt he belonged to them, even though in one sense he knew that he still did not belong to them. In the mercy of God, the man presently *became* a Christian, and now himself *belongs* to the church.

The applications of this sort of creative tension are legion. Yes, there need to be contexts in which unbelievers, or immature Christians who are still remarkably ignorant of the basics of what the Bible says, can ask frank questions about the Lord's Supper, homosexuality, and anything else they want to ask about, including the deity of Christ, what it means to confess God as triune, and much more. But there also need to be contexts where biblically faithful answers, *true* answers, are given to people who want to know what the Bible says or who are willing to be corrected by the Bible or who think their own reading of the Bible could be corrected by readings that are more informed, more mature, and more reasoned.

As I have said before, this is *not* advocating any claim about omniscient language. *All* faithful biblical interpretations spiral toward the truth, or approach it asymptotically (to use the categories developed in chapter 4), and never capture it perfectly. In some sense, *all* that I know from the Bible is provisional: if someone can show me from the Bible why it is wrong to confess Jesus as God, I shall gladly change my views. But the likelihood of this happening approaches zero: the matter has been worked over again and again in the history of the church, and from a child's first understanding through many years of reading the Bible, I have come to stable knowledge of what it says on these matters, as also on other questions (though I cheerfully admit there are areas where I am still very unsure how best to summarize and articulate what the Bible says). But none of these limitations makes it inappropriate to speak of creeds, moral absolutes, and truths that we can know and teach, so long as it is understood that we are not claiming omniscient or infallible knowledge.

---

[56] One recalls Paul's description of a biblically illiterate outsider who hears the intelligible gospel and sees it in the lives of believers and who in consequence is convinced by all that he is a sinner and that the secrets of his heart have been laid bare, and who in consequence falls down and worships God, exclaiming, "God is really among you!" (1 Corinthians 14:24–25).

5. Finally, something must be said about sectarianism. The leaders of the emerging church movement obviously think of themselves as transcending sectarianism, not least because they are, in their own view, crossing so many boundaries that they feel are outmoded and merely modern. I suspect they think of themselves as the least sectarian of Christian groups. Certainly McLaren has gone on record as eschewing sectarianism.[57]

Yet there are numerous instances in history in which restorationist or renewal groups, protesting perceived evils, soon became among the most sectarian of all—without so much as perceiving what is happening to them. Most of the emergent writers have gone to great lengths to say that unless Christians make the kinds of adjustments they are calling for—adjustments that they think are mandated by the assumptions of postmodernism—they will confine themselves to obsolescent enclaves. Such declarations are not calculated to enhance catholicity; they are the shrill cries of sectarians. On the American side of the Atlantic (much more so than in Britain), parts of the movement are driven by their own jargon: you must come to terms with emergent leaders, emergent friendship, emergent worship. Either you are part of the emerging movement, or you do not belong. Sectarianism will be the bitter fruit where the most prominent emerging leaders caricature evangelical convictions about substitutionary atonement as "a form of cosmic child abuse" (on which, see the next chapter). Who, then, really *belongs* to the wise and progressive church of tomorrow?

In the words of an anonymous Scottish preacher:

> You say I am not with it?
> My friend, I do not doubt it.
> But when I see what I'm not with
> I'd rather be without it.

Failure to Handle Facts, Both Exegetical and Historical, in a Responsible Way

A very difficult element to assess in the writings of the emerging church leaders is their actual handling of facts, evidence, the arguments of opponents, and the like. It is more difficult to assess, not because the evidence

---

[57] *A New Kind of Christian*, 46–47.

is wanting, but because sometimes the fault is apparent ignorance, sometimes misrepresentation, sometimes hyperbole taken to such an extreme that false portraits are being generated—and it is not always clear exactly which error is being perpetrated, even though it is transparent to anyone familiar with the sources that what the sources actually say—that is, the truth of the sources—is being handled very lightly. All of us make mistakes in judgment; sometimes we make mistakes in attribution; inevitably we sometimes skew the balance here and there. But when the pattern of distortion becomes endemic to a position, even the most charitable reading eventually turns sour.

What I have just said may seem ungracious, yet I do not see how I can say less. This is not to say that the emerging leaders are always wrong in their handling of facts or their use of Scripture, or that all of them are equally wrong; it is to say that the pattern of distortion is so persistent that after a while it becomes painful to read them. Perhaps the easiest way to make the point is by taking two recent books and indicating from each book the sort of thing I have in mind. For this we turn to the next chapter.

Chapter 6

EMERGING CHURCH
WEAKNESS ILLUSTRATED IN
TWO SIGNIFICANT BOOKS

In previous chapters I have interacted with a fairly broad range of sources produced by emerging leaders and those who are ideologically closest to them. In this chapter I shall focus on only two books. This has the advantage of following and evaluating a line of argument, the perspective of one writer at a time. Some of the problems already identified will rear their heads again: the reluctance to wrestle with the category of *truth*, the ungenerous characterization of opponents, the rather cavalier treatment of postmodernism. But in particular, evaluation of these two books discloses the persistent problem I mentioned at the end of the last chapter, viz., the distortion of facts, evidence, arguments, and Scripture that is prevalent in the writings of the leaders of the emerging movement.

The first of the two books (and the one that will capture the attention of most of this chapter) is *A Generous Orthodoxy*,[1] to which I have already briefly referred. It was written by Brian D. McLaren, whom most emergent leaders regard as their preeminent thinker and writer. The second, *The Lost Message of Jesus*,[2] was written by Steve Chalke with the help of Alan Mann.

---

[1] El Cajon, CA: emergentYS / Grand Rapids: Zondervan, 2004. In the discussion that follows, although I shall largely focus on this book, I shall draw on some of McLaren's other writings, both to represent his views as fairly as I can and to show that I am not drawn to a merely idiosyncratic specimen of his writing.

[2] Steve Chalke and Alan Mann, *The Lost Message of Jesus* (Grand Rapids: Zondervan, 2003).

Chalke is the most prominent figure in the corresponding movement in the United Kingdom.

A Critique of *A Generous Orthodoxy*

Though I have never met him, McLaren is, I suspect, a man it is very hard to dislike. There is a humorous cheekiness in him, a disarming self-deprecation, an over-the-top vitality to him. Not least when he is the most outrageous, you simultaneously want to wring his neck and give him a brotherly hug and say, "Aw, c'mon, Brian, be fair! That silly argument is unworthy of you!"—knowing full well he's likely to hug you back and say, with a twinkle in his eyes, "I know that. I'm not quite as stupid as you think. But I got you thinking about some important questions you've been ducking!" What do you do with a guy like that?[3] He writes (and it is one of his paragraphs with which I am in substantial agreement):

> Beyond all these warnings, you should know that I am horribly unfair in this book, lacking all scholarly objectivity and evenhandedness. My own upbringing was way out on the end of one of the most conservative twigs of one of the most conservative branches of one of the most conservative limbs of Christianity, and I am far harder on conservative Protestant Christians who share that heritage than I am on anyone else. I'm sorry. I am consistently oversympathetic to Roman Catholics, Eastern Orthodox, even dreaded liberals, while I keep elbowing my conservative brethren in the ribs in a most annoying—some would say *ungenerous*—way. I cannot even pretend to be objective or fair. This is simply an inexcusable shortcoming of the book that serves no good purpose, unless by some chance it could generously be included under the proverb, "Faithful are the wounds of a friend" (Proverbs 27:6 NASB). Even so, will I be grateful and gracious when this friendly wounding is generously reciprocated?[4]

---

[3] "I have gone out of my way to be provocative, mischievous, and unclear, reflecting my belief that clarity is sometimes overrated, and that shock, obscurity, playfulness, and intrigue (carefully articulated) often stimulate more thought than clarity" (*A Generous Orthodoxy*, 23).

[4] Ibid., 35–36.

Vintage McLaren, this. The over-the-top *mea culpa* disarms you, then he slyly provides a prooftext and hints that he may be obeying Scripture after all. It's almost enough to win you over. Yet sober reflection tires after a while of finding McLaren repeatedly painting all of confessional evangelicalism with the narrowness of the most conservative twig of the most conservative branch. The way he writes reminds me of the wild pendulum swings of the "angry young man" routine and is merely likely to introduce yet another wobble into churchmanship and theology. At what point is it the responsibility of Christian leaders to try to reflect the balance and holism of Scripture instead of glorying in one's extremism? True, "Faithful are the wounds of a friend"—but surely a real friend goes out of his way not to exaggerate what needs to be fixed, precisely because a friend wants to be winsome, to get things right, not merely score points, however witty they may be.

So I list a handful of examples, though I could cite scores from this book alone.

The Jesuses We Can Know?

The chapter "The Seven Jesuses I Have Known" sets up the approach. For the record, the seven Jesuses are the conservative Protestant Jesus, the Pentecostal/Charismatic Jesus, the Roman Catholic Jesus, the Eastern Orthodox Jesus, the liberal Protestant Jesus, the Anabaptist Jesus, and the Jesus of the oppressed. Some of these pen-portraits are better than others, but most of them do not offer what they promise. For instance, the Roman Catholic Jesus is not the Jesus taught by Roman Catholics in, say, their Catechism. Nor is he the Jesus experienced by most Catholics on the street in the most Catholic countries (where I have spent a good part of my life). McLaren's Roman Catholic Jesus "saves the church by rising from the dead"[5]—i.e., this is the *Christus Victor* theme. McLaren rightly admits that this vision is not exclusively Catholic. In popular Catholicism there is far more emphasis on the baby Jesus in Mary's arms. Nevertheless McLaren plays this *Christus Victor* theme into caring, giving, serving, sacrifice, and the like, as if these are peculiarly Catholic virtues. It even gets played into the Eucharist, which is "a constant celebration of good news, a continual rendezvous with the risen Christ and, through him, with God. That such

---

[5] Ibid., 53.

a rendezvous is possible is amazingly good news for everyone in the church."[6] But none of this is distinctively Roman Catholic. What Christian heritage would deny that the Eucharist is "a constant celebration of good news"? Is "a continual rendezvous with the risen Christ" a way of affirming transubstantiation, or is it purposely slippery, so that McLaren can simultaneously appear to be supporting a Catholic Jesus while distancing himself from what is peculiarly Catholic?

What about McLaren's construction of the liberal Jesus? He begins by quoting the old slogan, "Scratch the paint of a liberal, and you'll find an alienated fundamentalist underneath." I'm sure that some fundamentalists have alienated people and turned them into liberals, but I'm also sure that in the rise of theological liberalism, that is precisely what did *not* happen. Fundamentalism, in both its best and worst forms, was a response to the kind of unbelief that denied the deity of Christ, the virgin birth, and the physical resurrection of Jesus from the dead, but thought of itself as nicely Christian because it still espoused some elements of Christian ethics (e.g., all the slogans about love and sacrifice, but nothing on church discipline).

In McLaren's portrait of liberal Protestants, some, but not all, question whether some or all of the miraculous deeds in the Gospels and elsewhere actually happened.[7] But at least the liberals read these accounts for their moral lessons. So the account of the boy with the five loaves and two fishes tells us that we should give whatever little we have, and the healing of the paralytic encourages us to see our spiritual paralysis more clearly and believe it can be healed. "While I believe that actual miracles can and do happen," McLaren writes, "... I am sympathetic with those who believe otherwise, and I applaud their desire to live out the meaning of the miracle stories even when they don't believe the stories happened as written. (I find it harder to be sympathetic with those who take pride in believing the miracles really happened but don't seek to live out their meaning.)"[8] There it is again: another slam at "conservative Protestants" on the way by.

Worse, the handling of Scripture is poor. Is the account of the feeding of the five thousand (one of the rare incidents reported in all four canon-

---

[6] Ibid., 54.

[7] Ibid., 60.

[8] Ibid., 60–61.

ical Gospels) primarily about sharing one's lunch? I thought it was primarily to tell us who Jesus is and what he did and can do. Still worse, the liberal Christian heritage does *not* prove itself to be more generous or more engaged in self-sacrifice and good deeds than are confessional Christians. Inevitably there are individual exceptions, but numerous studies have shown that confessional Christians, precisely because they are confessional, are *more* likely to give generously, serve in tough places, build hospitals and schools, run shelters for battered women, and much more of the same than their liberal counterparts. Perhaps that is not the case for the Christians on the twig from which McLaren springs, but then he should refrain himself from projecting his twig onto most of the tree.

Worst of all, this picture does not wrestle with common liberal denial of irreducible elements of the gospel itself, the substitutionary death of Christ Jesus, who dies my death that I might live and rises again for the justification of his people—a resurrection without which, according to the apostle Paul, our faith is vain (1 Corinthians 15). Although some liberals, embarrassed by fundamentalist antics, doubtless thoroughly trusted the Christ of the New Testament while wondering if Jesus actually did multiply five loaves and two fishes, the influence of theological liberalism as a movement is, quite frankly, pernicious, simply another religion: the detailed evaluation of J. Gresham Machen still deserves close and thoughtful reading.[9]

In short, these "Jesuses" are misnamed. The Roman Catholic Jesus is not the Roman Catholic Jesus; the liberal Jesus is not the liberal Jesus. What McLaren does is pick up some element of his understanding of Jesus that he himself gleaned from these respective traditions, though in most cases he could as easily have gleaned them elsewhere. What is essential to or typical of the tradition is not explored.

Moreover, carving up the discussion of the kind of Jesus we *should* be trusting and following into these assorted traditions fits the postmodern agenda: different traditions read the source documents differently and experience God differently, and we can learn from all of them. Still, it would have been nice to see the way these assorted traditions present Jesus summarized for us in an accurate and evenhanded way. The sad fact is that,

---

[9] *Christianity and Liberalism* (Grand Rapids: Eerdmans, 1923)—both courageous and prophetic in its time.

despite the chapter title, McLaren has not known the Catholic Jesus or the liberal Jesus (or several others). Rather, he has constructed his own Jesus from disembodied slips of presentation he happens to have stumbled across within these various traditions.

More importantly, it would have been nice if there had been some evaluation of which of these traditions, whether at their most typical or at their best, most closely embrace the strengths of the other traditions while avoiding their worst weaknesses or even untruths, in the hope of uncovering not multiple Jesuses but the Jesus who actually exists. To this end, and most important of all, it would have been nice to see the extent to which the various presentations of Jesus actually conform, in whole or in part, to the Scriptures themselves—under the assumption, of course, that Scripture truly is the "norming norm," that it speaks the truth, and that what it says can be known (even if never exhaustively).

I wish there were space to interact with the next couple of chapters of McLaren's book, but I turn now to the bulk of his argument. In separate chapters McLaren explains (to use the subtitle of the book) "Why I am a missional + evangelical + post/protestant + liberal/conservative + mystical/poetic + biblical + charismatic/contemplative + fundamentalist/calvinist + anabaptist/anglican +methodist + catholic + green + incarnational + depressed-yet-hopeful + emergent + unfinished Christian." I have read these chapters with considerable care, and I must try to explain a little of why this is an attractive + manipulative + funny + sad + informed + ignorant + winsome + outrageous + penetrating + resoundingly false + stimulating + silly book. And I have used each of these words with more precision than McLaren has used with his.

Evangelical or evangelical?

Why does McLaren label himself an evangelical?[10] He is careful to distance himself from what he calls the "'Big E' Evangelical," which he associates with his youth, with "the Religious Right," and an array of other things he does not like. In what sense, then, is McLaren an evangelical? What he likes in evangelicalism, he says, is its *passion*: "When I say I cherish an evangelical identity, I mean something beyond a belief system or doctrinal array or

---

[10] *A Generous Orthodoxy*, chap. 6.

even a practice. I mean an attitude—an attitude toward God and our neighbor and our mission that is *passionate*."[11] So here McLaren rejects a definition of evangelicalism that is tied to historical movements (the sort of approach well exemplified by David W. Bebbington),[12] as well as any reference to a belief system (the sort of approach well exemplified in the contributors to *Evangelical Affirmations*),[13] or even to what "evangel" (i.e., "gospel") means in the New Testament.

What Does It Mean to Be Biblical?

Why does McLaren label himself biblical?[14] Some of what he says is insightful, but his barbs reflect, once again, his own tiny twig. I myself was never taught a dictation view of inspiration, nor was I reared on an eschatological system that made predictions about what would happen in the Middle East and that have turned out to be wrong. But what he wants the most is to emphasize the Bible's profitable purpose—all the good deeds and transforming character and conduct presupposed by a passage like 2 Timothy 3:16–17. All "truly biblical Christians (Protestant, Catholic, Orthodox, liberal, conservative, charismatic, whatever)"[15] have done these deeds: that's what makes them biblical. There is not a hint that biblical fidelity may be tied in some ways to questions of truth. The most important factor is reading the Bible as narrative, culminating in Jesus' new command "that fulfills and supersedes all Torah."[16]

> This narrative approach does not lessen the agony one feels reading the conquest of Canaan with the eyes of one taught by Jesus to love all, including enemies. But it helps turn the Bible back into what it is, not a look-it-up

---

11. Ibid., 117–18.
12. Of his many writings, see, perhaps, his contributions in Mark A. Noll, David W. Bebbington, George A. Rawlyk, eds., *Evangelicalism: Comparative Studies of Popular Protestantism in North America, the British Isles, and Beyond, 1700–1990* (New York: Oxford University Press, 1994).
13. Kenneth S. Kantzer and Carl F. H. Henry, eds., *Evangelical Affirmations* (Grand Rapids: Zondervan, 1990).
14. *A Generous Orthodoxy*, chap. 10.
15. Ibid., 165.
16. Ibid., 170.

encyclopedia of timeless moral truths, but the unfolding narrative of God at work in a violent, sinful world, calling people, beginning with Abraham, into a new way of life. This isn't the deterministic progress of Marxism or capitalism; this is the struggle of common people in the journey of faith, hope, and love. And it challenges us: to be truly biblical does not mean being preoccupied with some golden age in the ancient world and God's word to people back then. It means learning from the past to let God's story, God's will, and God's dream continue to come true in us and our children.[17]

There is insight, here, of course, but also knocking down of straw men and also some plain error. I do not know any thoughtful Christian from any camp who thinks being biblical means "being preoccupied with some golden age in the ancient world." On the other hand, it most certainly means coming to grips with "God's word to people back then," precisely because God's written revelation is an *historical* revelation.[18] Many Christian thinkers have recognized that the framework of the Bible constitutes a grand narrative, that the parts of the Bible fit into that narrative, that the Bible includes within its pages many discrete narratives, and that at many times across the centuries Christian thinkers were too quick to jump to atemporal emphases that lost the narrative thread and unwittingly distorted Scripture. Much of the biblical theology movement has been at the forefront of trying to sort this out and listen afresh to the biblical texts. But the Bible includes a lot of things in addition to narrative, or things embedded in narrative, or sometimes things that embed narrative: law, lament, instruction, wisdom, ethical injunction, warning, apocalyptic imagery, letters, promise, reports, propositions, ritual, and more.[19] The easy appeal to the overarching narrative proves immensely distortive.[20]

---

[17] Ibid., 171.

[18] There is a little more on this point in the final section of this chapter and in the next chapter.

[19] This point is poorly handled in many recent treatments of narrative. See, for instance, some of the essays in Joel B. Green and Michael Pasquarello III, eds., *Narrative Reading, Narrative Preaching: Reuniting New Testament Interpretation and Proclamation* (Grand Rapids: Baker/Brazos, 2003).

[20] See, for instance, the penetrating riposte of Daniel J. Treier, "Response to Laytham," *Ex Auditu* 19 (2003): 120–24.

Indeed, there is a sense in which the appeal to living the Bible's narrative is doubly distortive, because despite all his emphasis on the Bible's story line, McLaren remains deeply suspicious of any appeal to "metanarrative," even the Bible's metanarrative. I do not think his suspicions arise merely from the fact that the *word* "metanarrative" is in bad odor in many postmodern contexts. As soon as one speaks of the Bible's metanarrative, or of the "gospel" presented in Scripture, he wants to ask, Whose gospel? The prosperity gospel? The full gospel? The fundamentalist gospel? The Reformed gospel? This, he says, is the danger of metanarratives.[21] Well, I certainly won't go to the mat over the word "metanarrative," but I will over the notion it conveys, for two reasons.

First, McLaren's own presentation of what the gospel is, and of the Bible's story line,[22] is constantly making implicit and explicit claims regarding how the Bible is to be understood and therefore lived. After the condescending dismissals of all the "gospels" he doesn't like, he offers us, at the end of the day, his own understanding of the gospel. He cannot avoid it; that is why he keeps writing books. Are we not obligated to think through how faithful the prosperity gospel is, how faithful the fundamentalist gospel is, how faithful the emergent gospel is? Is this not bound up with our own reading and re-reading of the Scripture God has given us, which is framed into a massive story line?

Second, and more important, this means that the truth issue is back, that we can and must make some evaluations. (McLaren must recognize this if he is going to be as dismissive as he is about the various "gospels" he does not like.) As I have said, this does *not* mean that we are claiming infallible interpretations, anymore than McLaren is. It *does* mean that we can know some things of what Scripture says truly, even if nothing omnisciently. It *does* mean that he should be candid enough to see that, however humbly, he *is* making truth-claims about what Scripture says, about its

---

[21] See, for instance, Leonard Sweet, Brian D. McLaren, and Jerry Haselmayer, *A is for Abductive: The Language of the Emerging Church* (Grand Rapids: Zondervan, 2003), 191–93.

[22] This is best set forth, I think, in his book *The Story We Find Ourselves In: Further Adventures of a New Kind of Christian* (San Francisco: Jossey-Bass, 2003).

purpose, about what it demands, about how we should live—and these must then be shown to be anchored in Scripture. He cannot responsibly duck the exegetical questions and relegate the positions of others to the ash-heap of history while he escapes scrutiny by appealing to the postmodern.

Perhaps I should mention three more areas (of many I could choose) in which McLaren will impress many readers as being something other than biblical.

What to Make of the Atonement?

At numerous points in his writing, McLaren canvasses various theories of the atonement.[23] A theory of the atonement, we are told, "is a possible explanation for how Jesus' life and death play a role in the salvation of the human race."[24] But for McLaren the various theories he discusses cannot be dogmas or doctrines; they are at best windows that let you see a part of the sky rather than letting you see the whole sky. It is better to think of them as mysteries than as dogmas.[25] Moreover, in almost every theory McLaren lists, he tries to show what its alleged weak points are. Thus, substitutionary atonement doesn't address the question of why, if God wants to forgive us, he doesn't just do it. How can punishing an innocent person make things better? "That just sounds like one more injustice in the cosmic equation. It sounds like divine child abuse. You know?"[26] The ransom theory faces the problem that God seems to be making deals with the devil. The only two theories that are expounded at length yet do *not* receive criticism are what Neo calls the "powerful weakness" theory[27] and

---

[23] See, for instance, *The Story We Find Ourselves In*, chap. 20, pp. 100–108.

[24] Ibid., 102.

[25] Ibid.

[26] Ibid. These objections are placed on the lips of Kerry, who is the non-believer finding out about the faith. But the objections are never answered and are elsewhere voiced by McLaren himself, who makes no attempt either to show how those who support substitutionary atonement would answer such objections or to examine the extent to which substitutionary atonement is taught in Scripture.

[27] Ibid., 105.

a private theory of his own. The powerful weakness theory is expressed this way:

> It works like this: by becoming vulnerable on the cross, by accepting suffering *from* everyone, Jews and Romans alike, rather than visiting suffering *on* everyone, Jesus is showing God's loving heart, which wants forgiveness, not revenge, for everyone. Jesus shows us that the wisdom of God's kingdom is sacrifice, not violence. It's about accepting suffering and transforming it into reconciliation, not avenging suffering through retaliation. So through this window, the cross shows God's rejection of the human violence and dominance and oppression that have spun the world in a cycle of crisis from the story of Cain and Abel through the headlines in this morning's *Washington Post*. I don't know ... this theory might be nonsense, but maybe there's a grain of truth in it. The cross calls humanity to stop trying to make God's kingdom happen through coercion and force, which are always self-defeating in the end, and instead, to welcome it through self-sacrifice and vulnerability.[28]

As for his own private theory, Neo recalls the terrible suffering he underwent when he discovered his wife had betrayed him, and says,

> [E]ver since that day, when I think of the cross, I think it's all about God's agony being made visible—you know, the pain of forgiving, the pain of absorbing the betrayal and forgoing any revenge, of risking that your heart will be hurt again, for the sake of love, at the very worst moment, when the beloved has been least worthy of forgiveness, but stands most in need of it. It's not just something legal or mental. It's not just words; it has to be embodied, and nails and thorns and sweat and tears and blood strike me as the only true language of betrayal and forgiveness.[29]

But are any of these theories "biblical"? How do you know? And if several of them are, how do they relate to each other? Does the Bible say? How do you know? And if the Bible does not say, of what value are these theories anyway? How can McLaren know so much about theories of the atonement that have been developed in history, except by reading history? And

---

[28] Ibid., 105–6.
[29] Ibid., 107.

if he can learn these theories by reading history, cannot he at least attempt to read the Bible to try to discern the extent to which they are taught or sanctioned by Scripture? Note once again: I am not suggesting that any Christian or denomination has an *omniscient* understanding of the cross. I am saying, first, that nowhere in his writings (fiction and nonfiction) does he attempt to ground his treatment of the theories of the atonement in the Bible, and second, that he invariably takes the time to take cheap shots at substitution and other elements taught in Scripture. Nor is this paragraph an attempt to escape unpacking the ethical dimensions of the cross: I have recently taught 1 Peter in a couple of contexts, and that letter abounds with ethical implications that spring from the cross, and some Christian groups have overlooked them. Nevertheless the ethical argument of Peter does *not* sound like Neo's argument, and Peter finds *both* an example in the cross, *and* a sin-bearing substitution (carefully read 1 Peter 2:21 – 24, and note the allusions to Isaiah 53).[30] My point here is that McLaren's claim to be "biblical" rings a trifle hollow when crucial elements of what Christ accomplished on the cross, as taught by Scripture, are handled so cavalierly.

What about Hell?

When the horrible and frightening subject of hell comes up, the same sliding away from Scripture, without quite stating that Scripture is wrong, rises to the surface. For instance, after a sometimes moving anticipation of heaven, Neo sets forth the possibility of rejecting the grace of God in thoughtful terms.[31] The ostensible author, Dan Poole, quietly raises the question, "And what then? . . . What happens to them?" The chapter ends. The new chapter begins: "'Why do you always need to ask that question?'

---

[30] Among the more useful treatments of the last few decades, read J. I. Packer, "What Did the Cross Achieve? The Logic of Penal Substitution," *Tyndale Bulletin* 25 (1974): 3 – 45; Leon Morris, *The Apostolic Preaching of the Cross* (Grand Rapids: Eerdmans, 1965); Charles E. Hill and Frank A. James III, eds., *The Glory of the Atonement: Biblical, Theological and Practical Perspectives* (Downers Grove, IL: InterVarsity Press, 2004).

[31] *The Story We Find Ourselves In*, 167.

Neo asked, firmly but not angrily, his 'always' recalling our conversations back in 1999. 'Isn't what I just described to you *enough*?'"[32]

No, it's not enough, because Jesus himself says more about hell than anyone else in the Bible, and because other parts of the Bible dare to paint frightening pictures (e.g., Revelation 14:6–20). If someone reminds Neo of Jesus' words on this subject, Neo responds by ducking again: "Jesus is everywhere in this telling of the story, my friend"[33]—and runs off to retell in brief form the story on the large canvas without answering the question put to him. So Dan Poole has been rebuked for having the "need" to ask a question that Jesus himself dares to address. This strikes me as a kind of teacher's cheap shot: If you do not want to answer a question, make the student feel guilty for asking it. Perhaps on his twig McLaren had to deal with some Elmer Gantrys who took a vicious delight in describing the torments of the damned. But in today's Evangelicalism, we are, by and large, in far greater danger of saying much less than Jesus said on this subject than saying too much.

How is McLaren a "biblical" Christian here? Small wonder that numerous emerging leaders insist that the good news will focus on the importance of restoring one's lost relationship with God *rather than* salvation from God's judgment.[34] Yet the Bible dares to speak of the wrath of God in terms every bit as personal as it speaks of the love of God. It is not surprising that McLaren is not faithful to what Scripture says on the cross of Christ, since he is not faithful to the nature of the judgment from which we must be saved. His reading of the Bible's story line turns out to be so selective that the uncomfortable bits are discretely dropped.

Skirting Scripture on Ethical Issues

In line with several emergent writers, McLaren is also prepared to skirt what Scripture says about several "hot" ethical issues. For instance, emergent

---

[32] Ibid., 168.

[33] Ibid.

[34] This is typical of the literature. See, for instance, Richard P. Wager, "Hearing with Their Eyes and Seeing with Their Hearts: Ministry to the Senior High Bridger Generation" (D.Min. project, Trinity Evangelical Divinity School, 2001), 122.

writers not infrequently say that they want to be able to think through homosexuality for themselves and not simply be squeezed into a dogmatic conclusion.[35] In the Q & A session at his workshop at the 2004 Emergent Convention in which he was asked his judgment on the matter of homo-sexuality, McLaren said he did not want to answer directly.[36] He chose instead to make two other points. First, he said he is not entirely clear that what the Bible means when it speaks of homosexuality is exactly what we mean today when we speak of homosexuality, and therefore he wants to be very careful not to condemn what the Bible does not. Second, he wanted to stress the crucial importance of treating homosexuals as people, like other human beings in need of grace.

More recently, in *A Generous Orthodoxy*[37] he credits liberals with leading the way on a variety of ethical issues and then adds,

> And although the debate has been agonizing, liberals have blazed the trail in seeking to treat homosexual and transgender persons with compassion. Conservatives may follow in their footsteps in this issue just as they have in others, several decades down the road, once the pioneers have cleared the way (and once their old guard has passed away).[38]

Every step of this argument is either tendentious or manipulative or both.

1. Those familiar with the voluminous literature on homosexuality know perfectly well that to raise questions about whether what the Bible condemns is "homosexuality" as we understand it today is in fact one of the chief interpretive devices for taming Scripture on this subject, so as to make homosexuality acceptable. It is not homosexuality, some say, it is really pedophilia; it is not homosexuality that is repugnant in, say, Gene-sis 19, it is failure to observe the culturally demanded hospitality; it is not homosexuality *per se*, but promiscuous homosexuality. These arguments

---

[35] E.g., see the discussion in chap. 1, p. 16–17.

[36] Again, see chap. 1, p. 34–35.

[37] P. 138.

[38] Ibid. Some of McLaren's discussion at this point in the book is historically skewed.

really do not stand up to close scrutiny.[39] That McLaren gives them tangential support is deeply troubling.[40]

2. It is desperately important to treat homosexuals as people, Muslims as people, Westerners as people, Fundamentalists as people, emerging church leaders as people, and everyone else I can think of. Homophobia is inexcusable; it is sin against God. But many homosexuals label anyone "homophobic" who dares to make a case, no matter how careful, reasoned, compassionate, and humble, that the practice of homosexuality is wrong. I cannot be certain, but I suspect that nowadays there is more danger of

---

[39] Probably the ablest book, from the exegetical point of view, is that of Robert A. J. Gagnon, *The Bible and Homosexual Practice: Texts and Hermeneutics* (Nashville: Abingdon, 2001). For an extraordinarily careful and well-documented survey of the scientific evidence, see Stanton L. Jones and Mark A. Yarhouse, *Homosexuality: The Use of Scientific Research in the Church's Moral Debate* (Downers Grove, IL: InterVarsity Press, 2000). In brief compass, see John Stott, *Same-Sex Partnerships? A Christian Perspective* (Grand Rapids: Fleming H. Revell, 2000). For a book that is trying to combine faithfulness to Scripture with Scripture's pastoral sensitivity, see Christopher Keane, ed., *What Some of You Were: Stories about Christians and Homosexuality* (Kingsford, NSW, Australia: Matthias Media, 2001).

[40] McLaren's attempt to find an analogy in the Bible's silence on schizophrenia, supposing that Jesus' references to demon possession include the kind of phenomena that would today be labeled schizophrenic, is a nonstarter. For this to be a parallel, schizophrenia would have to be discussed and condemned in Scripture (the way the texts discuss and condemn homosexuality)—i.e., the texts would have to condemn *as schizophrenia* what we today would view as schizophrenia *qua* illness. Many (most?) Christians today who have thought long and hard about these things and tried to listen to what Scripture says acknowledge that there is such a thing as demon possession, and there are various forms of mental illness—schizophrenia being one of them—and that sometimes the distinction between the two is very difficult to discern. But if demon possession/schizophrenia really *were* a telling analogy, then it would mean that Jesus was "exorcising" people of something that was really nothing more than a mental illness. Perhaps McLaren has difficulty with demon possession because he has difficulty with the existence of a personal devil: see the documentation below.

homophobia-phobia than there is of homophobia. I know careful, responsible pastors who have received death threats, hate literature, and endless harassing phone calls, even major disruption of public services, for saying no more than what Scripture says. When I was asked to speak on this subject at a post-evening-service meeting at a church in London a year or two ago, the rector told me that of course he could not advertise the meeting in advance: he would simply announce it at the evening service itself. This would diminish the likelihood of major disruption.

3. Is it true that the liberals are leading in compassion on this issue? I doubt it. They are leading in the insistence that gay unions should be viewed as marriages, that gay men and women should be clergy, and much else. And of course, their own motives may be bound up with compassion. But if the Bible's prohibition is taken seriously, it is very difficult to read these movements as compassion. They sound more like unbelief and willful defiance of what God has said.

4. There is a sense in which it is highly regrettable that churches are drawing lines on this issue as opposed to more central issues: confession of the deity of Christ, for example, or the historical reality of the resurrection of Jesus Christ.[41] There is a great deal to be said for that view. On the other hand, there is also something to be said for the view that at some juncture churches have to decide whether they will, by God's grace, try to live in submission to Scripture, or try to domesticate Scripture. I suspect that in our generation, for better and for worse, the homosexuality issue is becoming one of those triggering issues (like indulgences at the time of the Reformation) that is forcing upon us some profound reflections on whether we will submit to Scripture or not. And quite frankly, on this issue, as on so many others, McLaren has given us very little evidence that he is fairly described as a "biblical" Christian.

Protesting the Protest?

Why is McLaren "post/Protestant"?[42] Protestantism is, after all, a movement of protest. The Roman Catholic Church at the beginning of the six-

---

[41] This is the argument of not a few contemporary confessional Christian thinkers—e.g., Carl Trueman, "Why You Shouldn't Buy the Big Issue," *Themelios* 29/2 (2004): 1–4.

[42] *A Generous Orthodoxy*, chap. 7.

teenth century, McLaren acknowledges, displayed some pretty awful features, especially the sale of indulgences. But things have moved on since then, he says: Protestants themselves pretty soon started protesting one another, ultimately creating some market-driven, commodifed forms of religion. Although they have paid more attention to the Bible than any other group, most of this energy has been spent fueling their efforts to prove themselves right and others wrong. Meanwhile, in recent years Roman Catholics have "pretty much agreed that the original Protestants were right about a lot of things. The average Roman Catholic today sees indulgences the same way Protestants will someday see their schmaltzy religious broadcasting or pop-atonement theology (what Dallas Willard calls 'the gospel of sin management'): with embarrassment."[43]

So in what way does McLaren see himself as a Protestant at all? He is a Protestant, he says, in the sense that he is committed to "pro-testifying"— something that Catholics, Protestants, and Eastern Orthodox are all doing when they are at their best. In that sense, his Protestantism, he acknowledges, is a kind of post-Protestantism.

Once again, there is a smidgeon of shrewdness. I have long thought and taught that religious TV selling vials of holy oil, or water from the Jordan River, is just as blind and wicked as the selling of indulgences half a millennium ago. But although this is typical of a disturbing percentage of kitschy religious broadcasting, is this typical of Protestantism? Of confessional Protestantism? Of confessional evangelicalism? I lecture or preach in scores of venues a year, and not one of them, as far as I am aware, thinks the practice a good thing. Most are openly scornful. More importantly, the Reformation was not primarily about indulgences. Indulgences triggered the Reformation, but the fundamental issues had to do with authority, the locus of revelation, the sufficiency of Christ's sacrifice on the cross, what it meant to be saved by grace through faith. The five "solas" were paramount for the Reformers and their heirs, and the denial or modification of them was paramount for the Catholic Counter-Reformation.

True, most Roman Catholics today are embarrassed by the heritage of indulgences (at least in the Western, North Atlantic church), but paid masses

---

[43] Ibid., 126.

to release souls from purgatory are still notoriously common in many parts of the Catholic world. As for the fundamental doctrinal issues that divided Reformers and Catholics half a millennium ago, although the polemic is today more courteous, the current pope and strong voices in the Curia such as Joseph Cardinal Ratzinger, are strictly Tridentine. Read the current Catholic Catechism on, say, justification. McLaren sidelines the entire Reformation debate by trivializing it: he makes it a matter of somewhat corrupt religious practice, not a matter of truth, of faithfulness to the Bible. Yes, Protestants have divided into many camps. In my experience, however, there is probably no more diversity in Protestantism than there is *within* the bowels of the Roman Catholic Church. But when it comes to the official voice of Rome versus the central confessions of Protestantism (however much neither side entirely lives up to its own standards), the issues *include* matters of religious practice and ethics, but they *focus* on mutually exclusive truth-claims. All of this McLaren sidesteps so that he can declare himself a Protestant or, under duress, a post-Protestant. Small wonder he has to redefine the word "Protestant" to make his case.

Let's look at it from the other side. In what sense does McLaren think of himself as a catholic (underlining the lowercase letter is his device)?[44] He begins by saying that one day he saw an Asian woman kneeling at the feet of a huge statue of Mary in Our Lady of Peace Roman Catholic Church in Santa Clara. "Sitting there," McLaren testifies (pro-testifies?), "I became a little more Catholic and a little more catholic, too."[45] Why?

Renewal and reforming movements, McLaren avers, often lead to exclusivism and elitism. Its leaders end up saying, "*We're* the only ones who have it right. Everyone else who doesn't join *us* is wrong, out, sub- or non-Christian."[46] By contrast, "to be catholic means to find another joy: the pleasure of accepting and welcoming the poor, the blind, the stumbling, the crippled, the imperfect, the confused, the mistaken, and the different. It doesn't

---

[44] Ibid., chap. 15. He switches back and forth, "catholic" referring to the universal church and "Catholic" referring to the Roman Catholic Church. I have followed his convention in this discussion.

[45] Ibid., 221.

[46] Ibid., 225.

mean that we lower our standards of authentic discipleship, rather that we raise our standards of Christ-like acceptance."[47]

Once again, the argument is deeply manipulative. I have found at least as much arrogance in the Catholicism that finds anyone not within its fold to be at best a "separated brother." Certainly there are Protestants who are narrowly elitist (as there are Catholics who are narrowly elitist)—especially far out on that little twig again. But insisting that some doctrinal issues *matter* is a pattern established in the New Testament itself, as Acts 15, Galatians 2, and 1 John, for example, make clear. In other words, even within New Testament times, not everyone who thought of himself or herself as a Christian really was. It is not, then, catholic to say they are; it is at best lack of discernment, and at worst defiance of what God has actually said in Scripture. Meanwhile, most confessional Protestants joyfully confess one holy catholic church, recognizing that there are regenerate people, justified people, saved people, redeemed people (all *biblical* terms) who are such by virtue of the gospel, regardless of the denominational label. But all of this McLaren seems to skate over in favor of an attitude.

And beyond his understanding (or perhaps I should say "feeling" or "aesthetics") of what it means to be catholic, he adds "six things (I could name many more) about Catholic Christianity that have enriched and continue to enrich my life in Christ":[48] Catholicism is sacramental, is liturgical, respects tradition, celebrates Mary, knows how to party, and can't escape from its scandals. Again, slipperiness triumphs. Consider, for example, sacramentalism. Orthodox Presbyterianism and evangelical Anglicanism confess themselves to be sacramental, but they mean something very different from what Rome's official documents mean. What does McLaren mean?

> A sacrament is an object or practice that mediates the divine to humans. It carries something of God to us; it is a means of grace, and it conveys sacredness. I care little for arguments about how many sacraments there are (although I tend to prefer longer lists than shorter ones). What I really like about the sacramental nature of Catholicism is this: through learning that a few things can carry the sacred, we become open to the fact that all things

---

[47] Ibid.
[48] Ibid.

(all good things, all created things) can ultimately carry the sacred: the kind smile of a Down's syndrome child, the bouncy jubilation of a puppy, the graceful arch of a dancer's back, the camera work in a fine film, good coffee, good wine, good friends, good conversation. Start with three sacraments—or seven—and pretty soon everything becomes potentially sacramental as, I believe, it should be.[49]

Quite apart from the fact that "sacrament" and its cognates have become astonishingly confusing terms,[50] once again McLaren is right, wrong, and silly. He is right (and countless theologians and pastors have underscored the point) that in God's universe everything should speak to us of God, prompt us to reflect on God, and mediate God's grace to us. At the end of the nineteenth century, C. H. Spurgeon (a Baptist in the Reformed heritage) was especially strong on this point. McLaren is wrong in thinking this extension is anywhere near what "sacramental" has meant in the primary historical debates. Indeed, it has often been shown that the heavier the emphasis on *all* things being sacramental, the more the peculiar theology of the sacramental traditions is undermined. If everything is sacramental, then nothing is (in the peculiar sense in which sacramentalism has historically been discussed). And it is silly to imagine that the magisterial office of Roman Catholicism would recognize McLaren's claim to be learning from Roman Catholicism if what McLaren has learned multiplies sacraments *ad infinitum*: Rome has no interest in thus weakening its historic understanding of the sacraments.

Each of the other things in Catholic Christianity that have enriched McLaren have similar problems. "Catholics celebrate Mary," he writes.[51] Of course, he does not want to worship her, but he has learned to delight in the fact "that Mary is highly favored, the Lord is with her, and that she is blessed among women." I learned all those things, too, in my secure Baptist home. I can remember expositions of the Christmas story in our family that had us thinking these things through from Mary's point of view:

---

49 Ibid., 225–26.
50 I discuss the problem in an excursus to chapter 6 of my commentary, *The Gospel According to John* (Grand Rapids: Eerdmans, 1991).
51 *A Generous Orthodoxy*, 228.

what a remarkable woman. But the more conservative the Catholic, the more likely it is that Mary is viewed, *at the very least*, as someone to be addressed in prayer, on the way to Christ and to God. Official Catholic doctrine insists she was conceived without sin, though Mary says that her soul delights in God her *Savior* (Luke 1:47). It is a dogma of the Catholic Church (i.e., something that one ought to believe to be a member in good standing in that church) that Mary went to heaven in bodily form and thus avoided decay, though there is not a whisper of this in the earliest documents. But never mind: McLaren has learned from Catholicism to venerate Mary.

In short, the doctrinal issues, the truth issues, are simply not brought up and examined. What is most admirable in Mary, according to the Scriptures, I want to affirm as loudly as he, and indeed this is what I was taught and what I teach. Maybe Mary was despised on his twig and he never quite got over it. But whereas I worry about people who have no respect for Mary, I worry no less about people whose appeal to Mary jeopardizes the exclusive sufficiency of Christ, finds in her a mediatrix, or addresses her in prayer because Christ himself seems too remote, people who think of her as coredemptrix with Christ and as the Queen of Heaven. I wish McLaren would spend some time examining the Catholicism of, say, Poland, in the light of the Bible. I have a lot of sympathy for men and women whose practice of religion is tied up with these things, when this is what they have been taught all their lives. I have less sympathy for those who teach such false doctrines, because they are not the *truth*.

What Is Fundamental?

Next, why does McLaren consider himself to be a Fundamentalist/Calvinist?[52] He is a fundamentalist in this way: "For me the 'fundamentals of the faith' boil down to those given by Jesus: *to love God and to love our neighbors*."[53] I think that this is among the shallowest and most distorted readings of Mark 12:28–34 now on offer. Jesus presents these commandments as the two that are most important in the law, not as the fundamentals of the faith. Those who recognize what Jesus says are "not far from the kingdom."

---

[52] Ibid., chap. 12.
[53] Ibid., 184.

What this means I have tried to elucidate in popular form elsewhere.[54] But to claim that these two laws are "the fundamentals of the faith" not only misconstrues the context of the passage where Jesus' utterance is found, it also overlooks the central themes of the canonical Gospels and, indeed, the entire New Testament. After all, two chapters earlier, Mark reports Jesus saying that he "did not come to be served, but to serve, *and to give his life a ransom for many*" (Mark 10:45).

Like the other Gospels, the gospel of Mark has been aptly described as a passion narrative with an extended introduction: the movement of thought is toward the cross and the resurrection. The narrative makes it clear that Jesus is himself the ultimate Passover lamb (14:12); his blood "is the blood of the covenant, which is poured out for many" (14:24). Small wonder Paul resolved to focus on "Jesus Christ and him crucified" (1 Corinthians 2:2), determined not to boast in anything except the cross of his Lord Jesus Christ (Galatians 6:14). This emphasis in no way means that the New Testament documents do not also include other emphases—ethical, cultural, eschatological, apocalyptic, and social. But for McLaren to assert that he is a "fundamentalist" because for him the first and second commandments are "the fundamentals of the faith"[55] is neither faithful to the use of the term historically, nor to the gospel and to what is most central in the New Testament.

---

[54] See the relevant sermon on the website of www.christwaymedia.com.

[55] The expression came into wide usage when R. A. Torrey edited four volumes entitled *The Fundamentals: A Testimony to the Truth*, recently republished (Grand Rapids: Baker, 1988 [1917]), which was a response to what was being denied by the liberals of the day. With only a few exceptions, the "fundamentals" were things that virtually all Christians had held to be true until liberals denied them. Later usage of the term, however, associated it with cultural withdrawal, religious conservatism, ignorance, and more recently, even hate. Nowadays the press lumps together Hindu fundamentalism, Islamic fundamentalism, and Christian fundamentalism without a vestige of remaining overtone of what Torrey and his fellow authors meant, which focused on distinctive Christian content. In any case, McLaren hijacks the term in order to invest it with the meaning he prefers, with the result that he can call himself a fundamentalist.

As for Calvinism, McLaren says that there are two ways for Reformed Christians to honor Calvin and his fellow Reformers: defend and promote their post-medieval formulations, or "follow their example in seeking to construct formulations of faith that are as fitting to our postmodern times as theirs were to their post-medieval times."[56] This is a bit like saying that an American is not someone who adopts the heritage of American values (however tweaked or gently modified), but someone who crosses an ocean to look for another country.[57] Moreover, the Reformers tried to make the Scriptures their formal principle and the gospel their material principle.

Undoubtedly all of this was cast in the categories and vocabulary of the debates at the time. Nevertheless, the Reformers envisaged ongoing attempts at reform to be ongoing attempts at better understanding holy Scripture, not least because the cultural questions would inevitably change. McLaren mentions none of this. Their theology is simply said to be valid for their post-medieval times, while postmodern theology is valid for postmodern times. But how does this interface with the truth-claims of Scripture, with the given of revelation? In other words, even in terms of the appeal for ongoing reformation, McLaren means something quite different from what the Reformers meant.[58] Unless you are a hard postmodernist, should you not try to assess the extent to which formulations of Calvin and his colleagues were faithful to their formal principle—i.e., to Scripture itself? Of course, if you are a hard postmodernist, it is impossible to avoid relativism. If you are a soft postmodernist, however, then you cannot duck such truth-claim issues.

---

[56] *A Generous Orthodoxy*, 189.

[57] Here McLaren depends on an essay by John R. Franke, "Reforming Theology: Towards a Postmodern Reformed Dogmatics," *Westminster Theological Journal* 65 (2003): 1–26, which McLaren calls "excellent" (*A Generous Orthodoxy*, 189 n.88) but whose description of Reformed theology has nothing in it that calls to mind the distinctive contributions of Reformed theology except for the belief that Reformation must be an ongoing task.

[58] This connects to my observation in the first chapter (p. 42) to the effect that the reformation envisaged by the emerging church movement rests almost entirely on the premise of cultural change and at best only marginally on the premise of bringing current aberrant theology into better conformity with the truth of Scripture.

And then, in what appears to be remarkable theological chutzpah, McLaren hijacks the famous TULIP anagram.[59] **T** will call to mind Triune Love instead of the typically Reformed emphasis on God's sovereignty; **U** now means Unselfish Election, since we must embrace election not to exclusive privilege but to "missional responsibility" (though in the best of Reformed theology I have never seen these opposed); **L** calls up Limitless Reconciliation; **I** now means Inspiring Grace; and **P** stands for Passionate, Persistent States. I suppose that having a TULIP entitles McLaren to say he is a Calvinist, for all the same reasons that he is entitled to call himself a Fundamentalist. But I would say to him, "If you believe these sorts of things are what the Bible teaches, you have every right to teach and explain and promote and persuade others of them. What you do not have the right to do is suggest that these emphases make you either a Fundamentalist or a Calvinist. Quite frankly, to anyone with a smidgeon of historical perspective, doesn't this sort of argument simply make you look a bit silly?"

Every chapter of this book succumbs to the same elementary analysis. Every chapter has some useful insights, and every chapter overstates arguments, distorts history, attaches excessively negative terms to all the things with which McLaren disagrees (even when they have been part of the heritage of confessional Christianity for two thousand years), and almost never engages the Scriptures except occasionally in prooftexting ways. Even the closing chapter, "Why I Am Unfinished,"[60] manages in brief compass to express attractive humility, misrepresent what "orthodoxy" has meant in the past, give a new definition of "orthodoxy," cite a couple of biblical passages that have nothing to do with what he is talking about,[61] and very

---

[59] Which of course does not derive from Calvin anyway, but springs from Dordt.

[60] *A Generous Orthodoxy*, chap. 20.

[61] Perhaps the most startling quotation is "beholding as in a mirror the glory of the Lord" (p. 292), which follows the New American Standard Bible for 2 Corinthians 3:18. I doubt that this is justifiable translation. But even if it is, McLaren's vision of God's self-disclosure in all of life, which can largely be substantiated on other biblical grounds, is not what is in view in this passage. The verse has little to do with glimpsing the glory of the God of creation in the brilliance of New Mexico sunlight. What is lost from the passage when it is misused in this way?

seriously understate what believers ought to know, should know, and can know, if we are to judge such matters not by postmodern epistemological preferences but by what Scripture actually says.[62] It is important to face the limitations of our knowledge; it is also important to celebrate the fact that one of the central purposes of the coming of the Son of God to this earth, of his death and resurrection, of the gospel itself, was to reveal and *make known* the things that had been much more hidden in earlier revelation (Romans 16:25–27).[63]

I wish these problems were located only in this book, so that one could say that this book is not typical of McLaren's work as a whole. But as far as I can see, he almost entirely loses sight of the gospel in *The Church on the Other Side*. In *The Story We Find Ourselves In: Further Adventures of a New Kind of Christian*,[64] Neo expresses many of the same sets of ideas we have just been exploring. Neo's strength is explaining some of the Bible's story line to unbelievers in a winsome way. Yet even here, parts of this ostensibly biblical story line are simply not biblical, not Christian. Neo is not very good at handling such biblical themes as idolatry and the wrath of God. For him, as we have seen, the theme of judgment is not tied to the cross in any biblically faithful way. Even though McLaren earlier assures us that salvation is by grace and through faith, here God's final judgment depends not on Christ's cross work, but on "how well individuals have lived up to God's hopes and dreams for our world and for life in it."[65]

Not for a moment do I want to loosen the necessary entailment of good works from the cross, yet to cast the final judgment in this way does not sound like "good news" at all: it sounds like a popularization of one strand of the so-called "new perspective" on Paul. As for Satan, he is not personal: in McLaren's hands, he becomes a personification of evil, "a horribly real

---

[62] See the brief discussion at the end of this chapter.

[63] On this issue, see D. A. Carson, "Mystery and Fulfillment: Toward a Larger Conception of Paul's Understanding of the Old and the New," in *Justification and Variegated Nomism, Vol. 2: The Complexities of Paul*, ed. D. A. Carson, Peter T. O'Brien, and Mark A. Seifrid; WUNT (Tübingen: Mohr-Siebeck, 2004), 393–436.

[64] San Francisco: Jossey-Bass, 2001.

[65] *The Story We Find Ourselves In*, 166–67.

metaphor for a terribly real force in the universe."[66] Or again, when he casts the ashes of a loved woman over the water near the Galapagos Islands, Dan Poole asserts that she "doesn't need these ashes anymore": her identity, her personhood, has been "uploaded like software, from the medium of molecules to a new medium." She has been "preserved, saved and cherished in the mind of God."[67] Despite the salutary emphasis on creation earlier in the book, this ending sounds a strangely Gnostic note, with neither place for nor emphasis on the resurrection.

A Critique of *The Lost Message of Jesus*

The second book I have in mind is *The Lost Message of Jesus* by Steve Chalke.[68] Chalke is an influential leader on the British side of the Atlantic,[69] but his book is warmly praised by Brian McLaren.[70] The title displays the confrontational stance I noted in the first chapter: *The Lost Message of Jesus* suggests that others have got it wrong and Chalke is going to tell us how to get it right. Like some others in the emerging church conversation, he used to preach what he now roundly condemns.[71]

The positive thrust of the book is its emphasis on the practical outworking of the great truth, "God is love" (1 John 4:8, 16). Christians are to love the loveless, embrace the untouchable, feed the hungry, forgive the unforgivable, heal the sick, and welcome the marginalized. How many prostitutes and homosexuals would feel welcome in our congregations? In Chalke's book, this vision of things is tightly tied to a rather narrow interpretation of the "kingdom," but many of his thrusts are well taken. On the other hand, I would love to take him to quite a few metropolitan churches

---

[66] Ibid., 103.

[67] Ibid., 193–94.

[68] Grand Rapids: Zondervan, 2003.

[69] Chalke is founder of the highly influential organization *Oasis* (which works closely with Spring Harvest, Youth for Christ, the Salvation Army, and *Youthwork Magazine*). He is an exhilarating speaker, as effective on television as in person.

[70] And others, including Tony Campolo and N. T. Wright.

[71] *The Lost Message of Jesus*, 184.

I know and introduce him to converted prostitutes and homosexuals whose lives have been transformed by the gospel.

But as he presents it, the cost of Chalke's thesis is disturbingly high. God is now defined in terms of one controlling attribute: his love. "The Bible . . . in fact never defines him as anything other than love. But more than that, it never makes assertions about his anger, power or judgment independently of his love."[72] The first of these two sentences is false: the Bible also defines him, even in 1 John, as "light," in whom "there is no darkness at all" (1 John 1:5), and elsewhere, repeatedly, as holy (e.g., Isaiah 6; Revelation 4). The second sentence is manipulative: it would be as true to say that the Bible never makes assertions about God's love independently of consideration of his holiness. For Chalke, holiness, domesticated by his controlling understanding of love, becomes a way of talking about God's pain as he gazes on a broken world. Chalke argues that God in Exodus 33 tells Moses that no one can gaze on his face and live, because it is so contorted with suffering: "No-one could bear to see a face wrung with such infinite pain and live."[73] This speculation is going to make it rather difficult to conflict with Exodus 32:10: "Now leave me alone so that my anger may burn against them and that I may destroy them."

Those who have problems with what the Bible says about the holiness of God almost inevitably have problems with what the Bible says about sin.

> While we have spent centuries arguing over the doctrine of *original sin*, pouring over the Bible and huge theological tomes to prove the inherent sinfulness of all humankind, we have missed a startling point: Jesus believed in *original goodness*! God declared that all his creation, including humankind, was very good. That's not to suggest that Jesus is denying that our relationship with God is in need of reconciliation, but that he is rejecting any idea that we are, somehow, beyond the pale.[74]

Actually, Jesus explicitly assumes that people are evil (e.g., Matthew 7:11, "If you, then, though you are evil . . .") and asserts that from the human heart come "evil thoughts, sexual immorality, theft, murder, adultery, greed,

---

[72] Ibid., 63.
[73] Ibid., 59.
[74] Ibid., 67 (emphasis his).

malice, deceit, lewdness, envy, slander, arrogance, and folly. All these evils come from inside and defile you" (Mark 7:21–23). Jesus, like Paul after him, knew his Scriptures (see Romans 3:9–20). The statement that God declared the entire creation "very good" was of course uttered before the fall (Genesis 1:31), yet Chalke slides over that fact as if it were inconsequential. But the issue is deeper yet. At the core of the Old Testament's treatment of our guilt is the issue of idolatry: we de-god God. What most draws God's wrath upon us in the Old Testament is idolatry, the relativizing of God, the elevation of the creature (as Paul puts it). And this is exactly the emphasis Paul makes when he deals with the biblically illiterate pluralists he confronts in Athens (Acts 17:29). In other words, in the Bible God's holiness is tied to our sin.

Inevitably, once these changes have been made to what the Bible actually says, other things then have to be redefined. Chalke is morally indignant at anything that excludes people. The Pharisees set the doorstep too high: "Jesus lowered the doorstep that the Pharisees had built, but as he did, he also lowered the mantle at the top of the doorframe so that anyone who wanted to enter had to stoop in order to get in."[75] I almost like the metaphor, though it would be closer to the truth to stop speaking of lowering the doorstep: at one level, Jesus insists that the real doorstep is impossible for anyone to navigate, but with God all things are possible. But the metaphor becomes dismaying when Chalke goes on to describe the role of the temple. "At the centre of this 'sin-busting', forgiveness-bestowing machine was what was known as the Holy of Holies, where God's presence was believed to be enshrined."[76] Chalke goes on to mock the entire apparatus, noting the excesses and distortions of the first century. But wait a minute—the design itself was God's, and it was meant to teach us some critically important things about his holiness and what is required to enter into his presence: a mediator and a sacrifice. Chalke's statement "believed to be enshrined" in this context is irredeemably cynical: this is where the glory of God actually manifested itself, both in the tabernacle and in the temple. Moreover, in the New Testament, Jesus is not presented as overthrowing the Law, but as *fulfilling* it. The New Testament repeatedly insists

---

[75] Ibid.
[76] Ibid., 104.

that Jesus fulfills the Old Testament patterns, that he is our high priest, and that his death is the death of the ultimate sacrifice, expiating our sin (Hebrews). But having come so far, Chalke does not hesitate to take the next step: any notion of penal substitution is both offensive and a massive contradiction of Chalke's understanding of the truth of God's love:

> The fact is that the cross isn't a form of cosmic child abuse—a vengeful Father, punishing his Son for an offence he has not even committed. Understandably, both people inside and outside of the Church have found this twisted version of events morally dubious and a huge barrier to faith. Deeper than that, however, is that such a concept stands in total contradiction to the statement "God is love". If the cross is a personal act of violence perpetrated by God towards humankind but borne by his Son, then it makes a mockery of Jesus' own teaching to love your enemies and to refuse to repay evil with evil.[77]

This sounds like McLaren's arguments. No wonder McLaren has endorsed Chalke's book. The judgment, the wrath, of God, spoken of repeatedly in Scripture, now becomes "a personal act of violence perpetrated by God towards humankind": it can scarcely be anything else, once you disbelieve what the Bible says about the odium of human guilt and shame, the offensiveness of idolatry to God, and the certainty and righteousness of judgment. "Surely he took up our infirmities and carried our sorrows, yet we considered him stricken by God, smitten by him, and afflicted. But he was pierced for our transgressions, he was crushed for our iniquities; the punishment that brought us peace was upon him, and by his wounds we are healed" (Isaiah 53:4–5)—all of this, which is the highest measure of God's love for us, is now nothing but the work of "a vengeful Father, punishing his Son for an offence he has not even committed." That which lies at the heart of Christian confessionalism is now "a form of cosmic child abuse."

I am not sure who coined the expression, but both Chalke and McLaren use variations of it. Certainly no thoughtful evangelical could use that expression to refer to what lies at the heart of evangelical confessionalism. No one who has sympathetically worked through what the Bible actually says about the death of Christ could deploy such condescension. No one who loves

---

[77] Ibid., 182–83.

evangelicals will use that language. Without exception, competent treatments of what is meant by substitionary atonement focus on the concurrence of the Father and the Son in the plan of the cross, on the different ways in which both Father and Son suffer, and on the resolution of the Son to do his Father's will. "A form of cosmic child abuse"? The first step in refuting an argument is to state it accurately, not in words that your opponent will understand to be both a massive distortion and only a whisker away from blasphemy. Rightly understood, God's love is all the more deeply cherished when the nature of Christ's sin-bearing act on the cross is understood in biblical terms.[78] But for Chalke, the cross is merely "a symbol of love. It is a demonstration of just how far God as Father and Jesus as his Son are prepared to go to prove that love. The cross is a vivid statement of the powerlessness of love."[79] Further, "The cross is often portrayed as the bridge over the chasm that separates heaven and earth. It is our means of escape. But the reality is that it stands at the centre of our decaying world—thrust into the dirt to proclaim 'God is here!'"[80] But as one review comments, "In other words, the cross is no more than Jesus identifying with our suffering, sharing in the pathos of it. It is difficult to see how this helps us anymore than my injecting myself with the HIV virus would improve the lot of a friend who has AIDS."[81]

Given this mindset, repentance has to be redefined as well. It no longer has to do with renouncing evil. The call to repentance is the call to fulfill our natural potential, to improve ourselves by acting like God.[82]

I have to say, as kindly but as forcefully as I can, that to my mind, if words mean anything, both McLaren and Chalke have largely abandoned the gospel. Perhaps their rhetoric and enthusiasm have led them astray and they will prove willing to reconsider their published judgments on these matters and embrace biblical truth more holistically than they have been doing in their most recent works. But if not, I cannot see how their own

---

[78] I have tried to deal with some of these issues in my book *The Difficult Doctrine of the Love of God* (Wheaton, IL: Crossway, 2000).

[79] *The Lost Message of Jesus,* 183.

[80] Ibid., 185.

[81] Review of *The Lost Message of Jesus,* by Andrew Sach and Mike Ovey in *Evangelicals Now* 19/6 (June 2004): 27.

[82] *The Lost Message of Jesus,* 121.

words constitute anything less than a drift toward abandoning the gospel itself. Chalke does so more straightforwardly; McLaren is smoother, tying his arguments to his understanding of the postmodern and the emergent, terminology that Chalke largely avoids. It will not do to argue, though some have tried, that whereas they may be a bit weak on the cross, they are closer to what the New Testament says about ethics. Why should it be any better or worse, someone might ask,[83] to deny one part of the gospel than another? Haven't those who have abandoned the ethics of Jesus denied the gospel as effectively as those who domesticate the cross? That, of course, is the answer typical of the "angry young man" syndrome: correct one error by telling everyone where they are wrong, and swing the pendulum so far the other way that another error is defended. The new error is compounded when it smirches everyone who disagrees with the blight of one particular twig. But surely the way to maturity, not to say biblical fidelity, is not pendulum-swinging reductionism, but the whole counsel of God, worked out, so far as we are able, in both theology and practice.

As far as I can tell, Brian McLaren and Steve Chalke are the most influential leaders of the emerging movement in their respective countries. I would feel much less worried about the directions being taken by other emerging church leaders if these leaders would rise up and call McLaren and Chalke to account where they have clearly abandoned what the Bible actually says.[84] But that, of course, involves truth-claims. . . .

---

[83] This case was forcefully put to me by an associate of Chalke at Heathrow Airport. He argued that in his Brethren youth in Northern Ireland, he never heard any serious calls for peace in that troubled corner of the United Kingdom. If he had to choose between the call to peace and substitutionary atonement, he'd rather go with the former. That seems self-righteous, to be prepared to define Christianity in terms of reaction to one's personal experience on a single matter. But if Scripture is the norming norm, why cast things in this antithetical way? Where is the wisdom in saying, "I'd rather be a heretic in area A than in area B"? Certainly there are many models of Christian leaders who both cherish the cross in biblical terms and strive for peace and justice.

[84] Indeed, after extended public debates, the British Evangelical Alliance has formally distanced itself from Chalke. This is simultaneously sad, necessary, and commendable.

Chapter 7

SOME BIBLICAL PASSAGES TO HELP US IN OUR EVALUATION

In this chapter I do not intend to lay out detailed biblical arguments to buttress what I have written in previous chapters. I intend, rather, to do two things. First, I shall provide a few lists of biblical references that have a bearing on the directions being taken by the emerging church movement, or conversation. Any comments I add will be minimal. Second, I shall briefly comment on a number of individual passages, indicating the relevance of the passage to the evaluations set forth in this book. I will *not* document again all the positions of the emerging church movement: that has been done throughout the book, and in this chapter I take such accumulated evidence as the given. I might have introduced detailed scriptural evidence throughout the evaluation provided by this book, but on balance I thought it might be helpful to introduce a little of the biblical evidence on the way by, anticipating this chapter when the accumulation of passages in one place may carry additional weight.

Some Lists of Relevant Texts on Truth, Knowledge, and Pluralism

In this section I shall provide three lists (italics added), all of them tied to issues about knowledge that have become skewed by hard postmodernism's pretensions. Several other subjects briefly addressed in this book might have also called forth useful lists (e.g., what the Bible says about the cross and the atonement, what it says about the devil, and so forth), but I have restricted myself to lists that bear most immediately on postmodernism's handling of truth, knowledge, and pluralism. None of the lists is exhaustive. What each list demonstrates is unpacked a little in the brief explanation at the end of the list.

On What Is True

And if it is *true* and it has been proved that this detestable thing has been done among you . . . (Deuteronomy 13:14).

O Sovereign LORD, you are God! Your *words are trustworthy*, and you have promised these good things to your servant (2 Samuel 7:28).

[The Queen of Sheba] said to the king, "The report I heard in my own country about your achievements and your wisdom is *true*" (1 Kings 10:6).

The king said to him, "How many times must I make you swear to tell me nothing but the *truth* in the name of the LORD?" (2 Chronicles 18:15).

Show me your ways, O LORD, teach me your paths; guide me in your *truth* and teach me, for you are God my Savior, and my hope is in you all day long (Psalm 25:4–5).

Do not snatch the *word of truth* from my mouth, for I have put my hope in your laws (Psalm 119:43).

All your *words are true*; all your righteous laws are eternal (Psalm 119:160).

My mouth *speaks what is true*, for my lips detest wickedness (Proverbs 8:7).

A *truthful witness* gives honest testimony, but a false witness tells lies (Proverbs 12:17).

Have I not written thirty sayings for you, sayings of counsel and knowledge, teaching you *true and reliable words*, so that you can give sound answers to him who sent you? (Proverbs 22:20–21).

Then they said to Jeremiah, "May the LORD be a *true and faithful witness* against us if we do not act in accordance with everything the LORD your God sends you to tell us" (Jeremiah 42:5).

"The vision of the evenings and mornings that has been given you is *true*, but seal up the vision, for it concerns the distant future" (Daniel 8:26).

"Now then, I tell you the *truth*" (Daniel 11:2).

"Thus the saying 'One sows and another reaps' is *true*" (John 4:37).

"As it is, you are looking for a way to kill me, a man who has told you the *truth* that I heard from God" (John 8:40).

"Yet because I *tell you the truth*, you do not believe me! . . . If I am *telling the truth*, why don't you believe me?" (John 8:45–46).

"But I *tell you the truth*: It is for your good that I am going away" (John 16:7 NIV).

"I am not insane, most excellent Festus," Paul replied. "What I am saying is *true and reasonable*" (Acts 26:25).

The wrath of God is being revealed from heaven against all the godlessness and wickedness of human beings who *suppress the truth* by their wickedness, since what may be known about God is plain to them, because God has made it plain to them (Romans 1:18–19).

But for those who are self-seeking and who *reject the truth* and follow evil, there will be wrath and anger (Romans 2:8).

I *speak the truth* in Christ—I am not lying, my conscience confirms it through the Holy Spirit (Romans 9:1).

Rather, we have renounced secret and shameful ways; we do not use deception, nor do we distort the word of God. On the contrary, by *setting forth the truth plainly* we commend ourselves to everyone's conscience in the sight of God (2 Corinthians 4:2).

But just as everything we said to you was *true* . . . (2 Corinthians 7:14).

We did not give in to them for a moment, so that the *truth of the gospel* might remain with you (Galatians 2:5).

When I saw that they were not acting in line with *the truth of the gospel* . . . (Galatians 2:14).

Have I now become your enemy by *telling you the truth*? (Galatians 4:16).

You were running a good race. Who cut in on you to keep you from *obeying the truth*? (Galatians 5:7).

Instead, *speaking the truth* in love, we will in all things grow up into him who is the Head, that is, Christ (Ephesians 4:15).

They perished because they refused to *love the truth* and so be saved. For this reason God sends them a powerful delusion so that they will believe the lie and so that all will be condemned who have *not believed the truth* but have delighted in wickedness (2 Thessalonians 2:10–12).

But we ought always to thank God for you, brothers and sisters loved by the Lord, because God chose you as firstfruits to be saved through the sanctifying work of the Spirit and through *belief in the truth* (2 Thessalonians 2:13).

This is good, and pleases God our Savior, who wants all people to be saved and to come to *a knowledge of the truth* (1 Timothy 2:3–4).

And for this purpose I was appointed a herald and an apostle—I am *telling the truth*, I am not lying—and a *true and faithful teacher* of the Gentiles (1 Timothy 2:7).

Opponents must be gently instructed, in the hope that God will grant them repentance leading them to a *knowledge of the truth*, and that they will come to their senses and escape from the trap of the devil, who has taken them captive to do his will (2 Timothy 2:25–26).

... always learning but never able to *acknowledge the truth* (2 Timothy 3:7).

For the time will come when people will not put up with sound doctrine. Instead, to suit their own desires, they will gather around them a great number of teachers to say what their itching ears want to hear. They will turn their ears *away from the truth* and turn aside to myths. But you, keep your head in all situations, endure hardship, do the work of an evangelist, discharge all the duties of your ministry (2 Timothy 4:3–5).

Paul, a servant of God and an apostle of Jesus Christ to further the faith of God's elect and their *knowledge of the truth* that leads to godliness (Titus 1:1).

He has surely *told the truth*! (Titus 1:13).

If we deliberately keep on sinning after we have received the *knowledge of the truth*, no sacrifice for sins is left (Hebrews 10:26).

Of them the proverbs are true: "A dog returns to its vomit," and, "A sow that is washed goes back to her wallowing in the mud" (2 Peter 2:22).

I do not write to you because you *do not know the truth*, but because you *do know it* and because *no lie comes from the truth*. Who is the liar? It is whoever denies that Jesus is the Messiah (1 John 2:21–22).

And he added, "These are the *true words of God*" (Revelation 19:9).

* * *

This list does not provide all the references to things that are said to be "true" or "the truth" or the like. I have not included the many times when "truth" words have to do with the faithfulness of someone or something, or with what is ultimate (e.g., Jesus is the "true vine," John 15). This list merely indicates some of the times the Bible says that words or propositions or reports or proverbs or promises or confessional statements are true. People can tell the truth and thus be true witnesses, or they can tell lies and thus bear false witness. Of course, this does not indicate that they can speak *all* the truth that omniscience could speak on any subject; it does mean that finite individuals can say something that conforms to the objective reality and that this can be believed and known by other finite knowers. The gospel itself can be articulated in words: it is new, good news, and it is *true* good news that can be believed and known. Indeed, it can even be obeyed, for this true good news brings entailments on how human beings should respond to it. The truth of the gospel must be defended, whether or not people refuse to receive or believe the truth.

Over against such truth is the lie, the false report, words that are false, the false tongue, false promises, false prophecy, false accusations, false apostles, false prophets (e.g., Exodus 23:1; 2 Kings 9:12; Psalm 119:104, 128; Jeremiah 14:14; 23:32; Ezekiel 21:23; Zechariah 8:17; Mark 13:22; 2 Corinthians 11:13; 2 Peter 2:1).

The bearing of these biblical passages on our discussion should be obvious. One remembers the student to whom I referred in the first chapter: he recognized that these sorts of passages exist in Scripture, but he admitted that they made him feel uncomfortable. Why? The reason was that he had bought into a harder form of postmodernism than can be sustained. There is *no* reason why we cannot speak of truth versus error, or truth versus falsehood, or true teaching versus false teaching, if we happily admit the insights of soft postmodernism. Only if we buy into the wretched antithesis discussed in chapters 4 and 5—which insists that to know anything truly we must know something omnisciently—does it make sense to assert that we have no ground for saying that something or other is the truth. We may confess it, choose to live it, advocate it, talk about its coherence, but not talk about its truth. Yet we have seen that if the antithesis is true, it is self-refuting. In the

Bible's many references to truth, it never hints that human beings are omniscient knowers: quite the contrary. The Bible's constant references to truth can scarcely be blamed on the absolutizings of some modernists.

If the emerging church movement, or conversation, wishes to remain faithful to Scripture, it must speak of truth and our ability to know it as sweepingly and confidently as Scripture does. If it does not, its underlying assumptions about epistemology remain fundamentally flawed. Equally, if Christians face nonbelievers who are hard postmodernists, part of a faithful Christian witness insists that there *are* truths to be believed and obeyed.

On Knowing Some Truths, Even with "Certainty"

The following list does not include the many passages where one person may "know" another or people may "know" God or "be known" by him. Still less does it include instances in which "to know" is a euphemism for sexual intercourse. All the entries in this list have to do with "knowing *that something-or-other,*" where the construction and context show that the content of what is known or believed to be true is a proposition. Even within such restrictions, the entries below mark only a very small part of all the biblical evidence.

* * *

"I *know* what a beautiful woman you are" (Genesis 12:11).

But Abram said, "O Sovereign Lord, how can I *know* that I will gain possession of it?" So the Lord said to him ... (Genesis 15:8–9).

"You *know* that I've worked for your father with all my strength" (Genesis 31:6).

"But I *know* that you and your officials still do not fear the Lord God" (Exodus 9:30).

"Now I *know* that the Lord is greater than all other gods, for he did this to those who had treated Israel arrogantly" (Exodus 18:11).

Moses said to the Lord, "You have been telling me, 'Lead these people,' but you have not let me *know* whom you will send with me" (Exodus 33:12).

Then Moses said, "This is how you will *know* that the Lord has sent me to do all these things and that it was not my idea: If these men die a natural death and experience only what usually happens to men, then the LORD has not sent me. But if the LORD brings about something totally new, and the earth opens its mouth and swallows them, with everything that belongs to them, and they go down alive into the grave, then you will *know* that these men have treated the LORD with contempt" (Numbers 16:28–30).

Acknowledge [lit., Know] and take to heart this day that the LORD is God in heaven above and on the earth below. There is no other (Deuteronomy 4:39).

"For I *know* that after my death you are sure to become utterly corrupt and to turn from the way I have commanded you. In days to come, disaster will fall upon you because you will do evil in the sight of the LORD and provoke him to anger by what your hands have made" (Deuteronomy 31:29).

He said to the Israelites, "In the future when your descendants ask their fathers, 'What do these stones mean?' *tell them* [lit., then you shall let your children know], 'Israel crossed the Jordan on dry ground'" (Joshua 4:21–22).

". . . then you may *be sure* [lit., know for certain] that the LORD your God will no longer drive out these nations before you" (Joshua 23:13).

But David took an oath and said, "Your father *knows very well* [lit., certainly knows] that I have found favor in your eyes . . ." (1 Samuel 20:3).

"My lord has wisdom like that of an angel of God—he *knows* everything that happens in the land" (2 Samuel 14:20—even if the claim is hyperbolic flattery).

"For I your servant *know* that I have sinned, but today I have come here as the first of the whole house of Joseph to come down and meet my lord the king" (2 Samuel 19:20).

"The day you leave and cross the Kidron Valley, you can *be sure* you will die; your blood will be on your own head" (1 Kings 2:37).

"Have the man come to me and he *will know* that there is a prophet in Israel" (2 Kings 5:8).

"They *know* we are starving; so they have left the camp to hide in the countryside" (2 Kings 7:12).

"Why is my lord weeping?" asked Hazael. "Because I *know* the harm you will do to the Israelites," he answered (2 Kings 8:12).

"Don't you *know* that the LORD, the God of Israel, has given the kingship of Israel to David and his descendants forever by a covenant of salt?" (2 Chronicles 13:5).

"In these records you *will find* that this city is a rebellious city, troublesome to kings and provinces, a place of rebellion from ancient times" (Ezra 4:15).

Know that the LORD has set apart the godly for himself; the LORD will hear when I call to him (Psalm 4:3).

The lips of the righteous *know* what is fitting (Proverbs 10:32).

"Then all mankind *will know* that I, the LORD, am your Savior, your Redeemer, the Mighty One of Jacob" (Isaiah 49:26).

"*Be assured* [lit., Know for certain], however, that if you put me to death, you will bring the guilt of innocent blood on yourselves and on this city and on those who live in it, for in truth the LORD has sent me to you to speak all these words in your hearing" (Jeremiah 26:15).

"And when I have spent my wrath upon them, they *will know* that I the LORD have spoken in my zeal" (Ezekiel 5:13).

"You will be consoled when you see their conduct and their actions, for you *will know* that I have done nothing in it without cause, declares the Sovereign LORD" (Ezekiel 14:23).

"All his fleeing troops will fall by the sword, and the survivors will be scattered to the winds. Then you *will know* that I the LORD have spoken" (Ezekiel 17:21).

"The great God *has shown* the king what will take place in the future. The dream is *true* and the interpretation is *trustworthy*" (Daniel 2:45).

"Seven times will pass by for you until you *acknowledge* [lit., know] that the Most High is sovereign over the kingdoms of men and gives them to anyone he wishes" (Daniel 4:32).

"Then I wanted to *know* the true meaning of the fourth beast" (Daniel 7:19).

"*Know and understand* this . . ." (Daniel 9:25).

"I will live among you and you *will know* that the LORD Almighty has sent me to you" (Zechariah 2:11; cf. 4:9).

"The *knowledge* of the secrets of the kingdom of heaven has been given to you, but not to them" (Matthew 13:11).

"Teacher, . . . we *know* that you are a man of integrity and that you teach the way of God in accordance with the truth" (Matthew 22:16—even though the context shows that they were lying through their teeth when they said this, the context also presupposes they should have been sincerely confessing this!).

"You are in error because you *do not know* the Scriptures or the power of God" (Matthew 22:29—a fine combination of propositional and experiential knowledge).

"But *understand* [lit., know] this: If the owner of the house *had known* at what time of night the thief was coming, he would have kept watch" (Matthew 24:43).

I too decided to write an orderly account for you, most excellent Theophilus, so that you may *know* the certainty of the things you have been taught (Luke 1:3-4).

Zechariah asked the angel, "How can I *be sure of* this?" (Luke 1:18).

"Rabbi, we *know* that you are a teacher who has come from God. For no one could perform the miraculous signs you are doing if God were not with them" (John 3:2).

The woman said, "I *know* that Messiah" (called Christ) "is coming. When he comes, he will explain everything to us" (John 4:25).

"Anyone who chooses to do the will of God *will find out* [lit., will know] whether my teaching comes from God or whether I speak on my own" (John 7:17).

"But we *know* where this man is from; when the Messiah comes, no one *will know* where he is from" (John 7:27—another instance of a false claim that nevertheless discloses the nature of the presupposed epistemology).

"When you have lifted up the Son of Man, then you *will know* that I am he and that I do nothing on my own but speak just what the Father has taught me" (John 8:28).

"We *know* he is our son, . . . and we *know* he was born blind. But how he can see now, or who opened his eyes, we *don't know*" (John 9:20).

"We *know* that God spoke to Moses, but as for this fellow, we *don't even know* where he comes from" (John 9:29).

". . . that you may *know* and understand that the Father is in me, and I in the Father" (John 10:38).

This is the disciple who testifies to these things and who wrote them down. We *know* that his testimony is true (John 21:24).

"People of Israel, listen to this: Jesus of Nazareth was a man accredited by God to you by miracles, wonders and signs, which God did among you through him, as you yourselves *know*" (Acts 2:22).

"Brothers, you *know* that some time ago God made a choice among you that the Gentiles might hear from my lips the message of the gospel and believe" (Acts 15:7).

"May we *know* what this new teaching is that you are presenting? You are bringing some strange ideas to our ears, and we *would like to know* what they mean" (Acts 17:19–20).

"You *know* how I lived the whole time I was with you, from the first day I came into the province of Asia" (Acts 20:18).

The commander wanted to *find out* exactly why Paul was being accused by the Jews (Acts 22:30).

"But we want to hear what your views are, for we *know* that people everywhere are talking against this sect" (Acts 28:22).

Now we *know* that whatever the law says, it says to those who are under the law, so that every mouth may be silenced and the whole world held accountable to God (Romans 3:19).

We *know* that the law is spiritual (Romans 7:14).

We *know* that the whole creation has been groaning as in the pains of childbirth right up to the present time (Romans 8:22).

And we *know* that in all things God works for the good of those who love him, who have been called according to his purpose (Romans 8:28).

We *know* that "We all possess knowledge" (1 Corinthians 8:1).

Those who *think they know* something *do not yet know* as they *ought to know* (1 Corinthians 8:2—which simultaneously pricks the pretensions of those who are proud in their little knowledge and rebukes them for not knowing more).

We *know* that "An idol is nothing at all in the world" and that "There is no God but one" (1 Corinthians 8:4).

But I want you to *realize* [lit., know] that ... (1 Corinthians 11:3).

For we *know in part* and we prophesy in part (1 Corinthians 13:9).

Always give yourselves fully to the work of the Lord, because you *know* that your labor in the Lord is not in vain (1 Corinthians 15:58).

For we *know* that if the earthly tent we live in is destroyed, we have a building from God, an eternal house in heaven, not built by human hands (2 Corinthians 5:1).

Understand [lit., Know], then, that those who have faith are children of Abraham (Galatians 3:7).

For of this you can *be sure*: No immoral, impure or greedy person—such a person is an idolater—has any inheritance in the kingdom of Christ and of God (Ephesians 5:5).

Convinced of this, I *know* that I will remain, and I will continue with all of you for your progress and joy in the faith (Philippians 1:25).

... our gospel came to you not simply with words but also with power, with the Holy Spirit and *deep conviction* (1 Thessalonians 1:5—here "conviction" meaning, not "conviction of sins," but "being convinced").

We had previously suffered and been treated outrageously in Philippi, as you *know* (1 Thessalonians 2:2).

We *know* that the law is good if one uses it properly (1 Timothy 1:8).

They forbid people to marry and order them to abstain from certain foods, which God created to be received with thanksgiving by those who believe and who *know* the truth (1 Timothy 4:3).

But *mark* [lit., know] this: There will be terrible times in the last days (2 Timothy 3:1).

Afterward, as you *know*, when he wanted to inherit this blessing, he was rejected (Hebrews 12:17).

. . . *remember* [lit., know] this: Whoever turns a sinner from the error of their way will save their soul from death and cover over a multitude of sins (James 5:20).

For you *know* that it was not with perishable things such as silver or gold that you were redeemed from the empty way of life handed down to you from your ancestors, but with the precious blood of Chirst, a lamb without blemish or defect (1 Peter 1:18–19).

We know that we have come to *know* him if we keep his commands (1 John 2:3—a matchless example of propositional knowledge, personal knowledge, and moral ground).

. . . even now many antichrists have come. This is how we *know* it is the last hour (1 John 2:18).

But we *know* that when Christ appears, we shall be like him (1 John 3:2).

This is how we *know* that we love the children of God: by loving God and carrying out his commands (1 John 5:2).

I write these things to you who believe in the name of the Son of God so that you may *know* that you have eternal life (1 John 5:13).

And if we *know* that he hears us—whatever we ask—we *know* that we have what we asked of him (1 John 5:15).

Yet these people speak abusively against whatever they *do not understand* [lit., know]; and what things they *do understand* [lit., know] by instinct, like unreasoning animals—these are the very things that destroy them (Jude 10).

"I will strike her children dead. Then all the churches *will know* that I am he who searches hearts and minds, and I will repay each of you according to your deeds" (Revelation 2:23).

* * *

This is only a small fraction of the relevant biblical evidence. Do not skip over it too quickly. Read all the passages, look up the contexts if you are unfamiliar with them, note the wide diversity of propositions that can be and should be and are known, and the equally diverse means by which these things are known. After you have read the passages a few times and pondered them, it is difficult to wonder what has gone wrong with both the episte-mology and the theology of those who are incessantly made uncomfortable by claims to human knowledge. When the Scriptures encourage us to know so much—when they can even say that they are written in order that we *may* know (1 John 5:13), indeed know the *certainty* of the gospel story (Luke 1:3–4)—only an oxymoronic humble arrogance (or is it arrogant humility?) could keep telling us that we can't know, making students uncomfortable with what Scripture actually says on these matters.

On Knowing Enough to Call Religions Idolatrous

We have observed that some leaders of the emerging church movement are reluctant to say anything adverse about other religions. This stance seems to be fueled by a cluster of commitments. Partly it is a matter of careful, cautious, courteous reticence, so that we do not needlessly offend con-temporaries who may read any criticism of another religion as a sign of impregnable intolerance. Partly it is the result of recognizing that there are in fact many good things in other religions; indeed, as we have seen, McLaren goes so far as to say that Buddhism has much to teach Christians in the domain of meditation. Partly it is the result of a postmodern reflec-tion on the dangers of absolutism. And perhaps above all it is tied up with the assumption that Christianity has as many horror stories as any other religion, as many things of which to be ashamed.

All of these matters I have addressed earlier in this book. Now I must briefly mention one more. Although in a handful of places in the Bible other religions receive some kind of honorable mention, even in such places the context provides serious limitations.[1] More importantly, there

---

[1] E.g., Proverbs 14:34 says, "Righteousness exalts a nation, but sin is a disgrace to any people"—which asserts rather more that God holds all nations to account than that all their respective religions are equally to be praised. In Acts 17:22 Paul tells the Athenian pagan philosophers that they are "very religious" (today we would probably have said "very spiritual"), but nevertheless ends up by describing their worship as "ignorant" (v. 23) and calling them to repentance (v. 30).

is one dominant way in which the Bible describes those who follow other gods, and on this point the writers of the emergent movement with whom I am familiar seem to be strangely silent. The Bible tends to call such people idolaters, and their gods idols. When Israel adopts some of these idols into their patterns of worship, the nation is not commended for its openness but condemned for its participation in idolatry. Some references: Leviticus 19:4; 26:1, 30; Deuteronomy 29:17; 1 Samuel 31:9;1 Kings 15:12–13; 21:26; 2 Kings 17:12; 21:11, 21; 23:24; 1 Chronicles 10:9; 16:26; 2 Chronicles 15:8; 24:18; 34:3–4; Psalm 96:5; 97:7; 106:36, 38; 115:4; 135:15; Isaiah 2:8, 18, 20; 10:10–11; 19:1, 3; 31:7; 45:16; 46:1; 48:5; 57:6; 66:3; Jeremiah 50:38; Ezekiel 6:4–5, 13; 8:10; 14:3–7; 16:36; 18:6, 12, 15; 20:7–8, 16, 18, 24, 31, 39; 22:3–4; 23:39, 49; 33:25; 36:18; 37:23; 44:10; Hosea 4:17; 8:4–5; 13:2; 14:8; Micah 1:7; Habakkuk 2:18; Zechariah 13:2; Acts 7:41; 15:20, 29; 21:25; Romans 2:22; 1 Corinthians 5:11; 6:9; 8:1, 4, 10; 10:7, 14, 19; 12:2; 2 Corinthians 6:16; Galatians 5:19–20; 1 Thessalonians 1:9; 1 Peter 4:3; Revelation 2:14, 20; 9:20; 21:8; 22:15. These passages are only a small part of the evidence. Many other passages describe the Baalim, for instance.

It is no answer to say that since covetousness is idolatry (1 Corinthians 5:10; Colossians 3:5), therefore we are all equally idolaters and so we should be loathe to label others idolaters unless we apply the same label to ourselves. Of course, anyone who does not love God with heart and soul and mind and strength, but has some stronger heart-commitment, has displaced God and is an idolater: that is why covetousness appropriately earns the label. But there is a profound difference. In the case of an idolater in the religious sense, the idols are part of the very religious system they cherish. In other words, the religious system itself is called idolatry. By contrast, if someone is a Christian but sometimes wrestles with a powerful and even life-controlling passion for, say, motorcycles, such that God himself is relegated to second-tier interests, although that sin is no less idolatrous than the pagan's idolatry, one cannot say that the very religious system of the Christian is idolatrous.

In other words, when some emerging leaders, such as McLaren, are asked questions about other religions, one of their first recourses is to list sins committed in the Christian heritage and compare them with sins committed in the heritage of the other religions. I have already indicated that the way these comparisons are set forth sometimes lacks evenhandedness. But in any case, this approach fails to ask fundamental questions about the nature of the respective religious systems themselves. The issues transcend sins committed on the horizontal level (as important these are) and raise fundamental questions about who God is. Here the Bible is far more straightforward. Can there be much doubt that if either Isaiah or Paul came up against, say, Hinduism, they would consider it a species of idolatry?

And what shall we say of the fact that of all the things in the Bible that are said to bring down God's wrath, idolatry is preeminent?

Brief Comments on Ten Texts

Some of the passages mentioned below I have briefly alluded to in the course of this book; others appear for the first time. In the former instance, it may be helpful to tease out a little more clearly than I was able to do earlier just what bearing the passages have on the emerging church movement; in the latter case, some fresh biblical considerations will be introduced. These comments are in no way to be confused with detailed exposition of the relevant passages. They merely point to some of the directions such exposition would take, were this book double its length. They are the merest summaries of some important things the Bible says that are being overlooked by large swaths of the emerging church movement and conversation.

1. Romans 1:18–3:20. Four features of these chapters have an important bearing on our reflections.

a. The main thrust of this passage is that all people, Jew and Gentile alike, are guilty before God and therefore subject to his wrath (1:18; 3:9). The catena of Old Testament quotations (3:10–18) that ends the passage needs to be pondered at length. In my experience, the hardest thing in the Bible to get across to postmoderns is what the Bible says about sin, transgression, evil, idolatry. I know full well that some of these words cannot even be used in some circles until they are carefully and faithfully defined within the framework of the Bible's story line. The fact remains that unless we share some level of agreement on what the problem is, we shall certainly not gain agreement on what the solution is. Take the time to read the following verses and ask, if you are a church leader, to what extent you integrate what the Bible says on these matters into your teaching, and to what extent these verses simply make you feel so uncomfortable that you maintain a guilty silence:

> What shall we conclude then? Do we [Jews] have any advantage? Not at all! We have already made the charge that Jews and Gentiles alike are all under the power of sin. As it is written:
>> "There is no one righteous, not even one;
>>> there is no one who understands;
>>> there is no one who seeks God.
>> All have turned away,
>>> they have together become worthless;
>> there is no one who does good,
>>> not even one."
>> "Their throats are open graves;
>>> their tongues practice deceit."
>> "The poison of vipers is on their lips."
>>> "Their mouths are full of cursing and bitterness."
>> "Their feet are swift to shed blood;
>>> ruin and misery mark their ways,
>> and the way of peace they do not know."
>>> "There is no fear of God before their eyes."[2]

b. Although the meaning of Romans 2:12–16 is disputed, it is crucial to see that when Paul speaks of Gentiles doing by nature the things required by the law, in the context he does not mean that some Gentiles are good enough to please God and so be saved. This makes no sense of the larger context, which reaches the sweeping climax we have already witnessed: "There is no one righteous, not even one" (3:10). In the immediate context, the point Paul is getting across when he speaks of Gentiles doing by nature the things required by the law (2:14) is this: even Gentiles, who do not have the law in written form (the way the Jews do), testify to their knowledge of substantial parts of the law by the way they sometimes obey what is written on their conscience and sometimes disobey it. "They show

---

[2] Romans 3:9–18, citing or alluding to, respectively, Psalms 14:1–3; 53:1–3; Ecclesiastes 7:20; Psalms 5:9; 140:3; 10:7; Isaiah 59:7–8; Psalm 36:1.

that the requirements of the law are written on their hearts, their consciences also bearing witness, and their thoughts now accusing [i.e., when they do wrong], now even defending them [i.e., when they do right]" (2:15). Thus the fact of not having the written law will prove to be of no excuse: all of us have the law in some sense, whether printed or, as it were, imprinted on our conscience. God will hold us to account for what we know, not for what we do not know: "All who sin apart from the law will also perish apart from the law, and all who sin under the law will be judged by the law" (2:12).[3] In other words, if Paul elsewhere tells us that everyone sins (3:23; cf. 3:10), here he tells us that whether or not we have the law of God in written form, the result is the same: we will perish. Only the basis for the condemnation will change.

c. All of this "godlessness and wickedness" has been done by human beings "who suppress the truth by their wickedness" (1:18). That is surely critically important. There is a loss of *the truth*, and the subsequent verses show that the truth that is lost is primarily the truth of who God is and what he has done—for a start, that he is the Creator-God to whom thanksgiving is due. The duty of sentient creatures is to recognize their creatureliness, for anything else is idolatry. And that which has prompted the suppression of this truth is sheer wickedness.

d. Because the fundamental wickedness and suppression of the truth is so deeply anti-God, surely it is not surprising that God's response is wrath (1:18). This is not the capricious bad temper of spoiled brats with their noses out of joint. It is the response, both judicial and personal, of the God whose very deity is being denied. So he operates, out of his wrath, to show these rebellious human beings the entailments: he gives them over to their own sins—including uncontrolled lust, shameful desires, and a depraved mind (1:24, 26, 28). In a profound sense, therefore, the most severe "problem" of fallen human beings is God himself, acting justly and entirely in line with his own character and glory as he confronts his rebel image-bearers. The plain fact is that "people are destined to die once, and after that to face judgment" (Hebrews 9:27).

---

[3] On this passage, see especially Douglas J. Moo, *The Epistle to the Romans*, NICNT (Grand Rapids: Eerdmans, 1996), 144–57.

We are now in a domain far removed from supposing that repentance means nothing more than living up to one's full potential. In some vague way, the idea is not wrong, in that we human beings are not living up to our potential as long as we are not the sinless image-bearers of God we were originally designed to be. But so sterile a formulation simply does not confront the sin problem with the starkness displayed in Scripture. It fails to recognize how ugly idolatry is. It refuses to see that our rebellion has justly attracted the wrath of God to us: "All of us also lived among them [the ways of this world] at one time, gratifying the cravings of our sinful nature and following its desires and thoughts. Like the rest, we were by nature deserving of wrath" (Ephesians 2:3).

2. Romans 3:21–4:25. Granted the flow of the argument in Romans so far, it is not surprising, but nevertheless spectacularly wonderful, that the answer comes next. The God who rightly confronts us in wrath because of our sin nevertheless meets us in grace because he is that kind of God. By grace all who believe in Jesus Christ are freely justified (3:21–24). God accomplished all this by Jesus' shedding of his blood in his death on the cross (3:24–25)—all done in such a way that God simultaneously set forth his own justice, while justifying the guilty.[4] Whatever wrath God had manifested in the past was restrained: it was mingled with "forebearance," sins being left "unpunished" (3:25). Now the punishment has been meted out—and God did this "to demonstrate his justice at the present time, so as to be just and the one who justifies those who have faith in Jesus" (3:26).

In fact, the principle of undeserved grace reaches back to the earliest Old Testament era: "Abraham believed God, and it was credited to him as righteousness" (Romans 4:3; see Genesis 15:6). Paul explains the entailments: "Now to anyone who works, their wages are not credited to them as a gift, but as an obligation. However, to anyone who does not work but trusts God *who justifies the ungodly*, their faith is credited as righteousness"

---

[4] I have argued elsewhere that this is the way the argument of the text runs: see "Atonement in Romans 3:21–26," in *The Glory of the Atonement: Biblical, Theological and Practical Perspectives*, ed. Charles E. Hill and Frank A. James III; *Festschrift* for Roger Nicole (Downers Grove, IL: InterVarsity Press, 2004), 119–39.

(Romans 4:4–5).[5] God credits righteousness to those "who believe in him who raised Jesus our Lord from the dead. He was delivered over to death for our sins and was raised to life for our justification" (4:24–25).

For me, the most troubling facet of the emerging church movement is the seeming cavalier manner in which the cross of Christ is handled by the best known and most responsible of the movement's leaders. Were this book to double its size, there would be space merely to survey the sweep of what Scripture says on this subject, virtually none of which seems to be referenced with any seriousness or exegetical competence by the emerging church leaders' published discussions.

3. John 3:1–21; John 4:1–42; and similar passages. One of the wonderful things about the earthly ministry of Jesus is the extraordinarily diverse way he handles people. He sees through all pretensions and is utterly removed from merely "canned" treatments of the gospel of the kingdom.

---

[5] Today (as in some other times) a number of disputes surround the interpretation of Romans 4. I have tried to justify my understanding of what Paul is saying in "The Vindication of Imputation: On Fields of Discourse and Semantic Fields," in *Justification: What's at Stake in the Current Debates*, ed. Mark Husbands and Daniel J. Treier (Downers Grove, IL: InterVarsity Press, 2004), 46–78. I hasten to add that neither a well-informed modernist nor a well-informed soft postmodernist will want to infer too much from the fact that the interpretation of certain texts is disputed. There is *no* cardinal teaching of the faith, including those articulated in the early ecumenical creeds (to which most emerging church thinkers subscribe), that has *not* been disputed. But both the modernist and the soft postmodernist will understand that it is possible to understand Paul's words, if not perfectly or omnisciently, then at least substantially and with asymptotic probability. That is the point of wrestling with the nature of responsible exegesis, of giving reasons for understanding a text this way or that way (and of course this holds true as much for narrative readings as for reading of any other sort: if they are not merest whimsy or subjectivism, the readings must be justified by the evidence). Only the hard postmodernist will demur from these obvious points, the theoretical foundation for which I have sketched in the previous three chapters.

Nevertheless, it is worth reflecting on how this rich awareness of the specific needs of individuals does not avoid confrontation. Jesus gently rebukes Nicodemus, in many ways an honest seeker, for his biblical illiteracy, even though he is the equivalent of a learned professor of Scripture: "You are Israel's teacher . . . and do you not understand these things?" (3:10). As gentle as he is with the Samaritan woman, Jesus will not allow her to duck her sexual promiscuity (4:16–18), and he certainly hits the mark, judging by her own self-assessment (4:29).

The evidence of these sorts of confrontations can be multiplied many times over, not only from the ministry of Jesus, but from the ministries of Peter, Paul, John, and others. Think, for instance, of Jude! The same Paul who exhorts a Timothy or a Titus not to be quarrelsome (e.g., 1 Timothy 5:1–2; 2 Timothy 2:23–25) can also insist that on occasion they must silence certain rebellious people, commanding them not to teach false doctrine any longer (1 Timothy 1:3; Titus 1:10–11). When they look to appoint elders, they must find those who not only display the requisite Christian character, but "who will also be qualified to teach others" (2 Timothy 2:2). Deacons, too, "must keep hold of the deep truths of the faith with a clear conscience" (1 Timothy 3:9). An elder "must hold firmly to the trustworthy message as it has been taught, so that he can encourage others by sound doctrine and refute those who oppose it" (Titus 1:9).

There is a place for moral commands (e.g., to those who are wealthy, not to put their hope in wealth, 1 Timothy 6:17), for constantly reminding believers of the basics, including great christological truths (2 Timothy 2:14 and context), for warning against false teaching and irresponsible handling of Scripture (2 Timothy 2:15–19; Titus 3:9–11), for preaching (2 Timothy 4:2), for linking conduct with "sound doctrine" (Titus 2:1–2).

This is not *all* that such Christian leaders must do, but even this abbreviated list goes way beyond the kind of discussion where every opinion carries the same weight as every other opinion, or where people are merely implicitly invited into our story. "Watch your life and doctrine closely," Paul writes. "Persevere in them, because if you do, you will save both yourself and your hearers" (1 Timothy 4:16). Paul does not offer an alternative, life *or* doctrine. We must persevere in both. Failure to do so calls in question not only our own salvation, but in the long haul, the people we are influencing, our "hearers."

4. Galatians 1:8–9 and similar passages. The language is stark and reinforced by repetition: "But even if we or an angel from heaven should preach a gospel other than the one we preached to you, let that person be under God's curse! As we have already said, so now I say again: If anybody is preaching to you a gospel other than what you accepted, let that person be under God's curse!" (Galatians 1:8–9). Not even apostolic status, not even angelic existence, stands above the immutable gospel. The point that Paul is arguing for in this letter is precisely the sort of gospel-related issue that has divided people across the centuries: whether or not justification comes to guilty men and women exclusively on the ground of the grace of God in the cross, or on the ground of such grace plus something further. Obviously, certain kinds of "generous orthodoxy" won't quibble about matters of that sort as long as we are all following Jesus. But Scripture does not see it that way: an apostle may even rebuke an apostle (2:11–14).

Of course, this is not the only doctrinal issue that calls forth similar language. In 1 John, the doctrinal component of the issue is christological. In 2 Corinthians, the opposing leaders present another Jesus (11:4) who seems to be tied up with triumphalism and power rather than with the cross, and Paul does not restrain himself from denouncing these people as imposters: "And I will keep on doing what I am doing in order to cut the ground from under those who want an opportunity to be considered equal with us in the things they boast about. For such persons are false apostles, deceitful workers, masquerading as apostles of Christ" (11:12–13).

At what point does an "orthodoxy" that is more "generous" than God's become heterodoxy? Not for a moment do I want a vote cast in favor of the narrow-minded, whining, fault-finding, picky, sectarianism with which Christianity has sometimes been afflicted. Rather, what is called for is biblical fidelity. One can be biblically unfaithful by being much narrower than Scripture; one can be biblically unfaithful by being much broader than Scripture. Both sides call it faithfulness; both sides are seriously mistaken. How can we know? By returning to Scripture, again and again, and refusing to be uncomfortable with the categories that God himself has given us, but seeking to learn and digest and believe and obey the whole counsel of God, as far as we see it, without flinching, without faddishness.

5. Jesus' parables of warning. Many of Jesus' parables have to do with explaining that the kingdom of God, against the prevalent expectation, was not about to come with a cataclysmic bang at that point in history, but was destined to be introduced slowly (e.g., parables of the mustard seed and the yeast, Matthew 13:31–33). Other parables demonstrate the power of the principle of reversal in the kingdom, flying in the face of many religious and social values, both then and now (e.g., the good Samaritan, Luke 10:25–37). But some of Jesus' parables, even if they touch on these two themes, bring with them an unmistakable accent of warning.

The parable of the sower (Matthew 13:3–9, 18–23; Mark 4:3–9, 13–20), for all that it explains how the kingdom advances—namely, by properly receiving the word, which then germinates and bears fruit—implicitly warns against unreceptive soil. Where the seed is snatched away and its tender stalks are squeezed to death or dehydrated before there is any fruitfulness (despite a good beginning), there we find people who are unresponsive in one fashion or another. If the kingdom grows like wheat sown in a field, there will also be a lot of weeds, and both will grow until the end (Matthew 13:24–30, 36–43). If good fish are collected, the bad are thrown away (Matthew 13:47–49). Sometimes the language of judgment is sterner yet: the five foolish virgins are shut out of the wedding banquet (Matthew 25:1–13); the ostensible servant who does not discharge his trust faithfully and honorably is cut to pieces and assigned "a place with the hypocrites, where there will be weeping and gnashing of teeth" (Matthew 24:51). These examples are merely representative of much longer lists.

One of the most striking of these parables is the sheep and the goats (Matthew 25:31–46). In the hands of some writers, what distinguishes the sheep from the goats is social concern: feeding the hungry, healing the sick, visiting people in prison—along with the dramatic addition of Jesus' words, "Truly I tell you, whatever you did for one of the least of these brothers and sisters of mine, you did for me" (25:40, 45). But that misses the point here. Certainly the Bible lays considerable stress elsewhere on compassion, justice, acts of mercy, kindness, and much else—as shown by Isaiah and Amos and the parable of the good Samaritan. But it has often been shown that in Matthew's gospel the expression "the least of these brothers and sisters of mine" can only refer to the least of his followers. In other words, the sheep and the goats are exposed for what they are by the way they treat the downtrodden of Jesus' followers.[6] The situation is exactly like that found in the book of Acts: when people persecute the people of Jesus Christ, they are persecuting Jesus Christ himself, prompting him to challenge a Saul on the Damascus Road, "Saul, Saul, why do you persecute me?" (Acts 9:4).

Yet the primary point in these parables I am citing is how many of them lay emphasis on the *dividing* effect of Jesus' ministry. In the case of the sheep and the goats, the latter will finally "go away to eternal punishment, but the righteous [the former] to eternal life"—with the same expression used for "eternal" in the two expressions. One senses that, in an effort to be magnanimous—in many ways, a very good thing—the pendulum swing now makes it almost impossible to pronounce condemnation on any position or stance or habit of life. I ask gently, is the emerging movement, wittingly or unwittingly, abandoning great swaths of biblical content, including some of Jesus' most sobering teaching?

6. Revelation 14:6–20. Now and then in the Apocalypse John provides us with contrasting sketches of the people of the Lamb (vv. 1–5) and the people of the beast (vv. 6–20). Once again, we must not avoid the staggering depiction of God's wrath and fury, now poured out undiluted (vv. 9–11) on all who worship the beast and its image—who, in the flow of the argument from chapters 12–13, are all those who do not follow the Lamb: everyone bears either the mark of the beast or the mark of the Lamb. The Bible here dares to use the language of torment, the smoke of which "will rise for ever and ever. There will be no rest day or night for those who worship the beast and its image, or for anyone who receives the mark of its name" (v. 11). When the final imagery of the chapter is set out, the punishment is shockingly violent (vv. 17–20).

None of these elementary observations on the text is meant to justify harshness, superciliousness, arrogance, haughtiness, or any form of religious cant. I suspect one should not teach much on what the Bible says about hell without learning to weep. But I have learned that one way I can

---

[6] Although some still try to avoid this exegetical conclusion, it is very difficult to do so responsibly. See D. A. Carson, *Matthew*, EBC 8 (Grand Rapids: Zondervan, 1981), 518–23.

check myself to see if I am deeply willing to teach the *whole* counsel of God is by listing the passages and themes that make me so uncomfortable (granted my own cultural locatedness) that I avoid them, or constantly stress what the passages *can't* mean so that I never get around to explaining and applying what they *do* mean. I must resolve this repeatedly and firmly, or I start to duck. This discipline is one of the surest ways of damping down the immaturity of theological pendulum swings, one of the most important disciplines to ensure that I am doing my best, by God's grace, to remain *under* the Word, rather than seeking to domesticate it to the service of the age. So there is the perennial challenge: try a little harder to get over your own background, and commit yourself to trying, so far as you are able, to teaching the whole counsel of God, *especially* the parts you yourself find least palatable.

7. 1–2 Corinthians. I might have chosen other New Testament letters, but I have selected the two letters to the Corinthians to make one observation and anticipate a second:

a. The forms of Paul's arguments in these letters betray a man with outstanding pastoral concern, but no less commitment to truth, good judgment, and balance. The apostle finds the church polarized on many issues. In some instances he handles this not by saying that both sides are right, or that the differences do not matter provided the two sides love each other, or that it is impossible to assert where the truth lies. Rather, he uses what might be called a "yes, but" form of argument. To each side of the dispute, he says, in effect, "Yes, yes, you are quite right—*but* there is something more to be said." For instance, some think that celibacy is the best option while others are pushing ahead with marriage. Yes, yes, Paul says, it is good for a man to be single, it is good not to have sexual relations with a woman (1 Corinthians 7:1, 32–35); *but* sex within marriage reduces immorality, and more importantly, both celibacy and marriage are "grace gifts" (*charismata*, 7:7). Some insist that eating meat offered to idols is blame free, since the informed conscience knows that an idol is nothing; others think that to eat such meat involves a person in idolatry and devil worship (1 Corinthians 8; 10). Here again Paul deploys his "yes, but" argument with telling effect, yet nevertheless points to certain circumstances in which eating such meat would involve idolatry. And of course, he can thank God that he speaks in tongues more than all of the Corinthians, *but* in the church he'd "rather speak five intelligible words ...

than ten thousand words in a tongue" (1 Corinthians 14:18–19).[7] These examples could be multiplied.

On the other hand, where a church member has been sleeping with his stepmother (1 Corinthians 5), there is no "yes, but" argument, no "on the one hand this, on the other hand that." Similarly for those preaching another Jesus in 2 Corinthians 11, those Paul labels "false apostles" (v. 13). Here there is straightforward condemnation, with reasons given and with exhortation to the church to exercise the needed discipline, with promise of apostolic sanctions if they fail to do so.

The distinction between these two approaches (and of course there are others) suggests that the apostle carries in his mind a well-thought-out set of principles that enable him to decide when one argument is called for and when the other. But even in the first form of argument, the "yes, but" form, Paul has a *correct* answer in mind, to which he is trying to win *both* parties. The two parties have a corner of the correct position, but are treating it as if it were the whole. Paul commends them where they are right, but seeks to broaden their horizons so that they will come to a more mature position. In other words, on some issues the *correct* approach, the *right* answer, the *wise* pastoral stance is to move the extremes to the mature and nuanced center. But on some issues the *correct* approach, the *right* answer, the *wise* pastoral stance is to draw a line in the sand and say, in unbending fashion, "This belief does not belong here; this practice does not belong here. It must be

---

[7] Incidentally, this chapter therefore says something about the importance of intelligibility in our corporate Christian meetings. It is right to appeal to mystery where one rightly recognizes the greatness of God and the limitations of our knowledge, owing not only to our finiteness and sinfulness but also to the fact that we can know only those things about God that he himself has disclosed. Some things are hidden from us (Deuteronomy 29:29). But to construct "mystery" by using symbols or candles or icons is not necessarily pointing to the transcendental. Church history has shown how often such devices actually domesticate God and turn him into a magic-purveyor. What is startling in 1 Corinthians 14, however, is how strongly the apostle underlines intelligibility as a primary characteristic of what takes place in public Christian meetings.

removed; it is not Christian." How shall we even begin to get such complicated matters right unless we think through what Scripture says on such matters, reading them and pondering them again and again?

b. Particularly telling is Paul's handling of the *truth* of the resurrection of Jesus (1 Corinthians 15). But this issue is so important that I have relegated it to its own point (the tenth, below).

8. Isaiah 6; John 8; 2 Thessalonians 2; and related passages. Isaiah the prophet is told that his faithful teaching will make the heart of his people calloused, make their ears dull, and close their eyes. Thus there is a sense in which Isaiah himself, precisely by his faithful ministry, is doing this to the people (Isaiah 6:9–10). Isaiah can accept this depressing responsibility, but not for long, so he asks how long he will face this dismal prospect (v. 11). God's answer is that Isaiah must continue in this vein until destruction rains down on the cities of Judah, houses are deserted, fields are ruined and ravaged, and the Lord has sent the people into exile (vv. 11–12). If even a tenth remain behind, Isaiah is to keep on doing the same thing; only at the end of the chapter is there a glimmer of hope that a shoot will one day spring up from this hacked-down stump (v. 13; cf. chap. 11).

Somewhat similarly, Jesus can tell some of his opponents, "Yet *because* I tell the truth, you do not believe me!" (John 8:45, emphasis added). It would be bad enough if Jesus had made this a concessive: "*Although* I tell the truth, you do not believe me." But that is not what Jesus says. Rather, it is precisely *because* he has spoken the truth that some people do not believe. So what is he supposed to do? Stop telling the truth? Tell them lies? Soften up his message so that they won't be offended? Give up on truth and tell stories instead?

When we reflect on how many of the emerging church leaders warn *against* using truth categories, can we help but sense the huge gap between their position and that of Jesus? The reasons why the truth was not acceptable to Jesus' hearers may not be exactly the same as the reasons why the truth is not acceptable to some contemporaries. Nevertheless, if we Christians are to take our cue from Scripture, this does not mean that we *stop* appealing to the truth, but that we recognize that sometimes the truth itself is what will actually repel people. There is nothing new in that; only the underlying reasons for the repulsion have a show of newness about them. But if we *stop* appealing to the truth when the truth repels, we go down a road specifically disallowed by Isaiah and Jesus. We may have to try extra hard to explain what truth is, to point out that we are not claiming to be omniscient, to point to the ultimate disclosure of the truth of God in the incarnation of his Son, and much more. But we cannot stop talking about the truth without abandoning Scripture or the gospel or the exemplary significance of Old Testament prophets and of the Lord Jesus himself.

We have already seen that those who suppress the truth are finally given over, by God himself, to multiplying sins and consequent wrath and judgment (Romans 1:18–3:20, above). The matter is put equally forcefully in 2 Thessalonians 2:10–12. Some people perish "because they refused to love the truth and so be saved." If that is their committed stance, God confirms them in it as an act of judgment: "For this reason God sends them a powerful delusion so that they will believe the lie and so that all will be condemned who have not believed the truth but have delighted in wickedness."

Yet how many emerging leaders want us to stop talking about the truth?

9. John 20:29. The context tells us how Jesus showed himself to Thomas after the resurrection, inviting him to touch the marks of the wounds in his hands and his side. The nature of this doubt and what prompted Thomas' remarkable confession, "My Lord and my God!" (20:28), are worth careful exploration. But here I will focus on verse 29: "Then Jesus told him, 'Because you have seen me, you have believed; blessed are those who have not seen and yet have believed.'"

This verse is often misunderstood. It has been taken to mean that faith without evidence is superior to faith with evidence. Proper faith should therefore be unconcerned with truth, evidence, reasons for belief, and the like—it should simply believe, and such belief will be blessed by God. But this interpretation of the passage is not reading it in its context. It sounds more like postcritical thought than first-century thought.

The point is that the resurrection of Jesus is a *historical* event, and the only access we have to historical events are through the original witnesses and the records they have left behind. Jesus graciously offered Thomas concrete evidence of his own resurrection, evidence so tangible that Thomas could not discount it. He believed and began to see something of the implications. But many others would come to faith in the resurrected Jesus who would *not* see him. The resurrected Jesus remained on this earth for only forty days before his ascension. He no longer accords the same sort of proof that he accorded to the first apostles and their friends, the "more than five hundred" of whom Paul writes (1 Corinthians 15:6). Yet their faith, too, is blessed: "blessed are those who have not seen and yet have believed" (John 20:29).

But on what basis do they come to faith? Is this merely an existential leap? Far from it. Verse 29 is integrally related to verses 30–31: "Jesus did many other miraculous signs in the presence of his disciples, which are not recorded in this book. But these are written that you may believe that Jesus is the Messiah, the Son of God, and that by believing you may have life in his name." In other words, later generations come to faith by means of the historical witness of the first generation, the generation that included Thomas. He saw, and he believed, and these things have been written so that we may believe too. Here, then, is emphasis not only on the truth of Jesus' resurrection, but on the historical nature of that truth and the need for reliable witnesses to that truth and for faithful recording of that truth in written form.

This matter becomes clearer yet when we reflect on our final passage.

10. 1 Corinthians 15. Influenced by their culture, at least some of the Corinthian Christians had not left place for believing that there would be a general resurrection from the dead at the last day. For them, immortality was a good thing, resurrection an incoherent thing. Prolonged unbelief in this arena, however, would sooner or later evoke unbelief with respect to the resurrection of Jesus himself. Then where would the gospel be?

So Paul teases out some of the implications of the supposition that Jesus did not rise from the dead (vv. 12–19). He lists several of them, of which we select four:

a. The apostles and all the other first-generation believers who have testified that they saw or touched or ate with the resurrected Christ turn out to be a nasty bunch of false witnesses. Either they are deluded, or they are willfully deluding others—but they are not to be trusted, for they are exposed as "false witnesses about God" (v. 15).

b. This means that the heart of the first Christian preaching is false and useless. The earliest Christian proclamation has been gutted. This means that the Corinthians remain in their sins (v. 17). In other words, Paul supposes that the Bible's analysis of the human dilemma remains correct. But since the only solution to our sins is Jesus' death and resurrection, then if the resurrection has not taken place, there is no solution, so we are all damned: we remain in our sins.

c. Further, this means that the Corinthians' faith is "futile" (v. 17). In other words, the Corinthians' faith is valid *only if its object is true*. Faith is *never* validated in the New Testament when its object is *not* true. Indeed, New Testament faith is strengthened when its object is validated, supported by witness, shown to be revealed by God, impregnably real, true. Such an understanding of "faith" is utterly at odds with the use of "faith" in most of Western culture.

d. Believing in something false about the future, but only for this world before the end comes that will expose the falseness for what it is, does not make us heroic believers, believing against the evidence, hoping against hope, receiving temporary blessings even if no eternal ones. Far from it: such short-term delusion, mislabeled "faith," means "we are to be pitied more than all others" (v. 19). Paul has no conceptual space for the stance that doesn't care if faith's object is true so long as we find it beneficial in some way. In the apostle's eye, that makes us objects of pity, nothing more.

The gospel is deeply and unavoidably tied to truths, truths of various sorts. Our ability to know such truths (never exhaustively) and obey them turns on many factors: direct revelation from God (not least in matters concerning the nature and character of God), the illumination of the Spirit, and, for the ineluctable *historical* elements of the gospel, on historical witnesses and the records they have left. And we increase such biblical faith by being crystal clear on the convincing nature of the evidence so graciously provided. Alternatively, the same presentation may simply repel some who hear us, precisely because it is the truth itself that guarantees unbelief in the hearts and minds of some.

Final Reflections

These biblical texts have been lightly marshaled and represent only a tiny fraction of all the biblical evidence. Still, it is enough to make us recall the famous passage by G. K. Chesterton about the sophisticated unbelief in his day. The reasons why people distance themselves from the truth may be a little different at the beginning of the twenty-first century from those advanced at the beginning of the twentieth century, but Chesterton's comments are no less relevant today than when he wrote them:

> What we suffer from today is humility in the wrong place. Modesty has moved from the organ of ambition . . . [and] settled upon the organ of conviction, where it was never meant to be. A man was meant to be doubtful about himself, but undoubting about the truth; this has been exactly reversed. We are on the road to producing a race of men too mentally modest to believe in the multiplication table.[8]

---

[8] G. K. Chesterton, *Orthodoxy* (Garden City, NY: Doubleday, 1957), 31–32.

Chapter 8

A BIBLICAL MEDITATION ON TRUTH AND EXPERIENCE

A good deal of the discussion in this book could be recast as a debate between the claims of truth and the claims of experience. From the side of the emerging church movement, traditional evangelicalism appears to be hard-edged and inflexible because it constantly thinks in truth-categories and does not perceive the legitimate place of experience—not least the fact that the personal experience of the knower plays a part in what he or she thinks is the truth. From the perspective of the traditional Christian, the emergent Christian may appear to be so committed to new experiences and subjective evaluations that the truth can easily be left behind.

Certainly some kinds of appeal to experience lend themselves to distorting the truth. Many revivals, genuine movements of God, end in disarray because Christians begin to pant after the experiences associated with them rather than the gospel and the Christ of the gospel that alone anchor them. Even the most sympathetic observer of the Welsh Revival of 1904–5 recognizes with regret the sad way it staggered to a close, however glorious its beginning.

Still, we need to be careful. The Bible itself appeals to experience in various ways. In Galatians 3:1–5, confronting Gentile Christians who are being drawn into the view that submission to the Mosaic law would make them better Christians, or might even be necessary to their being true Christians, the apostle Paul asks a series of frankly experiential questions: "I would like to learn just one thing from you: Did you receive the Spirit by observing the law, or by believing what you heard? Are you so foolish? After beginning with the Spirit, are you now trying to attain your goal by human effort? Have you suffered so much for nothing—if it really was for nothing? Does God give you his Spirit and work miracles among you because you observe the law, or because you believe what you heard?" (NIV).

This is not the only place where Paul can appeal to the *experience* of conversion and the changes it brings as part of his argument (e.g., 1 Corinthians 6:11). Elsewhere he prays that believers might have the power to grasp the limitless dimensions of the love of God, without which there is no maturity—and what he has in mind is certainly more than a merely intellectual apprehension of the doctrinal formulation of the love of God (Ephesians 3:16–19). And what shall we say of the Psalms, with their kaleidoscopic reflections of the full range of human experience, including hope, despair, fear of death, friendship, adoration, love, indignation, betrayal, and wonder?

Of course, truth and experience do not have exactly the same sort of footing. Truth itself, *rightly understood*, may correct experience, but not the other way around. On the other hand, experience may prompt us to revise our previous understanding of the truth. Truth in the Bible is often propositional (though it is often more than that), but mere knowledge of merely propositional truth does not necessarily save us: just ask the Devil himself. Both truth and experience, wrongly functioning in our lives, can be corrupting; our memories of our experiences may easily become idolatrous, making it necessary to turn our backs on some of these memories (Philippians 3:13–14), and knowledge may become that which puffs up, while love builds up (1 Corinthians 8:1).

So it might be useful to finish this book by thinking our way through one particular passage where an emphasis on truth and an emphasis on experience come together in remarkable ways. Once we have worked through the passage, we shall briefly reflect on the bearing of that passage on the emerging church movement.

2 Peter 1

[1]Simon Peter, a servant and apostle of Jesus Christ,

To those who through the righteousness of our God and Savior Jesus Christ have received a faith as precious as ours:

[2]Grace and peace be yours in abundance through the knowledge of God and of Jesus our Lord.

[3]His divine power has given us everything we need for a godly life through our knowledge of him who called us by his own glory and goodness. [4]Through these he has given us his very great and precious promises, so that through them you may participate in the divine nature, having escaped the corruption in the world caused by evil desires.

[5]For this very reason, make every effort to add to your faith goodness; and to goodness, knowledge; [6]and to knowledge, self-control; and to self-control, perseverance; and to perseverance, godliness; [7]and to godliness, mutual affection; and to mutual affection, love. [8]For if you possess these qualities in increasing measure, they will keep you from being ineffective and unproductive in your knowledge of our Lord Jesus Christ. [9]But if any of you do not have them, you are nearsighted and blind, and you have forgotten that you have been cleansed from your past sins.

[10]Therefore, my brothers and sisters, make every effort to confirm your calling and election. For if you do these things, you will never stumble, [11]and you will receive a rich welcome into the eternal kingdom of our Lord and Savior Jesus Christ.

[12]So I will always remind you of these things, even though you know them and are firmly established in the truth you now have. [13]I think it is right to refresh your memory as long as I live in the tent of this body, [14]because I know that I will soon put it aside, as our Lord Jesus Christ has made clear to me. [15]And I will make every effort to see that after my departure you will always be able to remember these things.

[16]For we did not follow cleverly devised stories when we told you about the coming of our Lord Jesus Christ in power, but we were eyewitnesses of his majesty. [17]He received honor and glory from God the Father when the voice came to him from the Majestic Glory, saying, "This is my Son, whom I love; with him I am well pleased." [18]We ourselves heard this voice that came from heaven when we were with him on the sacred mountain.

[19]We also have the prophetic message as something completely reliable, and you will do well to pay attention to it, as to a light shining in a dark place, until the day dawns and the morning star rises in your hearts. [20]Above all, you must understand that no prophecy of Scripture came about by the prophet's own interpretation of things. [21]For prophecy never had its origin in the human will, but prophets, though human, spoke from God as they were carried along by the Holy Spirit.

How Does the Apostle Begin?

Peter makes no mention of where his intended readers live. If he envisages the same readers as those mentioned in his first letter ("God's elect … scattered throughout the provinces of Pontus, Galatia, Cappadocia, Asia and Bithynia"), they live in a large part of modern Turkey. Judging by chapters 2 and 3, they are in danger of being seduced by false teachers, especially with respect to certain teaching regarding the second coming.

Peter introduces himself, first, as a convert: "Simon Peter," he calls himself, daring to mention both the name that was his before he knew Jesus, and the name that the Lord Jesus gave him. Second, he introduces himself as "a servant," in solidarity with all of the people of God. Perhaps by this period in his life, the apostle has a knack for this light touch, both true and humble, for when he addresses elders, he similarly appeals to them as a "fellow elder" (1 Peter 5:1). Third, he introduces himself as "an apostle" and thus in solidarity with Jesus Christ himself.

The way Peter refers to his readers is similarly thought-provoking. First, they are "those who *through the righteousness of God* … have received a faith as precious as ours" (2 Peter 1:1). The language is stunning: we might have expected Peter to say that Christians received this precious faith through the mercy of God or through the grace of God (and both claims would be true), but here he says that Christians have received this precious faith "through the righteousness of God." The language is somewhat reminiscent of the opening verses of 1 John, where we are told that God "is faithful *and just* [righteous] to forgive us our sins and to purify us from all unrighteousness" (1:9). When he forgives us our sins and grants us saving faith, God is not being slovenly in integrity or merely indulgent, like some good-natured grandpa who is happy to overlook the waywardness of his grandchildren. No, he is just and righteous in forgiving them precisely because he has provided "Jesus Christ, the Righteous One" as "the propitiation for our sins" (2:1–2 KJV).

Second, Peter refers to his readers as "those who through the righteous-ness *of our God and Savior Jesus Christ* have received a faith as precious as ours" (2 Peter 1:1). This is not only a wonderful affirmation of the deity of Jesus, but in the context of the entire letter—which repeatedly warns its readers against licentiousness, immorality, godlessness, and rebellion—the phrase underscores the fact that the Jesus whom we profess as our Lord (if we are Christians at all) is God, *and he is righteous*. Rebellion against him is doubly foolish and dangerous: How shall one successfully strive against God? And how shall we get away with unrighteousness when "our God and Savior Jesus Christ" is righteous?

Third, Peter's addressees are "those who through the righteousness of our God and Savior Jesus Christ *have received a faith as precious as ours*." This "faith" is doubtless both the subjective act of believing and the substance that is believed (as in our expression "the Christian *faith*"), and the grateful and reverent way Peter refers to this faith is a model for us. But the focus of the expression is on the implicit contrast between Peter and his readers. His readers have received a faith as precious *as ours*: almost certainly Peter is thinking of the divide between Gentile and Jew. The Peter who went up on a rooftop in Joppa to pray was still instinctively unwilling to tear down the barriers between the races (Acts 10). Even the Peter who, under complex pressures as he works beside Paul in Antioch, still felt that there were occasions when the Jew-Gentile divide needed preservation (Galatians 2:11–14) could scarcely have penned these words. But at this stage in his spiritual maturation, Peter fully and gladly recognizes that the faith of his (largely Gentile) readers is as precious as his own. If reconciliation to the living God is achieved exclusively through Jesus Christ, then God himself has "canceled the written code, with its regulations ...; he took it away, nailing it to the cross" (Colossians 2:14 NIV), as Paul put it. "Mr. Gorbachev, tear down this wall!" intoned President Reagan. But in the cross, a much more formidable wall has been torn down, with the result that at this stage of his life, Peter could join with Paul in saying, "Here there is no Greek or Jew, circumcised or uncircumcised, barbarian, Scythian, slave or free, but Christ is all, and is in all" (Colossians 3:11).

"Grace and peace be yours in abundance," Peter greets his readers (2 Peter 1:2). The pair of nouns "grace and peace" were common in Christian greetings and resonated with Old Testament associations: grace is tied to God's unmerited favor under the terms of the covenant, and peace is the holistic well-being that God's grace ultimately achieves for us. Let grace and peace "be yours in abundance," Peter writes, which displays the apostle's prayer that his readers will experience these blessings in *increasing* measure (compare Philippians 1:9–11). Let grace and peace be yours in abundance "through the knowledge of God and of Jesus our Lord"—with God and Jesus here being distinguished, even as they were united in verse 1. No matter: all the blessings Peter envisages come to us from God through Jesus Christ.

Thus Peter greets his readers, allusively introducing the impregnable gospel that has saved them and their growing experience of it. Now he turns to his fundamental appeals, grounded in both experience and truth.

Experience

1. The reality of our experience is grounded in God's transforming power (1:3–4).

The point is that the one who calls us (whether God or Jesus) also enables us: "His divine power has given us everything we need" (v. 3). Grace follows through (cf. Philippians 1:6). God may not give us everything we lust after, or everything we need for every conceivable purpose, but everything we need "for a godly life" (v. 3). If you want to be a neurosurgeon or a deejay or a billionaire, God may or may not give you everything you need. But if you adopt the perspective that what is of ultimate importance lasts into eternity, what you *need* the most is eternal life and godliness—and we are assured that God has given us all we need "for life and godliness" (NIV).

After all, these things are bound up with the gospel itself. Otherwise put, they come to us "through our knowledge of him who called us" (v. 3). And how did he call us? He called us "by his own glory and goodness." The combination might strike us at first as a little odd, but it has excellent antecedents. After the incident of the golden calf (Exodus 32), Moses prayed that God would show him his *glory* (Exodus 33:18). God replied, "I will cause all my *goodness* to pass in front of you" (33:19). But this is not changing the subject: the next chapter finds Moses looking out of the rock at the trailing edge of God's *glory* and receiving fresh copies of the law, the demonstration of God's *goodness*.

John's gospel picks up on the same twinned themes. Again and again we are told that Jesus manifested his glory to his disciples, not least in his "signs" (e.g., John 2:11). Ultimately, however, Jesus manifests his glory in the odium and shame of the cross, the highest demonstration of God's goodness. In the Synoptic Gospels, Jesus shows something of the unshielded radiance of his *glory* in his transfiguration, but inevitably he moves steadfastly toward the cross and resurrection.

Peter was one of only three apostles who witnessed the transfiguration. It should not surprise us that for him, "glory" remained an important theme: the word is used eight times in 1 Peter and four times in 2 Peter, and this chapter makes a direct allusion to the transfiguration (2 Peter 1:16). But Peter is also an incomparable theologian of the cross, demonstrating with particular vigor both the theological and the ethical dimensions of Christ's death (see especially 1 Peter 2:19–25). The word here rendered "goodness" means something like "moral excellence" in this context. And we have been called, Peter insists, by the glory and goodness of the One who called us (again, it is far from certain that Peter would want to distinguish between God and Jesus at this point).

Anyone who has been involved in bringing the gospel to people who have never heard of it before can testify to what this means in practice. God has disclosed himself in Christ Jesus in great glory and goodness: there is something so utterly attractive about him that people turn away from what held them before, drawn to his glory and goodness. I remember a Pakistani Muslim, reading and rereading John's gospel, pondering all that was embraced when the Prologue insists that Christ Jesus, the Word-made-flesh, was "full of grace and truth" (John 1:14). I recall the conversion of an Iranian who, having stolen a Gideon Bible from a hotel room, read and reread the Gospels, utterly captured by this person Jesus. God calls his people "by his own glory and goodness," manifested supremely in the glory and goodness of his Son.

Indeed, through these—i.e., through his glory and goodness—"he has given us his very great and precious promises" (2 Peter 1:4). What are these promises? In the context, they must be *gospel* promises, the promises that flow out of the good news. After all, we have already been introduced to the righteousness of our God and Savior Jesus Christ, by which we have received a precious faith (v. 1). We have been told that we have been given everything we need for a godly life through our knowledge of the one who has called us (v. 3). And now we are assured that we have been given these "great and precious promises" *in order that* ("so that") through these promises we may "participate in the divine nature, having escaped the corruption in the world caused by evil desires" (v. 4).

The promises afforded by the world are at best of transient significance. Work hard, and you will succeed; be faithful, and you will build a solid home; save, and you will have enough to live on in your old age; play for publicity, whether by being great and good or by being outrageous, and you will have fame. But we all know that these promises are frequently broken. Work hard, and you *might* succeed. Alternatively, you might get fired or contract cancer and die young or get killed in a hunting accident. Be faithful, and you will build a solid home—unless, of course, your spouse is unfaithful or your kids somehow hit the skids and cause you endless pain or you happen to live in a part of the world that is ravaged by war and tribalism. Even when these promises work out, they are at best transient. The hunks and beauties of today's football field, today's catwalk, today's big screen will all die. If they live long enough, they will die weakened, perhaps emaciated, likely in some pain, or doped out so as to be largely unaware of their surroundings. On an eternal scale, the world's promises are not very reassuring.

By contrast, the promises God makes in Scripture are rich and enduring. Hundreds of years before Christ, God promised to enter into a new covenant with his people (Jeremiah 31:31–34; Ezekiel 36:25–27), and he kept his promise. Jesus promised his followers "rest"—not only the well-being believers enjoy now, and the "rest" from their works (Hebrews 4:1–13), but the ultimate rest of the new heaven and the new earth. Jesus promised that he was going away to prepare a place for his people; he promised to receive them at the end, so that they might be where he is, forever (John 14:1–4). He promised he would build his church and do so with such vigor and certainty that the gates of hell would not be able to prevail against it (Matthew 16:17–19). Jesus promised to bequeath his Spirit to us (John 14:15–27; 15:26–27), and he kept his word. He promises to be with us until the end of the age (e.g., Matthew 28:20). God promises not to allow his people to endure a temptation beyond what they will be able to bear (1 Corinthians 10:13). He promises us resurrection life on the last day (1 Corinthians 15); he promises to complete his work in us (Philippians 1:6).

These and countless other gospel promises have been given to you, Peter tells his readers, in order that "through them you may participate in the divine nature, having escaped the corruption in the world caused by evil desires" (2 Peter 1:4). Some think they will participate in the divine nature by chanting mantras or obeying laws or being absorbed into nature or having mystical experiences. But Peter insists that Christians participate in the divine nature *through the gospel promises.* Our hope, finally, rests on promises—promises that are to be understood and trusted because God spoke them and his authority and sovereignty stand behind them. Claiming not to know the substance of these promises would be folly past measure—as would claiming to know them but not trusting them, or (better put) knowing them but not trusting the One who has made them.

At this juncture, then, we must ask what Peter means when he speaks of participating in the divine nature. This precise expression is found only here in the New Testament, so we cannot go and look up a list of parallel occurrences of these words to help us get a better handle on what they mean. They cannot possibly mean that we become gods ourselves, with all the attributes and characteristics of the God of the Bible: Old Testament and New Testament writers alike would shrink in horror at the proposal, such is their understanding of the uniqueness of God. Nor can it mean that we are somehow simply absorbed into God: that idea better suits pantheism than the vision of God set forth in the Bible. This passage is often appealed to in Eastern Orthodoxy, which makes much of "participating in the divine nature," seeing it more as a function of the incarnation than of the cross.

Yet there are several factors that help us understand at least a little more closely what Peter has in mind. First, the notion is tightly linked with moral transformation. The aim is to participate in the divine nature, "having escaped the corruption in the world caused by evil desires" (v. 4). We need a God-given transformation to escape the corruption of this world, of course, but it is also true to say, as here, that escaping the corruption in the world caused by our evil desires is necessary for full participation in this divine nature.

Second, although no other passage in the New Testament displays exactly this form of words, quite a few passages deal with similar themes. We become children of God, not by human procreation, but by new birth, by believing or receiving Christ (John 1:12–13)—and this new birth is later unpacked for us as simultaneously a cleansing and a reception of God's life by means of God's Spirit (John 3:3, 5, in language drawn from Ezekiel 36 and elsewhere). In his first letter, Peter himself has spoken gratefully and pointedly about the new birth (1 Peter 1:3). On the night that he was betrayed, the Lord Jesus prayed to his heavenly Father, asking that his followers might so be perfected that they become one, in a way entirely akin to the way the Father and the Son are one—and what could be a stronger sign of participating in the divine nature than that? (John 17:20–26).

Third, if we are going to participate in the divine nature, we had better remember that Jesus Christ—God and human being—commands our "participation" with him at many levels. Elsewhere Peter himself tells us we participate in Christ's sufferings so that we "may be overjoyed when his glory is revealed" (1 Peter 4:13; cf. Philippians 3:10–12).

In other words, what is envisaged here is not escape from human existence, but transformation by the power of God, the life of God, the divine nature of God—and as, by grace, we flee from sin, our participation in this divine nature becomes all the more overwhelming. God's power has given us everything we need for a godly life (2 Peter 1:3), and indeed we have been called to such living through God's great and precious promises, through which we participate in the divine nature, having escaped the corruption of the world caused by our own evil desires.

I could regale you with many wonderful accounts of conversion. I know a Canadian who by his mid-thirties had spent more time in prison than outside prison, and he deserved every sentence he received and then some. But he was converted and transformed. Released, he began to read and study and witness, to grow with other Christians. Eventually he went to seminary and, in order to get a passport so that he could serve overseas, petitioned the Canadian government for a Queen's pardon—and, astonishingly, received it. He spent most of the rest of his life ministering in Latin America, much of his ministry focusing on inmates in the toughest prisons.

I could tell you about a hockey player whose ankle the Lord broke three times before this player would bend the knee. His life was transformed, and he spent half a century in cross-cultural ministry.

I could tell you about the miners of Wales who, transformed by the power of the gospel at the time of the Welsh revival (1904–5), ditched about a third of their vocabulary, with the result that the pit ponies could no longer understand the men who formerly had spoken to them only in profanity and vulgarity.

The gospel is powerful; it transforms us, for God gives us everything we need. And as we turn from the sins that ensnared us, we participate fully in the divine nature. Here, then, is an appeal to experience—but a reminder that if Peter's readers—and we—have enjoyed such experiences and anticipate yet fuller participation in the divine nature, the reason is God's transforming power. That is the first point Peter makes: the reality of our experience is grounded in God's transforming power.

2. The reality of our experience is attested by spiritual growth and productivity (1:5–8).

"For this reason"—i.e., because God has given us everything we need for godly life—Peter says, "make every effort to add" a long string of virtues to your character (vv. 5–7). Use every ounce of energy ("make every effort") to grow experientially in certain well-defined, godly ways. The flow of Peter's argument demands that three things be said.

First, this is one of many passages in the Bible in which God's work in us and for us becomes an incentive to us to make every effort to grow in godliness and obedience to Christ. In other words, the dominant biblical pattern is neither "let go and let God" nor "God has done his bit, and now it's all up to you," but rather, "since God is powerfully at work in you, you yourself must make every effort." Elsewhere, the apostle Paul exhorts the Philippians to "continue to work out your salvation with fear and trembling, for it is God who works in you to will and to act to fulfill his good purpose" (Philippians 2:12–13). So here: God has given us everything we need for a godly life, including precious promises and participation in the divine nature; for this very reason we should make every effort.

Second, the string of virtues we are to add to the faith with which we begin the Christian pilgrimage is fascinating and probing:

a. To faith we must add *goodness*—i.e., virtue, moral excellence.

b. To goodness we must add *knowledge*—not merely morally neutral cerebral substance, but the intellectual substance that enables and fructifies moral discernment.

c. To knowledge we must add *self-control*—not only in such domains as sex, food, and drink, but also in every other domain of life, including what we say, our temper, our use of time, our workaholism. "For the Spirit God gave us does not make us timid, but gives us power, love and self-discipline" (2 Timothy 1:7).

d. To self-control we must add *perseverance*—not just patience, which has overtones of passive endurance, but active resolve, enduring advance, unmoved by difficulties, tears, obstreperous people, or setbacks. In the deepest sense, Christians do not give up (cf. Mark 13:13; Romans 5:1–3; 8:31–39; Colossians 1:21–23; Hebrews 3:14; Revelation 2–3).

e. To perseverance we must add *godliness*—reverence for God, yes, but more than that, an awareness of God in all of life, and therefore the conduct that works itself out in the conscious presence of God. Today we might speak of God-centeredness.

f. To godliness we must add *mutual affection*, for this vision of discipleship is not "Lone Ranger" mythology, but a family (cf. Hebrews 13:1; 1 Peter 1:22; 1 John 4:20).

g. To mutual affection, we must add *love*. Indeed, the greatest of the three cardinal virtues—faith, hope, and love—is love (1 Corinthians 13:13), for of the three, only love is a fundamental attribute of God himself.

All of these "additions" spring from the initial faith, and we must make every effort to add them.

Third, the additions are not ends in themselves. "For if you possess these qualities in increasing measure, they will keep you from being ineffective and unproductive in your knowledge of our Lord Jesus Christ" (1 Peter 1:8). In other words, the increasing development of these listed virtues leads to greater effectiveness and productivity. They fructify (I love that old English word; we ought to bring it back; it means "make fruitful") the Christian's knowledge of our Lord Jesus Christ.

So that is the second appeal to experience that Peter offers: the reality of our experience is attested by spiritual growth and productivity.

3. The reality of our experience is attested by our unflagging perseverance (1:9–11).

Suppose that someone does *not* pursue the qualities listed in the previous verses. What does this say? Peter tells us that "if any of you do not have them, you are nearsighted and blind, and you have forgotten that you have been cleansed from your past sins" (v. 9). A pedant, I suppose, might ask, "Which—nearsighted or blind?" But both expressions are obviously metaphorical, and each contributes something a little different from the other.

To be nearsighted in this context means that if you are not pursuing these qualities, you do not see the gospel very clearly. You have lost a sense of proportion; you cannot see how things are shaping up long-term, down the road, in the middle- and far-distance. You have foolishly focused on the immediate, against the explicit instruction of the Lord Jesus Christ (Matthew 6:19–21).

To be blind means that you do not see reality at all.

The dangers of gospel near-sightedness and moral blindness are real. The proper approach is found in the next verse: "Therefore, my brothers and sisters, make every effort to confirm your calling and election" (2 Peter 1:10). God calls us and provides everything we need (v. 3). But God's call and supply become, once more, an incentive to mighty effort—in this case, the effort "to confirm your calling and election." The confirmation of genuine call and genuine election lies in the transformation of character. It is found not only in faith, but in goodness, knowledge, self-control, perseverance, godliness, mutual affection, and love. "For if you do these things, you will never stumble, and you will receive a rich welcome into the eternal kingdom of our Lord and Savior Jesus Christ" (vv. 10–11). The alternative is wandering away, by which we show that we never really did belong to God's people, despite initial appearances (1 John 2:19).

So by making every effort to add to our faith the qualities Peter prescribes, we confirm our calling and election—and the result is Christian growth and stability ("you will never stumble") and a rich welcome into the eternal kingdom of our Lord and Savior Jesus Christ.

In short, the reality of our experience is attested by our unflagging perseverance.

To sum up: the reality of our experience as Christians is grounded in God's transforming power, is attested by spiritual growth and productivity, and is attested by our unflagging perseverance.

But if Peter appeals to his readers' experience, he appeals no less to the truth itself.

Truth

1. Our confidence in the truth is stabilized by constant review (1:12–15).

The fact that Peter has given all these exhortations to his readers and has spoken of God's gracious calling and election of them does not mean he thinks he is saying something brand new. Far from it: he understands that part of his ministry is to remind Christians of what they already know. "So I will always remind you of these things," he writes, " even though you know them and are firmly established in the truth you now have" (v. 12). In fact, Peter feels a special urgency to keep repeating these things, because he knows he himself does not have all that much time left: "I think it is right to refresh your memory as long as I live in the tent of this body, because I know that I will soon put it aside, as our Lord Jesus Christ has made clear to me" (vv. 13–14—the last clause doubtless alludes to the events reported in John 21). Moreover, so committed is Peter to the importance of repetition and review that he has even made preparation for it to continue after he himself has gone: "And I will make every effort to see that after my departure you will always be able to remember these things" (v. 15).

This emphasis calls forth two further observations.

a. Some things are worth repeating; some things are learned well only with constant review. That is true, for instance, in language learning, especially in the early phases. Christian leaders must remember this. We may be reluctant to deal with some basic Christian theme, thinking it to be old hat. We may find ourselves hunting for what is novel or even esoteric. But the most important things *need* to be repeated. There, too, lies the importance of memory work (or, as the Bible puts it, hiding God's word in our hearts—see Psalm 119:11). This was the strength of the liturgical year: good things need to be reviewed. Nowadays we are so fond of the novel that even our children's Christmas pageants manage to incorporate space visitors and rocket ships, while fewer and fewer people know what actually happened on that first Christmas two thousand years ago. None of this means we should be boring in our teaching, of course. The competent teacher and preacher learns how to teach old things in such a way as to make them fresh. But wise preachers and teachers *plan* for repetition.

b. What Peter's readers already know and are firmly established in, and what Peter commits himself to repeating, is "the truth" (2 Peter 1:12). Part of any Christian teacher's job, whether in a seminary classroom or a Sunday school classroom, is to grasp the substance of Christian truth and teach it again and again. Yes, we understand that across the centuries the hearers of the Christian message have spoken different languages, lived in different cultures, and brought different sets of baggage to the task of understanding and applying Scripture. Nevertheless, there is content that we may substantially know and are committed to repeating. Judging by the flow of the argument, Peter holds that it is precisely by such repetition of Christian fundamentals that his readers are encouraged to "make every effort" to add certain qualities to their faith and to confirm their calling and election (vv. 5, 10)—just as he is committed to "make every effort" to continue this heritage of teaching and review (v. 15).

2. Our confidence in the truth is established on historical witness (1:16–18).

Peter gives further reflection on the *truth* of the gospel. This truth came to the first generation not as a philosophical system, but as historical events. These events really happened; in that sense the reports that describe them are *true* reports. That is Peter's point:

> We did not follow cleverly devised stories when we told you about the coming of our Lord Jesus Christ in power, but we were eyewitnesses of his majesty. He received honor and glory from God the Father when the voice came to him from the Majestic Glory, saying, "This is my Son, whom I love; with him I am well pleased." We ourselves heard this voice that came from heaven when we were with him on the sacred mountain (vv. 16–18).

Transparently, Peter is referring to what he saw when Jesus was transfigured. Perhaps he fastens on that particular event because in some ways it points to several turning-points in the history of redemption.

a. The transfiguration points back to the incarnation: in some ways it enabled Peter, James, and John to glimpse something of Christ's genuine glory, now veiled in flesh.

b. It points forward to Jesus' death and resurrection. As the Son, Jesus comes to do his Father's will: that is his mission. The glory of the mount anticipates the glory of the empty tomb and the subsequent ascension.

c. It points to the parousia, the appearance of Jesus at the very end of history, when he will appear in unshielded glory and bring in the consummation.

The crucial thing to observe is that Peter wants his readers to understand that what he observed *really happened*. What he is saying *is the truth*. The reason why he wants people to believe certain things and act in certain ways is not simply because they are part of a confessional community or because it is good for them or because this happens to be their particular heritage of spirituality, *but because this is the truth*. As in 1 Corinthians (briefly discussed in the previous chapter), so here: Christian faith and conduct are grounded in *truth*, faith is established by assuring people of the *truth* to be revealed, and the historical components of the Christian faith depend on the *truthfulness* of the first witnesses and their reports. Our confidence is established on historical witness.

3. Our confidence in the truth is grounded in biblical revelation (1:19–21).

Peter writes, "We also have the prophetic message as something completely reliable,[1] and you will do well to pay attention to it" (v. 19). We are to pay attention to it "as to a light shining in a dark place, until the day dawns and the morning star rises in your hearts." This colorful language probably means, in this context, that by paying attention to the word of the prophets (the Old Testament prophets are primarily in view), light dawns on us and the darkness recedes. As we pay attention to Scripture, it illuminates us, it forces our darkness to recede, and its truths and values and direction—in short, its gospel revelation—get inside us and transform us. For this very thing Jesus himself prayed on the night he was betrayed (John 17:17).

We can have confidence that in the same way that the apostles told the truth of the things that they witnessed (2 Peter 1:16–18), so the Old Testament prophets were not simply putting their cultural spin on things. True, the prophets inevitably spoke out of the language and culture in which they were embedded, but nevertheless God so superintended the entire process that what they produced sprang from God himself: "Above all, you must understand that no prophecy of Scripture came about by the prophet's own interpretation of things. For prophecy never had its origin in the human will, but prophets, though human, spoke from God as they were carried along by the Holy Spirit" (vv. 20–21).

Our confidence in the truth is grounded in biblical revelation.

---

[1] This rendering captures what the original means. Some render the original "we have the word of the prophets made more certain"—but the context shows that this does not mean that the word of the prophets was intrinsically uncertain yet has somehow now been "made more certain" by the transfiguration and other later revelatory events. Rather, the idea is that the word of the prophets in Scripture is certain, but that what later fulfills it, to which the apostles bear witness, makes its authority and truthfulness all the more transparent. We Christians become all the more certain of the truthfulness and reliability of this word as we see it come to its fulfillment.

Final Reflections

So which shall we choose?

Experience or truth? The left wing of an airplane, or the right? Love or integrity? Study or service? Evangelism or discipleship? The front wheels of a car, or the rear? Subjective knowledge or objective knowledge? Faith or obedience?

Damn all false antitheses to hell, for they generate false gods, they perpetuate idols, they twist and distort our souls, they launch the church into violent pendulum swings whose oscillations succeed only in dividing brothers and sisters in Christ.

The truth is that Jesus Christ is Lord of all—of the truth and of our experience. The Bible insists that we take every thought captive to make it obedient to Christ (2 Corinthians 10:5).

If emerging church leaders wish to become a long-term prophetic voice that produces enduring fruit and that does not drift off toward progressive sectarianism and even, in the worst instances, outright heresy, they must listen at least as carefully to criticisms of their movement as they transparently want others to listen to them. They need to spend more time in careful study of Scripture and theology than they are doing, even if that takes away some of the hours they have devoted to trying to understand the culture in which they find themselves. They need to take great pains not to distort history and theology alike, by not caricaturing their opponents and not playing manipulative games. And above all, they need to embrace all the categories of the Scriptures, with the Scriptures' balance and cohesion—including, as we saw in the previous chapter, what the Bible says about truth, human knowing, and related matters.

If they manage this self-correction and worry less about who is or who is not emergent and rather more about learning *simultaneously* to be faithful to the Bible and effective in evangelizing the rising number of alienated biblical illiterates in our culture, they may end up preserving the gains of their movement while helping brothers and sisters who are more culturally conservative than they are learn to reconnect with the culture.

INDEXES

Scripture Index

This index includes all Scripture references apart from chapter 7.

INDEX OF NAMES

SUBJECT INDEX

We want to hear from you. Please send your comments about this
book to us in care of zreview@zondervan.com. Thank you.

GRAND RAPIDS, MICHIGAN 49530 USA

ZONDERVAN.COM/
AUTHOR**TRACKER**